UFO OF GOD

UFO OF GOD

The Extraordinary True Story of Chris Bledsoe

**A spiritual journey of missing time,
clouds of fire, healings, and transformation.**

CHRIS BLEDSOE

Cover Design: David Broadwell
Interior Design: Creative Publishing Book Design

ISBN Paperback: 9798986571119
ISBN Hardcover: 9798986571126
ISBN eBook: 9798986571102

To my family

FOREWORD

Jim Semivan
Former CIA, Clandestine Directorate
of Operations

If there is a generally accepted truism in the study of UFOs and the phenomenon it is that the whole subject area is extraordinarily complex and perhaps, ultimately, insoluble. This situation may change, of course, but I think not without the help of the phenomenon itself. And that prospect—a formal introduction or, perhaps, a long, Socratic dialogue—does not appear to be in the cards. So far, we are engaged in a one-way conversation with the phenomenon despite the messages and admonitions it occasionally dispenses to contactees, experiencers, and abductees. UFOs have appeared often enough in our history that they are now indelibly stamped on our imagination. But, they offer no calling card or fixed address except the occasional remark that they hail from a distant galaxy or planet or from another reality.

To add to this muddle, the science necessary to explain the phenomenon and/or place it in context and the philosophy to understand it ontologically are simply not available or exist only in a nascent form. And perhaps more importantly, worldwide governments, scientists, and academicians are simply not displaying the courage and fortitude needed to finally accept that this phenomenon is a clear and unalterable part of our reality. Despite the recent U.S. government acceptance that there is possibly more to our consensus reality than we care to acknowledge, the subject is still seen as fringe, to be discussed only with a good deal of trepidation and skepticism. What should be "the story of the millennia" is too often relegated to the alternative press, informal government seminars, or used as titillating fodder for late night television. What the folklorist and ethnographer David Hufford terms the "tradition of disbelief" is still encouraged despite overwhelming evidence of the reality of the paranormal, psychic phenomena and UFOs. But not having a context or branch of science to specifically place the phenomenon is certainly not an excuse to ignore it.

But we should not bury ourselves in pessimism. Despite the opaque nature of the phenomenon we should find hope in the work of the many and varied intrepid researchers and historians doing credible research. And more importantly, we should look to the experiencers, those special few whose stories engage and enlighten us and offer a glimpse into the wilderness of mirrors that is the phenomenon. Eventually, if we begin to pay more attention, we may finally get to a place where we know where to start asking the right questions.

I first met Chris Bledsoe through a mutual friend, Larry Frascella, who insisted that I meet with Chris given that our respective experiences with the phenomenon shared some similarities. Larry graciously arranged a meeting in New York City that included my wife, Debbie, a psychologist, and Chris's wife, Yvonne, and two of their children. During our meeting, both families shared our experiences in great detail along with the emotional and psychological effects these experiences have had on both of our families. (Whether the phenomenon appears to one person or a few, the aftereffects of the experiences are always absorbed and dealt with by the family writ large.) The meeting was emotional for all of us but the effect of sharing our stories created a bond that remains strong to this day.

What followed and continues to this day are occasional private conversations with Chris that I always find stimulating and illuminating. Chris also sends me truly wondrous videos of the orbs that are a regular occurrence at his home. Chris is one of the most humble, honest, compassionate, and loyal people you could ever meet. People that know Chris far better than I tell me he held these same attributes before his experience which I do not doubt. With Chris, you always get the truth and you always feel the love. As clearly demonstrated in this book, Chris's experience changed him drastically. Still the same nice guy, for sure, but he has also become more "spiritual" in the sense that he is more in tune with the concept of the eternal and abiding Love that governs the universe. This becomes apparent in any conversation you have with him; there is no guile, no attempt to appear special in any way, and always a dedication to remaining on a morally and ethically centered course.

What happened to Chris on January 8th, 2007 was life-altering and seminal in his later development as a teacher and healer. His experience was fantastic, as remote from our consensus reality as any one person could possibly expect. And his experience seemed to hit most if not all the variables of a classic contact and abduction experience: lost time, orbs, saucers, up close and personal contact with an alien presence, healings, absurd visuals, and, of course, the appearance of The Lady, to name a few. When Chris first told me his story, I was gobsmacked. The narrative was truly incredible. And I knew it was an honest recollection of the events that happened to him and his son, Chris Junior. And I am not alone in this view. Chris has probably been visited officially and unofficially by more "government types" and UFO researchers than any other contactee or experiencer. There's a reason for this: the story Chris tells touches very close to home for many government officials, scientists, and academics who have either had a similar experience themselves or who are aware of some elements in Chris's story that they have either personally seen or experienced before, officially or unofficially. The Invisible College indeed took notice...and so should you.

I am not a researcher, but like many of you who have purchased this wonderful book, I am a devoted student of the phenomenon. And while there are many students of the phenomenon who claim to have an understanding of all the variables and subsets of the subject, no one, to my knowledge, has come up with an adequate theory or hypothesis to explain all of the weirdness, absurdities, and high strangeness associated with this phenomenon. Chris has his own ideas about the phenomenon as expressed in this wonderful retelling of his story, and I share many of them. To me though, one of the most compelling aspects of Chris's story is his depiction of "The Lady," a truly enigmatic figure with the obvious religious and cultural correspondences. She has appeared before, often in quasi-religious contexts, and her role is always as a protector, guide, and hierophant of the otherworld.

The recent U.S. government interest in UFOs and the phenomenon is also, I think, a notable vindication for Chris and his family, a late but important acknowledgement that like many other U.S. government and worldwide experiencers, they have smacked headfirst into a part of our reality that has refused to stay hidden. Now our role is to try and discern their message.

I also want to add a final note about the importance of family and how in this book Chris has taken great pains to describe how his and Chris Junior's experiences had unintentionally severely strained the bonds of a very close-knit family. Confusion, loneliness, desperation, frustration, and fear usually follow the types of trauma experienced by Chris and Chris Junior and these feelings always reverberate through the family and the community. They are experienced as a family and they are overcome, blessedly in this case, as a family. And it is a testament to Chris's honesty and strong moral center that he acknowledges the pain his family suffered and the despair he felt at having no solution to relieving this family pain. And I want to personally acknowledge Chris's family—Yvonne, Chris Junior, Jeremy, Ryan, and Emily—for standing by their dad and showing him the love and understanding that he so desperately needed to heal, remarkably, even in the midst of their own personal crises. I am blessed to know and love them all.

Jim Semivan
January 2023

INTRODUCTION

Col. John B. Alexander, PhD
Retired U.S. ARMY

Welcome to the great adventure. What you are about to encounter is a byzantine entanglement of phenomena that defy both explanation and imagination. Importantly, the events continue to morph and unfold, often in unanticipated directions as external observers become participants and report their own independent observations. Do not be surprised if you, the reader, become one of them.

If you have heard something about the UFO experiences of Chris Bledsoe, you may have many questions. The foremost might be, "Can they be real?" The short answer is, YES. The more complete answer is far more complicated and profound. In fact, as many have learned, just being exposed to his observations may well lead to your own, firsthand experiences. That has already happened to several witnesses. Please consider, what you are about to read has implications well beyond what any of us understand today. As some of us believe, there are spiritual consequences related to these observed phenomena that exceed the limits of our current knowledge.

Since I have a solid scientific background, some explanation of why I am such an ardent supporter of Chris, and his family, might be in order. Chris Bledsoe first came to my attention several years ago at the home of a mutual friend in Bucks County, Pennsylvania. At that time, I recorded a long interview with him. Over hours, Chris painstakingly detailed much of what you are about to read. In fairness, that interview led me to ask many of the same questions that most readers would have.

A short time later, in 2015, my wife, Victoria, and I were fortunate enough to travel to North Carolina and visit Chris, Yvonne, and their children. Their modest home was located on a five-acre lot in a transitional area between small residential settlements and more rural and farming areas. Geographically, they were located south of the sprawling Ft. Bragg (soon to be Ft. Liberty), where decades earlier I had been assigned with the 7th Special Forces Group. Contiguous to the base is the well-known military-supporting city of Fayetteville. On the drive from the airport, we noted that not far from their home was a Bledsoe Street, so named as Chris's ancestors had lived in that area for more than a century.

With noisy dog kennels situated on one side, there were numerous tall protective deciduous oak trees and thick green hedges adorning the acreage. Near the center of the property was a unique hollowed out Northern Catalpa tree with clearly visible charred stains on the inside. That tree will come to prominence in later chapters, but suffice it to say you could feel there was something different about it. While visiting, we had the opportunity to observe firsthand some phenomena they had alluded to and sense that indeed, something there was different, almost magical. Hell, we even saw smoke on film although it was not physically present in the air that night. Many more of the details of that visit are related in this book.

The most significant was the observation that we jointly made occurred while standing in the field above the banks of the Cape Fear River where Chris had his first encounter January 2007. Worth telling again is the event that totally changed my perception and convinced me that Chris was telling the truth. During the late afternoon that mid-October day we visited the location where the major original event occurred. After traversing the muddy road to the river, we returned to our rental car that was parked on higher ground just a couple of hundred meters from the bank. It was just getting dark. Victoria and Emily, Chris's daughter, were seated in the back of the car talking while Chris and I leaned against the left front fender discussing the precipitating extraordinary events of January 2007.

In the middle of that discussion, and without warning or introduction, Chris suddenly mentioned to me, "Oh, I think they are here." Seconds later a bright luminous object spontaneously burst into view directly above us and immediately went streaking off. That, my second-ever UFO sighting, was brief but significant and indelible. The temporal relationship between Chris's pronouncement and the appearance of the object firmly convinced me of the authenticity of his experiences. While I could not describe the structure of the object, the reality and brilliance were undeniable.

Our collegial relationship has sustained for years and Chris has continually updated me with videos he has taken of orbs. Significant events happened as this book was being written in October, 2022. One Tuesday afternoon (Pacific Time) I called Chris to discuss an upcoming television filming. While on the phone with me, Chris went outside and had a most unique observation. There, in the darkness (he was on East Coast Time) he observed several orbs and recorded them as he described them to me on the telephone. Importantly, on the recording includes parts of our discussion while he was watching those orbs moving in front of him. Thus, there was no doubt about the timing and authenticity of the event. Notably, he sent me the recording just a few minutes after we hung up. Amazingly, a similar occurrence was captured two days later in another of our calls. This is not unique to me as Chris has had similar coincidental observations with other people as well.

The near-omnipresence of orbs (balls of light) in many, if not most events, is extremely significant. For Chris, and many other observers, there appear to be an obvious connection between their conscious thoughts and the sighting and activity of these orbs. Some intuit communications and even what may be described as a spiritual interaction between the human observers and the orbs. The impact can be profound in nature. As one who has engaged in experiments employing telepathy with dolphins and whales in their natural habitat, I am postulating that these interactions between humans and orbs may be an embryonic form of advanced interspecies or interdimensional communication. Missing is a Rosetta Stone that provides the key to our human understanding of the information.

Near the beginning of all my presentations is a chart that lists many phenomena including UFOs, remote viewing, post-mortem communication, psychokinesis, spontaneous healing, near-death experiences, interspecies communications and even cryptozoology. The implication is that these, and other phenomena, have a common factor in human consciousness. While normally reported and examined separately, the events described in this book by Chris Bledsoe encompass many of them. Rarely have we encountered observations of so many separate elements rolled up into a single case. This is one of those exceptional instances. And, it is the confluence of so many multifaceted phenomena that lends credence to the hypothesis that consciousness is at the heart of these events that Chris illuminates. Readers should know that these concepts are directly related to spirituality.

Nearly a century ago, it was Nobel Laureate physicist, Max Planck, who stated, "I regard consciousness as fundamental. I regard matter as derivative from consciousness. We cannot get behind consciousness. Everything that we talk about, everything that we regard as existing, postulates consciousness." Echoing that thought, my friend, Larry Dossey M.D., in 1987 first addressed nonlocality of consciousness and wrote, "nonlocal consciousness and spirituality are seen as a complementary dyad." It is the complex and interwoven nature of the multifaceted events that Chris enumerates in this book that lends credence and supports the postulations of those eminent scientists.

Strap in for a wild ride. As several explorers before me have stated, "You are a spiritual being having a human experience." This book, UFO of GOD, will be an important addition to your repertoire.

Shanti, Shanti, Shanti
Col. John B. Alexander, PhD

CHAPTER 1

At dusk we stood around the Burning Tree, a blackened, cavernous tree that somehow remained alive after mysteriously catching fire three times. I was shivering with my hands pushed deep into my pockets. Autumn was coming. The investigator handed me a small square box and a digital recorder that were attached by a three-foot-long black wire. Holding one in each hand, I leaned against the scorched hollowed opening as the group of us stood there listening to the contraption as it droned and whirred. The investigator took notes and timestamps of changes in its staticky flow, her pen tapping at the clipboard.

"Jason," echoed into the darkness.

We looked at each other wondering who just said that, but it came from the box. My friend's eyes welled with tears. His son Jason had recently died from a heroin overdose. My friend was so distraught in the aftermath of the loss of his son that he gave up on life entirely, attempting suicide twice.

We could hear crickets chirping over the sound of the box as we tried to give him some privacy. Hearing Jason's name out loud was a shock and we could see the deep bond that still existed between father and son. I looked over at him and could see he was trying with all his might to keep his emotions in check. Then I eyed the charcoaled opening of the tree and the investigators' contraption in my hand, trying to suss out words in its chaotic woosh.

"Pope. Danger. Heads-up. Danger pope. Warn pope."

Again, we were shocked, looking around for who could have said it. The investigator coolly asked where the danger was coming from.

"Philadelphia."

I never knew such a machine could speak so clearly and responsively. Whoever, or whatever, was speaking to us had an urgent message and given its willingness to bring Jason into the picture, seemed to be going to great lengths to get our attention. I stepped away for a minute to text my friend Larry Frascella who lived outside of Philadelphia. Larry was well connected and had resources. He called right back and asked me to tell him everything, instructing me to keep asking questions and get as many details as possible. The pope was to visit Philadelphia in just a week's time. I brought the phone close to the voice box so Larry could hear it as we asked what building the danger was coming from. The burned-out husk of a tree held still in front of us.

"Congress. Hit."

Upon hearing this, Larry suggested I come up to Pennsylvania and see if I could figure anything else out, and he would do what he could to adjust the pope's itinerary. The investigator asked the voice box if Larry was doing the right thing in regard to getting involved. The machine rasped back.

"Help, help, help. Chris. The pope. We need him. We need him."

On Monday, plane tickets for my wife, Yvonne, and I arrived in the mail. Larry had deep pockets and a longstanding interest in experiences like mine, and it was clear he was taking this warning seriously. On Thursday, September 22, 2015, Yvonne and I boarded a plane for Philadelphia. We were met by a man standing in baggage claim holding up the name Bledsoe on an iPad. The gentleman gathered our belongings and escorted us to a waiting black limousine. Everything with Larry was first class. Yvonne and I sat in the backseat holding hands and looking out the window as we drove forty-five-minutes to Larry's palatial residence located just outside the city.

The pope would be arriving in Philadelphia on Saturday and stay through Sunday. We had three days to figure out what was happening. Was there to be an assassination attempt? Was Christ's representative on earth, as the catholic doctrine describes him, in harm's way?

Larry is a serious man. He was devoted to helping in any way he could, as well as to understanding the phenomena. We had met three years previously at a party he threw to bring together like-minded people who were serious about investigating UFOs: researchers, scientists, experiencers, government officials, wealthy donors, and others. There was no one in the community he couldn't get ahold of.

After Yvonne and I placed our bags in the guest room Larry had set up, I was walking through the house and was shocked when I turned a corner and saw Colonel John B. Alexander standing there. I froze in my tracks, everything people had told me about the infamous colonel raced through my mind. He was the keeper of all the secrets. The man whom George Clooney portrayed in the movie *The Men Who Stare At Goats*, which was based on the best-selling book about John's stint in the army's efforts at harnessing paranormal techniques. The man who in 1987 was in a secret meeting with Uri Geller held on the third floor in the U.S. Capital building in a secured classified briefing room. The man whom, I was told, could make anyone disappear (which I felt could not possibly be true, but the fact that I heard it stayed with me). A retired U.S. Army Colonel and PhD, John Alexander was known for having had a hand in almost every top-secret paranormal military project. He was with billionaire Robert Bigelow the day Bigelow bought Skinwalker Ranch and he spent the first night there outside. To me, there was no more dangerous and imposing figure in the UFO world than Col. Alexander, and there I was standing face-to-face with him.

I didn't know what to do or say, so I just gave him a great big bear hug. Surprised, he just smirked and said softly, "It's nice to meet you". We sat and talked that night about the issue of the pope and about some of my experiences with UFO phenomena. We brainstormed potential routes the pope might take between speaking events, factoring in the kinds of security concerns only the colonel would have known to expect.

The next day, Larry, John, and I drove around the city in Larry's Mercedes Benz and walked around the streets as much as we could. I looked long and hard at different colonial brick buildings, statues of men in tri-corner hats, at dive-bars, and churches, trying to bring myself back to the feeling I had listening to the voice box at the Burning Tree. Where had those voices been pointing us? I reminded Larry and John of the transcript of what they had said:

"Congress. Hit."

The pope was due to speak at Congress Hall, but it was swamped with tourists and hard to get a read on the situation. We knew we needed a major breakthrough and hard evidence if we wanted to get the pope to skip a speech out of security concerns. The pope's visit had no doubt taken at least a year to plan, and the U.S. Secret Service would be there in addition to Pope Francis's regular security detail, the Pontifical Swiss Guard. Time was ticking and we had done all we could in the city that day, so we headed back to Larry's.

When we arrived at the house, John pulled me aside and with whispery words told me he wanted to conduct a special exercise. He led me down to the basement telling me it should be the quietest place in the house. I followed him down a narrow flight of stairs to an insulated room covered with dark carpeted walls. With every step I could feel my heart beating louder in my ears. The room was full of plush leather recliners and had a large screen on one wall. I was relieved to see it was Larry's entertainment theater. John said he wanted me to try a remote viewing session—something I had never done before much less heard of. Remote viewing is the ability to describe a person, place, event, anything that is remote from you, that you have absolutely no access to, and no one has told you anything about. It can be past, present, or future, and time and space are not relative factors.

John dimmed the lights and had me lean back in a comfortable chair. He guided me into a meditative state. Images started flowing through my head. I described them as best I could: water, bridge, highway, metal, boat ramp. John was taking notes and occasionally asked a question. I made a drawing of the boat ramp I had envisioned while still in the meditative state. I thought about Pope Francis and this ambiguous feeling of responsibility to do something. I focused as intently as I could on what I saw, but those words were all I could summon. I thought about this high-ranking government official sitting next to me and believing in me. And why an individual of such prominence would show me so much respect and give me so much attention. A man with his background, education, and security clearance credentials obviously knows more than the average person when it comes to scientific study of the paranormal.

When I finished the remote viewing session, John called a friend of his. Without telling me, he had called Joseph McMoneagle, Remote Viewer 001. This was the number assigned to Joe through the U.S. government's classified remote viewing program. Joe was a decorated retired U.S. Army Chief Warrant Officer. He had received the Legion of Merit medal for exceptionally meritorious conduct in the performance of outstanding services and achievements for his work in remote reviewing. Joe had been involved in remote viewing operations and experiments conducted by U.S. Army Intelligence and the Stanford Research Institute (SRI) dating back to 1978. John asked Joe if he would do a remote viewing of the current situation. This entailed following a more stringent set of protocols than I was given. I was a complete novice and had no training or idea what I was doing. Joe obliged the request and the remote viewing process yielded information that was similar to mine. The Ben Franklin Bridge, which was the closest to the pope's speaking engagements, seemed to best fit our combined information. This was a dangerous choke point in the itinerary. Larry made a call to a contact within the CIA.

Security tightened on the Walt Whitman and Betsy Ross bridges, and vehicle traffic was completely shut down on the Ben Franklin Bridge. Compared to his two previous stops in New York City and Washington D.C., the pope's parade was shortened while in Philadelphia to a simple tour around Independence Hall.

Federal prosecutors ended up indicting a local man with plotting to assassinate the pope near the Ben Franklin Bridge. Whether this arrest had anything to do with us, I do not know. It was obvious though the serious attention that was given to what I had encountered only days earlier at the Burning Tree. I had just participated in an investigation of a plot to assassinate the pope and was left with my mind swirling, wondering, How did I get here?

CHAPTER 2

Somewhere down a dirt road in North Carolina, a pile of trash burned behind a mobile home. Strange smoke wisped up through the pine branches that hung over my family's clearing. I was two-and-half years old and drawn to what I did not understand.

Mother might have been away in town at the laundromat. Dad might have been undertaking some improvement to our prefabricated home, which had all the soundness of a tin can. As always, there was work to be done. My occupation was of no less importance: grow up and stay out of harm's way.

The gray-yellow smoke rose from a lump of rubble and trash in the far corner of the yard. I stayed next door with my grandparents during the day while my mom and dad were at work. I wandered out the back door and tottered to it over the dusty dirt past shoulder-high weeds. Something was happening there. I recognized some of the objects in the smoldering detritus of our life: a can of beans, some corn husks that had blown off to the side, a blackened pack of Lucky Strikes. The flames looked dim and tame in the morning light, and I got closer, wanting to know what was happening, how it got hot and withered in different ways, why Dad would put such a pretty thing so far away. I stepped into it.

Pain screamed up my legs. I screamed back at the pain to make it stop as flames crawled over my pants. Out of nowhere, my granddaddy tackled me to the ground, smothering both me and the flames at once with his hulking chest. Darkness, a new kind of pain, his sweat and smell, the hard dirt he pressed me to.

A new knowledge.

The third-degree burns would have been much more serious if I were not so young, the doctors said. My skin was already in the process of growing and re-growing anyway. If it is possible to become comfortable with pain, or heighten one's tolerance of it, my apprenticeship began early and intensified year by year. At six years old, I fell off a bunk bed and hit my mouth on a table. Half my teeth were knocked loose and I needed twenty-four stitches. Jeffrey MacDonald, the doctor who sewed me up, yelled and cursed at me while he stitched. Three years afterward he was famously charged with the murder of his wife and two daughters at Fort Bragg. One force harms, another rescues. The blood I've spilt in Cumberland and Robeson counties could make a creek run red, but healing has always found me. This book is an account of the fires I've wandered toward, what I've learned from them, and the people and forces that kept me safe.

My mother, Carrie Faye, and father, Ted, both grew up with deep roots in the areas surrounding Saint Paul's and Fayetteville, North Carolina. Like myself, they both grew up with little money and worked hard all their lives. My mother's grandfather was known as a healer in the surrounding community. In Saint Paul's, a small township between the two major cities in the area, my mother grew up with her mother, depending on each other to make a living. My grandmother worked at cotton mills, my mom worked behind the soda counter at the Rexall drugstore, at the Winn-Dixie grocery, and for twenty-one years at the A&P as a bookkeeper.

My father and the Bledsoe name came from the late medieval Bletsoe family in Bedfordshire, England, where the mother of King Henry VII was born, Lady Margaret Beaufort, in Bletsoe Castle. My father's ancestors arrived in the area around Fayetteville when it was still referred to as Cambellton, after the Scottish town Campbelltown where many of the recent settlers had come from in the early 1700's. The Bledsoe's had accumulated hundreds of acres over the years, but by my grandfather's generation it had been divided up several times among descendants, so my father grew up in Grays Creek, a small farming community south of Fayetteville. These lands that had passed in and out of my family are the same on which I played, farmed, hunted, and fished. If memory is passed down in DNA, I have spent my life in a landscape my body was born knowing.

Growing up deep in the country, miles from other houses, the natural world was more than just a backdrop. At most, one or two cars would go by the house on any given day. Like all the animals among us, we lived by the land's generosity and punishment. When my granddaddy tackled me to put out the fire, he began a rough initiation into the joys and dangers of nature. I spent my childhood with more tools than toys, a small black-and-white TV set that got two channels on a good day, and four family members in a ten-by-forty-foot trailer. The outdoors were an extension of the living room, dining room, and bedroom: stepping out the trailer door was merely an entrance to another room, no more or less dangerous, no more or less hospitable than our family's structure.

There was always work to be done, and this brought me closer to the land. I tended my grandmother's vegetable garden, I fed and tended dozens of hogs as well as horses and goats, I watched my father practice his trade, carpentry. Dad gave me a full slate of responsibilities around the house from a young age. I had to mow with a push lawnmower, and heaven forbid I allow our four-and-a-half acres of grass to grow too long. Four days out of a week I had to wrestle with that grass. It was difficult and exacting work that never really finished. There was always something else to do. Worst of all was the upkeep of Dad's hunting dogs, who had to be fed and watered every day, and have their pens shoveled and cleaned twice a week. I have shoveled train cars full of dog manure in my life. To this day, I cannot stand the smell of it;

the kennel smelled worse than a farm. It exhausted me, but I learned. An old saying goes "tell me and I forget, teach me and I understand, involve me and I learn," and as my father's only son I was involved in most of his wide-ranging projects and ambitions. I was as much a full-time employee as a son. He trusted me with a circular saw as an eight-year-old, so that was when I learned how to use one. Everything was trial-by-fire, and I learned early the importance of managing risk and taking responsibility for my own well-being.

Daddy was a truck of a man at six-foot-three and two hundred fifty pounds. All muscle. He was loved and respected in the community as a hunter, fisher, and builder. He and my mother met in high school, one year apart and in neighboring school districts. She was a cheerleader from St. Paul's rooting for the people he was playing against in basketball, but she noticed him. He would walk the thirteen miles between their towns most days to visit and court her. They were high school sweethearts and married just after mother graduated in her senior year. My older sister was born a year later, and I came along three years after. My father wanted more than anything to get out of farming and into building and carpentry, and taught himself the skills necessary to do that while my mother took shifts at the grocery store and raised us. Neither of their families had much money; so they worked constantly, often leaving my sister and me with my dad's mother.

Early on, Dad took me hunting and fishing. That was his life, same as most of the men in our community when they weren't working. He did everything from breed and train hunting dogs to cleaning kills and cooking venison. It was thrilling and beautiful out in the country. Tagging along with them, I could go deeper into the woods and travel farther down creeks and rivers than I had before. They sent some of the dogs around the edge of a clearing into the woods to flush out any deer. They were well-trained dogs and Dad taught me how to use them, marshaling them around the landscape, carrying out our orders. I would watch the pack of them flush and round up animals that thought they were on the verge of escape, only to be met by a barrage of gunfire. We heard them barking as they ran through the brush in a wide loop toward us. If bucks were there, they would come flying toward us. When we weren't out hunting or nothing was in season, he would take me down the road to go golfing. He taught me well in this respect too, and I won a junior invitational in high school.

Nights I would spend under the wide window at the back of the trailer looking at the moon and stars. As clean and organized as we kept the trailer, the cramped space hardly offered room enough for our own bodies. At times the smells of the kennel and livestock would leak through the walls. I would spend hours visiting my friend the moon. I was holed up in the back corner of the unit watching something bright and unfettered swing across the night sky. No two nights' moons were the same. Always a new path, a new brilliance, a new angle of scythe-shaped crescent or bloating gibbous.

On overcast nights I would look for its soft glow behind the clouds, reaching toward me, me reaching toward it. My fascination with the moon made an impression on my mother, and she bought me glow-in-the-dark balls to play with. Their phosphorescence captured my gaze, and I would set them in the sun during the day so they would absorb enough sunlight to glow at night. I don't know why I became so infatuated with the moon, but it was my first encounter with a shape that would appear to me throughout my life in stranger and stranger ways.

What fun we had as children we had to make ourselves, and our mobile home and clearing in the woods became a neighborhood hangout among local children. Quickly the weeds and grass around the house were trampled to dusty dirt by the games we spent all day playing. But only when there was no work to be done. The adults would play the Grand Ole Opry from open windows and we would all listen as we played outside. That compact surface was home to hopscotch, tag, and many of my best memories. One of my favorite games was to draw circles alone in the dirt and pretend they belonged to the parts of a spaceship. Some intuitive instinct led me as I drew them. As with the moon, no two circles I drew were the same, though none were as perfect as the whole and new moon at the extremity of its cycle. The recurring importance of this shape in my life matches the nature of the shape itself: how orbits repeat themselves indefinitely, how the constancy of its curve makes one portion of its arc indistinguishable from any other, how a circle in three dimensions makes a sphere, and how the matter of all planets, moons, and stars gathers itself into that shape. A golf ball soaring over a fairway or rolling predictably across a green was another iteration of the moon, its dimpled surface like its craters. Like the ducks and doves my father hunted, or the Fort Bragg military aircraft that would sometimes fly overhead, flight sparked my curiosity. It was here that I discovered the power and pleasure of thoughtfulness, and it was here that I discovered my ability to accomplish and understand the same things my father did. My mind thrived daydreaming on this dirt floor chalkboard.

Drawing circles in the dirt was also a creative outlet for my imagination, which had developed largely without books, television, and films. Mother had a record player and would sometimes listen to Perry Como, Elvis, and other music from the fifties. She would cook the fresh turnips and collard greens we could always get from the garden. Because she worked at the Winn-Dixie and the A&P, she had access to all the bread, snacks, and meats that were still good but too old to sell. From the hogs and Dad's hunting excursions, we always had meat in the freezer. Twice a month, we would go to the cookout Dad helped host at the hunting club. Home could be harsh, but it was good, honest living. I was behind in school the first few years, but after third grade I only ever brought A's and B's home on my report card. This was despite rarely if ever doing homework at home on account of the constant demand to attend to chores. The last two years of high school I got permission to leave school early to work construction jobs for my dad. I had wanted to go to college after I graduated, but Dad needed me at a jobsite the following Monday morning.

Later on this would translate to a deft intuition for all things mechanical. From the age of nine I operated a word-of-mouth business where people would ask me to repair their toasters, washing machines, and other appliances. I would also enable car radios to receive FM signal in addition to AM. I could crack open any kind of mechanical panel and know how it worked and how to fix it. My mother would have to hide screwdrivers from me growing up so I wouldn't take apart everything in the house. I saw patterns and logic within machinery that no one else did. The system of a carburetor paralleled how my father built a set of cabinets and how he arranged a fox hunt with his friends. The boundary between nature and the human world has always been fuzzy to me. The running of electrical wires and a spider's web share a logic.

When my father decided to build a permanent home on the same lot as the trailer, he involved me in every step of the process. At nine years old I was digging foundations and learning how to frame a house, to work with teams of friends and neighbors, to be scrappy and useful to the people around me. Gradually, my father turned this into a business, and it would become my career too.

Despite my comfort with the outdoors, eerie things happened in my childhood that unsettled me. One night at our church, Cape Fear Baptist Church, where kids would meet to play, I was alone waiting for mother to pick me up. It was just after Christmas, 1971, and we attended church there for the same reason we did most things in the county: it was the only one nearby. I was leaning against a young dogwood tree, not wanting to go back to the church in case she showed up and I wasn't exactly where she told me to wait for her. She was as protective as a mother hen, fierce about keeping me out of danger. I could never go to sleepovers at friends' houses, they had to come to mine. I waited a long while outside for her to show up, stargazing. The familiar sound of her baby blue Chevelle slowly rose in the night air. When her headlights started to crest the horizon, I suddenly locked eyes with an owl two feet from my face. It was massive, eyes big as saucers. I was entranced, and not at all frightened. As the car slowly illuminated us, neither of us looked away. I didn't know how long it had been there watching me. When I got in the car and told mother, she said she saw me under the tree but no owl.

A few days later on New Year's Day, Dad took me out to the five thousand acres of the surrounding area he and his hunting friends had rented to hunt whatever was in season: deer, raccoons, rabbits, quail, ducks, bears, and whatever else was out there. They had a hunting club and were celebrating the season that had just ended the day before. My cousin Kenny and my neighbor Vance came along to play while Dad and his hunting friends spent the morning repairing the roads that ran through the property, which was part of their agreement with the property owner. Since it was a holiday, my grandfather came along and was cooking a hog for the hunting party. Kenny, Vance, and I decided to go dove hunting. They were nine and I was ten. We walked over half a mile from my grandfather at the grill to a cornfield by some woods where we thought some of the birds might pass by. The guns we had were tall enough to stand to our shoulders, and loaded heavy with twenty-gauge birdshot. We took our posts about a hundred yards apart from each other, all along the same side of the corn field, which wasn't entirely cut down but had lanes through it to attract the doves. We stood still, waiting and watching.

One came by, first by Vance who shot at it a few times from his bolt-action shotgun, which was difficult to fire quickly. It kept coming, next toward me. I was big enough now to not be knocked back and I got two rounds off at the steel-grey turtle dove with a soft white underbelly. After I shot, it started to come down, gliding until it reached some bushes in the forest line at the opposite side of the field. Its small red feet grasped for a perch. I ran quickly toward it to put it out of its misery. I broke open the Stevens double-barrel shotgun sending the spring-loaded spent shells on to the pine leaf-strewn dirt. I fumbled in my hunting vest pocket for two more shells. It was darker in the trees; it would be hard to find it if it were still and on a high enough branch. One shell clicked into the barrel, but in my rush to find the floundering bird I dropped the second shell.

I bent down to reach for it. I rose back up, about to place it in the other barrel -a flutter, a footstep, a deafening crack, and what felt like the full-force of a sledgehammer into my back I went face-first into the dirt.

∞

My back had been torn into by more than three hundred pellets of lead birdshot, leaving a baseball-sized crater of gore just inside of my left shoulder blade. I knew people did not survive this kind of thing because animals didn't either. I had seen countless animals suffer deaths by these same guns. Death was nothing remarkable to me. It was a process that happened to different things at different times. First, the blood came out, maybe there was some twitching and gasping, and hopefully whatever we were hunting did not struggle too much, or worse, get away from the dogs.

I gasped out, "Who shot me? Why did you shoot me?"

It turns out Vance had sprinted after me, hoping he would be the one to find the bird, wanting to finish off the dove he thought he had shot before me. When he got into the woods, he thought he saw the bird, but it was me popping back up from picking up the shell I dropped. He didn't want the struggling bird to get away so he shot over me. But I rose up as he shot.

Kenny and Vance started fighting about whose fault it was. That's how dead I looked. They argued about who was going to go get help, which was really a fight about who had to watch me die. They fought loud, screaming at each other in the high strident voices of nine-year-old boys. They kept on at it, both refusing to leave, both refusing to stay alone with me. There is not much I remember besides pain and a floating sense of being outside my own body that I had given up on reentering.

Vance's father was with my grandfather checking on how the hog was coming. From a half-mile away, he had somehow heard them screaming at each other, and came up the road in his old farm truck. The '65 holly green and Wimbledon white workhorse Ford, full of dirt, papers, and car parts came down the cut lanes of the cornfield looking for the source of the noise. Wordlessly, he came straight at me, slung me over his shoulder and rushed me to the hospital as fast as that truck could go. Bleeding in the front seat, I remember him stopping briefly to tell my grandfather what had happened, who was devastated and sure I was a goner. My grandfather then went to tell my dad. I remember the farmer's rough hands on the wheel, the truck bouncing down the dirt road, and again that sense of defeat, that all this would be over soon. When we got to the hospital, my dad wasn't far behind.

I was wheeled in and out of surgery several times. Over three hundred pellets entered me, and seventeen are still inside my chest, shoulder, and arm. One came out of my chest recently, almost of its own accord, as if it simply felt like carrying on with its existence elsewhere. I can feel another one on its way to surfacing just under my heart. Nobody could explain how my vital organs weren't damaged. The X-rays showed the leaden spheres were inoperable, embedded a half inch from my spine, right next to my heart, deep in my neck. In the body of a slight ten-year-old, these organs are closer together, and the crater bored into me went deeper and broader than if I had been full grown. Something kept me alive, and I credit that protective force to the giant owl that surprised and entranced me. An omen from God, from nature, or from the land that made me communicated that I would be kept. Outside of the church, my head among the branches of a dogwood, a friend was with me when I thought I was alone. Silently, secretly, I was watched that night; I do not believe that force has abandoned me since.

The year I was born, John F. Kennedy asked congress to send a man to the moon. He asserted human hands would touch the lunar surface and bring its substance back to earth. Of course, asking congress to pursue this mission had political and military motivations, but it was also a kind of prayer. Could we set foot on that heavenly body? Could I? Over the course of my childhood, the space race—this national prayer—guided scientists, astronauts, and engineers to make the impossible possible. Doubt and fear came alongside this hope, but enough people believed to make it happen. All of earth had a stake in this mission's daring hope and existential fear. Like splitting the atom, would this leap from one sphere to another unleash a force that could never be taken back?

CHAPTER 3

It was job site after job site. In high school I had my own framing crew and left school early most days to work at Dad's sites as an independent contractor. I spent afternoons and weekends measuring and cutting the two-by-fours that together added up to the bare bones of a house. Usually we would arrive at a site that had recently been cleared of forest and prepped for development. New roads, sewage lines, and power lines marked the way to these interior frontiers. Sometimes it was forest that had never been logged before. Our crew showed up and made it into a place for people to live. We traded parcels of trees, shrubs, and dirt for mailboxes, porches, and chimneys. As the country grew people needed houses. Dad and I knew how to make them.

A new development arrived at our doorstep. Local golfer and Fort Bragg army veteran L. B. Floyd purchased the land our trailer was on to build a golf course. We simply moved a quarter mile down the road. Once the trees were cleared, they brought in bulldozers and backhoes to contour the fairways, bunkers, and greens according to L. B.'s designs. When the fairways were all dirt because the grass had not yet grown in, Dad and I would practice hitting through what was once a dense pine forest. I liked the focus and technique required by the game. It bore a similarity to the work I'd done in carpentry: measure twice, cut once. Practice your game, swing fewer times, win. I liked the arc of the ball in the air, how far it could go with so little effort. Playing there was a way of reconnecting with our old life, each other, and the outdoors. There was always wildlife around: a group of deer strolling along a forest line, bluebirds dipping along the grass catching bugs. Unlike hunting, golf was always in season. I worked hard at getting better and got a lot of advice from L.B., who coached two of his own children to professional careers. L.B. liked having kids around the clubhouse to caddy, work, and learn how to play. His son Raymond Floyd won The Masters in 1976 and his daughter Marlene made it on the LPGA tour.

Between the golf course, work, school, and all of my duties at home, I was very sealed in my world. It was not until I got my driver's license at sixteen that I even learned how to navigate from Hope Mills to the nearest city, Fayetteville. It finally occurred to me that the deafening, trailer-shaking booms I would hear as a child were due to the military aircraft from Fort Bragg breaking the sound barrier over our heads. When there was no work or school, I would golf or go hunting with Dad. Once I got to town, I was amazed to realize how many of the structures he had played a part in building.

Maybe it was a limited childhood experience: I did not tour Europe or learn foreign languages, but I still had enough to discover. Nature is inexhaustible. You can never love your family too much. Work hard enough and a round of golf and a good story is all you need for fun. These are some of the principles I've held to that have led me through a full and blessed life.

Like my dad, I met the woman who would become my wife in high school. I had started to make a decent amount of money for myself from framing houses and working on people's appliances, car radios, and electronics. With that money I bought a new red 1979 Trans Am when I was only seventeen. I'd had it for just a few weeks when the engine started knocking while I was on a double date with my future wife and some friends, on the way to see a movie. I pulled into a service station, popped the hood, and went to check what was going on. There was some steam hovering around the humming black hoses and machinery. A powerful, brand-new car, somehow waylaid. I went to check the radiator. Suddenly I was struck by a jet of superheated green liquid that blew the radiator cap twenty feet away from the car. The left side of my face, my left arm, and my shoulder all had severe burns from the scalding liquid.

For two weeks in the hospital afterward, I bathed in iodine every day. The pain of the burn, along with the pain of the treatment, were among the worst of my life. They scrubbed my skin off with disinfectant and I watched long strips of it peel away. What little was left of me dreaded those baths. So, fed up with the brutal treatment, I walked out of the hospital with just my gown on. I borrowed a dollar from a lady and called my cousin to come pick me up. I got home but Mom made me go back to the hospital. This time around, they acknowledged the pain I was in and put me to sleep before removing my skin. As when I was burned at three years old, a transition occurred with this great wave of suffering. If I was treated like a young adult at thirteen, now I was a man, working and hurting like a man. Again, I had been marked.

After my senior year, my wife and I got married and would have lived together in the area if a recession had not come and left us with little to no building projects. I had thought about going to the University of North Carolina in Chapel Hill, but the money wasn't there. Dad said, wait a few years. Housing loans rose to twenty-one percent and no one wanted to build. Because Dad had a good reputation as a builder and many employees who needed work, he won a contract to build Housing and Urban Development apartments an hour and a half away in Wilmington, North Carolina. Naturally, I had to go where the work was too and stayed with the rest of his hundred-and-ten-member building crew in a hotel Dad rented out just for his employees. Over the next five-and-a-half years, we built over six hundred condo units in the Wilmington area.

∞

Marriage was new, and my wife and I were doing the best we could given the distance my work imposed on us. I was living on the beach and she was back at a mobile home in Fayetteville. It was difficult to balance work with visits. We both wanted the housing market to pick up so we could spend more time together, but the usual problems kept cropping up. We were just twenty years old but had been together four years.

Eleven months into our marriage, I was on a small island off the coast of Wilmington hunting and running dogs. That night there was a keg party at the hunting club, and I made the drive back to see her and my friends. When I got home, my wife was not there so I assumed she had already gone on to the party. As I got out of my car, at the edge of the small crowd surrounding the keg, I saw her talking to a former high school sweetheart of hers. This upset me and was exactly what I had feared. I did not want to go to the party feeling this way, and I did not want to cause a scene, so I got back in my car and headed home. I sped away for a few minutes. I calmed down. I stopped in the same church parking lot where I had seen the owl ten years before. Then I decided to turn around and give the party a shot. I had driven all the way from Wilmington. They were just talking after all, and it was a small community. Those chance conversations and reminiscences likely could not be avoided no matter how hard one tried.

On my way back, still close to the church, I saw a smoking car turned over on its side off the side of a bend in the road, its wheels still spinning. Shocked and terrified, I pulled over, jumped out and looked for anyone to save. It was dark. I could hear the car's engine still running but I didn't see anyone. The porch light of a house in the distance flipped on and I went up to ask the family who emerged whether they saw who was in the car. They said no and I went back toward the wreck and saw in the light from the light on the porch a small form in the grass.

On the grass, thrown from the car, lay a mangled and bleeding body. I ran over to it. I held it in my arms, at a total loss for what to do, watching this suffering thing draw its final breaths. I looked over at the car again.

It was my wife's. This body was my wife's.

She was my wife.

It still hurts. I drank and blamed her death on my suspicion and jealousy. I wondered how things might have gone that night if I had stopped and turned around sooner, if I hadn't allowed myself to get that upset, if I'd been more present as a husband those last several months. There was no end in sight to my misery. The trauma of those moments holding her and not knowing who she was while her life left her has stayed with me all my life. Always, the memory comes back as fresh and painful as when it happened. I drank to escape those feelings but held onto my job building condos on the beach. There were fewer reminders of my old life there, and I had some friends from work.

I lived south of Wilmington on Carolina Beach, a mile-wide strip of land with the Atlantic on one side and the broadening Cape Fear River on the other. At nineteen I was working on the peak of a roof of a three-story beach house, which itself was standing on pylons. The scaffolding I stood on gave way and fell from the house, bringing me down with it. I fell four stories through the network of metal bracings and makeshift plywood floors like a Plinko chip. The bracing's metal bars cut open my arm, stomach, and chest. My T6 vertebrae was fractured. Time passed, I got better, and went back to work. There was no other option. My apartment faced the ocean and its uninterrupted horizon. Grand tapestries of weather rolled by nonchalantly. On stormy days waterspouts wormed their way up to the clouds amid gray rainy chaos. Waves crashed in. Beach grass swayed. Tourists dropped their ice cream cones and winced at their sunburns.

I wound up on the other side of those two years scarred but mostly intact. A friend of mine invited me to lunch one day to set me up with his sister Yvonne, who was home visiting from East Carolina University. Maybe he had a high opinion of me, or maybe he didn't like the guys she was seeing in college. It didn't matter to me. It was love at first sight. Like mine, her dad turned out to be a builder who liked to hunt and fish too. We hit it off at that lunch but she went back to college and I didn't see her for a while. I kept working on the beach building condo after condo.

One day I decided to go see my dad at the sporting goods store he had opened up that had become a local hangout for fishermen and hunters. He was there behind the counter talking to a businessman who happened to be Yvonne's dad. I brought up that I would like to see his daughter and he gave me a ride to their house. I walked in their front door and the businessman introduced me to Yvonne not knowing we had already met. Again, we hit it off and I asked her out on our first date that very night.

∞

On January 30th, 1911, a man by the name of Sam D. Page walked into a crowded octagonal church in Falcon, North Carolina. The church was built from timber that had been uprooted by a tornado and was in that shape because it reminded its builder of revival tents. Sam had been named the head of the first general convention of the new Pentecostal Holiness Church, which that day was officially merged with the Fire-Baptized Holiness Association. Like the tabernacle they were in, the worshippers used all the scrappy ingenuity they had to build a new structure from old wreckage.

Sam D. Page was Yvonne's relative, and he had a leading role in the establishment of the church, which now has over a million members internationally. To this day, the church has been a huge presence in Yvonne's family. As we dated, it became clear that if I wanted to have a life with her, I would have to have a life with the church as well.

I had grown up Baptist mainly because that denomination offered the closest church to our trailer. We were Christians but didn't follow anything resembling the restrictive codes followed by the members of the Pentecostal Holiness Church, which forbid alcohol and smoking. On the other hand, Baptist services were stiff and reserved compared to the passionate eruptions that characterize most pentecostalist churches. In the Baptist church I was raised in, you could hear a pin drop every time the preacher wasn't preaching or the people weren't singing. In the Pentecostal Holiness Church, they believed in baptism by the holy spirit and that speaking in tongues was a result of God's presence in someone. I heard stories of ecstatic brushes with the holy spirit: Yvonne's aunt running backwards over the tops of the pews with her eyes closed. Maybe there was something to their approach that I had to experience to know what it was like.

My many near-death experiences caused my interest in the church to deepen, starting with the omen of the owl outside the church just a few days before I was shot. These experiences raised questions in me that I still wrestle with. Why did I survive being lit on fire at three, getting half my teeth knocked loose at six, getting shot at ten, third degree burns at seventeen, falling four stories through scaffolding at nineteen? What meaning could be gleaned from so many near misses and so much pain? What could I expect from the rest of my life if this pattern were to continue? I had still been drinking while we dated and she tolerated it as long as I went to church on Sunday, though things quickly got more serious between us. We got married that same year in 1983 and moved in together in Carolina Beach. The waves and weather came and went, and we lived happily together.

Weekends we would go back to the Fayetteville area and visit our parents. About a year into our marriage, Yvonne took me to the local Fayetteville airstrip and bought me my first flying lesson as a present. It was a fluke, but it was love at first sight with flying too. Every weekend I returned to the airstrip to build up my hours-in-air so I could earn my private pilot's license. It took months, but I was hooked.

There was a certain mix of peace and delight that came with flying that was unlike any feeling I had known. I think I found peace in the sky *because* it was so dangerous. It never ceases to amaze me how something as thin as air could support thousands of pounds of metal and fuel. No two flights were ever the same, the scale of vision always too large and intricate to bore me: an odd pattern of clouds, wind from an unusual direction for that time of year or that time of day, connecting places I had been to before with how they looked from above. From ten thousand feet, I read the region that was my family's home like an ever-changing text. As long as the flight lasted, I didn't have to worry about anything other than keeping the plane in the air.

My staying with Yvonne was important. We were both in our mid-twenties, and instead of getting a house somewhere where one of us would inevitably get stuck, the first home we bought together was an eight-by-thirty-two-foot camper. If work became unsteady and we had to move, I wanted to be able to take her with me. An opportunity came up in Myrtle Beach to build a six-story high-rise and a marina, so that was where we went. Together.

My mom's family was from the area so we were able to stay on my Uncle Gus's farm out in the country. While I was down on the water building a lighthouse, Yvonne helped my seventy-year-old uncle run a roadside vegetable stand. She was a young city girl driving around with him in a dirty old truck. For fun, I learned how to fly gliders too, which are light-weight, long-winged aerobatic aircraft that don't have engines. Halfway between a hang-glider and Cessna, they would get towed up into the sky by a plane and then set loose. They were thrilling to fly, and much safer to do corkscrews and barrel-rolls in than a real plane. There was my marina, carving into the shoreline. I didn't think about timecards or erosion issues or appointments with coast guard inspectors: I watched it all slide by under me, replaced by the next beach, the next pier, the next swamp.

Yvonne and I spent the next four years traveling around the region in our camper, going wherever there was work. A training tower for the Marines here, an apartment complex there. I was twenty-six and already gaining a good reputation for myself as a builder. If we were too far from the Fayetteville area to visit our folks, we would rent a plane and fly back. There were airstrips and enthusiasts everywhere we went; they have always been a welcoming and passionate community.

Eventually we built ourselves a house back in Fayetteville. I bought an old 1946 Aeronca and restored it in my garage. Like my neighbors' washing machines and refrigerators, I couldn't wait to take it apart and see how it worked. It was a single engine plane with a propeller on its nose and seating for two up front. I took its wings off and made sure every part was in working order over the course of a few months. An old-fashioned plane, all it had for navigational instruments was an altimeter and a compass.

Once I took Yvonne out with me for a ride. It was foggy and the weather was bad. By the look of her beside me I could tell she was not thrilled: with me, with the weather, with the plane I had spent so long taking apart and putting back together. In the fog, I lost track of where I was and had to look at the VFR chart, which is essentially a map of the region that showed major landmarks, roads, and water towers. They are made for pilots who have to navigate by eyesight alone or don't know where they are. I had the chart open on my lap in the cockpit when some turbulence hit and it got sucked straight out the window.

Yvonne looked over at me. I smiled at her as though everything was fine then looked straight ahead. With the engine roaring and our headsets on, there was an amusing lack of control over what was happening. At least in retrospect. A passenger would do best to support the experienced pilot no matter how out-of-control things appeared; a pilot would do their best to seem calm and collected no matter how out-of-control things actually were. Between us was the fear of physical danger and the comfort of being beside each other, both confronted by the same blank formlessness. All I saw was white around me and, in the rare gap between clouds, characterless treetops below. I cautiously descended a few hundred feet keeping an eye on the altimeter.

Maybe something tall in the distance was a water tower. It was my best shot at finding out where I was. As we crept toward it, we passed a highway, though I wasn't sure which it was. The old lightweight plane maxed out at seventy-five miles an hour, so many of the cars below were outpacing us toward our destination. Neither of us said anything. Eventually we got close enough to read the town's name on the water tower. I remembered how to get back home from there.

I bought a faster plane after that, a blue and white M20-E Mooney that could chug from Fayetteville to Disneyworld in an hour and a half. Yvonne and I would go all over the country traveling. My work hours became more flexible and I was starting to make more money. I felt great flying. I wore aviators, grew a mustache, and might have been mistaken for slimmer Mike Ditka on the airfield. We would fly far away to visit some park, some state fair, anything we wanted. We had a small blue tent and no obligations besides church, work, and each other.

By 1987 I had enough hours flown under my belt to take the commercial pilot's test. I could make great money working for an airline and do what I loved more than anything for work. Also, I would get to fly the big birds. I was going to take the test to have the option, but Yvonne came to me with some news. She was pregnant with our first child. I wanted to fly, but I had some long talks with my family and her and remembered the first years of our marriage traveling around in the trailer. Home was wherever we found ourselves together. Being away three or five nights a week, sleeping in hotels, missing our children's plays, games, and events: this career would keep me from everything I had built my life around as well as the values I was raised with. I stayed in construction, and I stayed with my family.

CHAPTER 4

After my first son, Chris Jr. (or as we call him, Junior), was born in 1989, I went to work managing construction and hog farms around the region. It paid the bills and allowed us to move out of our camper and into a brick and mortar home. We had a pool and more space than Yvonne and I knew what to do with. I was proud of us.

It was about this time I started having symptoms of irritable bowel syndrome, or IBS, as my gastrologist told me at the time. It is not an easy disease to treat or live with, and it began to cause some problems at work and at the Pentecostal Holiness Church, where I had begun to serve as Deacon—twice on Sundays and on Wednesday nights. The problems were namely that I had to spend so much time in restrooms, the discomfort it caused me, and the fact that it could be a difficult and embarrassing problem to explain.

Not much is known about what causes IBS and Crohn's disease, but stress made it worse. More and more often in those years, I had to spend nights away from home. I would get a call from one of the hog farms and I would have to drive the three or four hours to check on what was happening. Again, I could never avoid the smell, just like when I was a kid shoveling manure from Dad's hunting dogs and living next to goats and pigs. Driving up to one of these massive complexes, you could smell them ten minutes away. In the parking lot you could hear the din of squealing and the ventilation system used to keep the pigs cool, given that they don't have sweat glands.

I felt responsible for those seas of pink swine. I felt even more responsible for my newborn baby alone with Yvonne. Since the components of these mechanized farms largely controlled the well-being of the animals, the hogs were sometimes in distress because of what was going wrong with the equipment. I would try to fix whatever it was as fast as I could, but sometimes I would have to wait for a part, or it would take a couple of days to hire the people that could address the issue. Working with the machinery of maximum-efficiency pork production was often ghastly. It was a job where success was uneasy: the lives of those animals differed so greatly from the hogs my grandpa raised behind our mobile home, wallowing all afternoon in the heat to cool down. Those nights away from home I would spend in a nearby motel, phoning Yvonne if it wasn't too late by the time I got there. Once a job was finished, I might have a few days at home with Yvonne before another crisis at another farm. Another motel, another hoard of suffering trapped animals.

Meanwhile, my time commitment at the church was ramping up. I studied the bible day and night like I never had before. I experienced some of the richest religious moments of my life and learned a great deal about faith. It was a passionate and supportive community, full of diverse opportunities to engage with other congregants and with God. There were concerts and camp meetings that I attended with increasing frequency.

I tried as hard as I could to keep up with all my responsibilities, but the harder I tried the more my IBS symptoms started acting up. People at work and church became used to me bowing out of events or arriving late, though they never knew explicitly why. It wasn't easy but I was making it work.

In 1991 the Environmental Protection Agency effectively shut down the hog farms because pollutants from the waste lagoons had been leaking into drinking water and the air surrounding the sites. Around the same time, my dad realized that several hundred thousand dollars were missing from his construction company's account books. His house and business were both on the line. Luckily I was able to assume that debt, take over his company, and eventually successfully sued to get the money back. None of this happened without a great deal of stress and uncertainty that caused my symptoms to worsen. From then on I worked as a foreman and sold the houses we built. I was still busy but I had more control over my schedule and could stay closer to Yvonne, Junior, and Jeremy, who was born in 1991.

My father-in-law passed away suddenly in 1994. Since he was my flying buddy, I stopped flying and started fishing with my dad on weekends. I wanted to spend time with him while I could, and it always felt good to be with family. My family kept growing with Ryan in 1993 and Emily in 1996. My reputation in the area started to grow and business took off. I once sold six houses in one day, meeting people who drove by and letting them pick out a lot. Unfortunately, business started to take off too quickly, and I did not have the business skills to scale properly.

All through the nineties, at any given time we would have about seventy active home construction sites and thirty renovation projects. The amount of detail that I personally had to keep track of—supplies, codes, drainage, personnel management, and beyond—was staggering. It was an impossible amount of things to keep track of, and each of them was vitally important to at least one person. Home-buyers needed somewhere to live. My workers needed jobs. My suppliers needed to get paid. I had to ensure that everything was up to code so I wouldn't lose my license. I should have started saying no to projects, but it was difficult to turn down business. Just like when I was a kid, if there was a way to make extra money, I would do what it took.

It turned out I could not solve everything by elbow grease alone. My symptoms kept worsening and we had four young children at home. It was unsustainable. When the market took a major downturn after the attacks on September

11th, it was the beginning of a long downward spiral. My health, career, and reputation all started to go downhill. As houses went unsold, interest on loan payments began to accumulate, and within a short two years, the company had burned through all of its cash reserves. Early on, it was clear that this was going to happen, but there was no way to stop it apart from hope that people would want to buy houses again. Local people were especially discouraged as Fort Bragg locked down and ramped up training activity.

This powerlessness took a toll on me, and my IBS became debilitating. I could not leave the house. If I tried to, I couldn't get more than a few minutes down the road before I had to turn back. Every day was the same inescapable story, no matter how much I wanted to save the company. I was the guardian of the livelihoods of over a hundred people, many of them close friends and family, and I was failing. Trying to manage so many job sites over the phone was endlessly frustrating. My intestines were swelling to the point that my medications' effectiveness was waning. On top of this, I was so busy that I had to miss doctors' appointments and rarely was able to eat the foods that were healthy for me.

My gastrologist passed away in 2003, so I went to my primary doctor for my medication. Overwhelmed in his exam room, I wept in front of him. He told me I would not live much longer if I didn't sell the company. Even if I did live a long time, it would continue to be an intolerable existence. Hardly a life worth living. He prescribed me an antidepressant and referred me to a psychiatrist so I could find more ways of reducing my stress levels.

The psychiatrist was smoking in his office when I first met him. At the time, I thought it was an amusing eccentricity of his. He started me off on lithium and over the course of the next several months kept prescribing me additional ones. I held onto the business and everything got worse. I started to feel strange in addition to suffering from IBS and business stress. Eventually this psychiatrist had me on five medications. I was wary, but I had always trusted doctors and saw no reason to give up on a treatment that might turn around. By the summer of 2003, I was bedridden and unable to work due to the fact that the concoction of medications I had been taking reached a critical toxic level. Yvonne and the children came home one afternoon to find me lying on ground unconscious on the vacant lot next to our home. What I did not know at the time was that the medications the doctor was prescribing were slowly poisoning me to death.

I woke up in an emergency room, somehow looking down on my body from above. Doctors in the hallway were talking about me, saying I was the hundred-and-thirteenth patient of the same psychiatrist to be admitted to the hospital. I had no idea how he had avoided losing his license or reputation. Officially, it was lithium toxicity, which over the course of the past several months had slowly built up to dangerous levels in my blood. In addition to the injury done to my brain by the lithium, the interactions between the other medications amounted to a major mental setback.

Only a week after I was hospitalized, I heard that the psychiatrist had died from what I can only assume was a similar quack regime of psychoactive medications. He was unwell himself and has surviving family members, so I refrain from naming him. None of his other patients came forward publicly either, so I was left to account for the past months and my recovery thereafter without being able to name explicitly what had happened.

My children and family were frightened by what had happened. Something had to change. Back at home in bed, recovering from lithium toxicity and dogged by Crohn's, I signed the papers to sell my company. Yvonne and I hoped this would come as a relief and a much-needed respite from the tumultuous past several years. The debt from the houses I didn't sell, the faces of the men I had to tell there was no work to be done, the eerie developments half-filled with unsellable houses falling into disrepair: there was no getting away. The buyers out-lawyered me, expenses kept piling up, and by 2005 we had nothing.

Crohn's kept me from working, which created more stress and in turn made the Crohn's worse. Laid up in bed, I fell into a depression. I went from overseeing the construction of a hundred houses a year to having to sell my own house. No one understood how or why this could have happened, least of all the employees and relatives who depended on my success for their livelihoods. Yvonne did not want to explain that I was occupied in the bathroom twenty to twenty-five times a day, so rumors abounded about me and why I had lost the company. People assumed that because I had sold the company I was cashing out and retiring early; in reality, I hardly broke even, had four children to raise, and was barely getting by. The kids had grown up in a big house with a pool. When it sold, we moved back into an old, dilapidated double-wide I had remodeled on my dad's property. At forty-four I was starting from scratch, the same as when I was ten years old, looking for any and every opportunity to make a little money.

A lot older and a little wiser, I was blessed to have a family I could lean on, and we grew closer in that time, not only because of the physical proximity enforced by living in our upgraded double-wide. We all were trying hard to make the best of things. Despite my depression and Crohn's, I was determined to keep us afloat by hook or by crook. The precipitous decline of my kids' quality of life weighed on me, but I kept moving somehow. We spent all of 2006 in that home without kitchen cabinets: there simply wasn't the time or money to get them installed. I went to surrounding neighborhood's offering to clean their gutters, start a project, do anything that could earn us money. Because of the rumors surrounding the sale of my company that I had gambled it all away, betraying all of my employees and relatives for selfish and sinful reasons, it was difficult to find any kind of work. I was a pariah. To my shame, the kids would go to school without lunch money, but never complained. All of it seemed futile.

By 2006, Dad could see that I was not getting out much and was worried about my well-being. Having always been my boss, it was natural for him to take control. Eventually he confronted me and told me something had to change. He found a new job site on the coast, a beach house that needed framing. Same job, skills, and employer as when I was sixteen. I was afraid of my symptoms worsening and letting more people down. The beach was far enough away from Fayetteville though that I felt I could get somewhat of a fresh start. I put aside my pride and took the job.

Junior quit school to come work with me while we framed the house over the course of a couple of months toward the end of 2006. We lived together in a nearby rented beach house. Yvonne and the other kids appreciated having more space at home, and Junior and I enjoyed working with each other. It was a million-and-a-half-dollar house, so it was a big framing job. We worked with a crew of six or so guys, day by day piecing together the walls, floors, and roof with two-by-fours. Every angle had to be correct, every floor level, every dimension executed exactly according to plan. Otherwise, this creates major problems down the road for the rest of construction. This project set Junior behind in school, but he learned the trade that would become his career.

We finished framing the house by Christmas and went back home to be with Yvonne, Ryan, Jeremy, and Emily. There was nothing particularly festive about those holidays. Still, we held onto each other. The kids had gone from hosting pool parties to not having lunch money. It was uncertain whether I would get another project from my dad to work on. My Crohn's had not let up and it seemed like it never would. The future was uncertain and I was as broken a man as I had ever been.

CHAPTER 5

*Then I looked, and behold, a whirlwind was coming out
of the north, a great cloud with raging fire engulfing itself;
and brightness was all around it and radiating out of its
midst like the color of amber, out of the midst of the fire.*

—Ezekiel 1:4

Two weeks after Christmas, on January 8th, 2007, our lives
changed forever. It was a Monday. We were due at the site to
meet the contractor and finish up any loose ends and get paid
if it all looked right. It was a cold day and a quick inspection:
it looked fine and we got our check that morning. I had been
on both sides of this kind of transaction hundreds of times, so
having a frame job pass muster was nothing new to me. I was
depressed by my lack of job prospects beyond this. I would
have to return home that night with nothing to wake up for
in the morning besides my own miserable existence chained
to the toilet. But Junior and the guys were in a celebratory

mood, having been paid and not having another job to get to. After the crew got back to Fayetteville and cashed their checks, they called me up asking if Junior and I wanted to go fishing.

I knew of a good fishing spot on the Cape Fear River back toward Fayetteville on the same land my dad's hunting club rented. Along with the three sub-contractors, we each got our fishing poles and got ready to head down to the river together. One-by-one they piled in my red Ford pickup. The roads there often got muddy and impassable, and I was the only one with four-wheel-drive.

A while after turning into the property, we came to a broad field, at least four acres wide and surrounded by pine forest. The dirt road crested the hill at the center of the field and then descended toward the river toward a hole in the edge of the forest. In the pine-dominant forests in this part of North Carolina, the thickest and most hostile places are along the forests' edges. Bushes, briars, and weeds thrive along these boundaries because there is enough sunlight to reach them. Beyond about ten or fifteen feet into these woods, these plants lack the sunlight they need because of the year-round coverage by the evergreen canopy. One sees a fern here and there, but otherwise it's as open as a living room. The grill of my truck nosed its way through a thick tunnel of branches on the road to the river.

Fishing and palling around with the guys were the last things I wanted to do, but I wanted Junior to enjoy the result of his labor and sacrifice of his education. Even though I needed his help on the framing job, I regretted setting him so far back in school, especially because so many of my business problems would never have happened if I had gotten a business degree. I would have delegated more of my work, set firmer boundaries regarding which projects I took on, not taken every failure personally. The list goes on, yet at this point I would do anything that could give my kids a less impoverished life. It had become a habit of mine to keep my sadness to myself; this day wouldn't be much different from any other supervising their work at the job site. However, here, I could give myself as much space from them as I wanted. I could walk around and remember old hunting trips from when I was a boy, before life had ground me down, before I'd failed my family and friends. I would avoid where I got shot. As long as my stomach didn't act up, this might pass for a good day.

If you don't hunt or fish, you may question the appeal of going out to the middle of nowhere on a cold day. The guys had a small cooler of beer, sure, but that wasn't the draw. I myself hadn't drunk in years because Crohn's prevented my doing so. Neither is it a question of pursuing a rewarding hobby or enjoying each other's company, though I'm sure those can be pleasant aspects. It's about freedom: from work, bosses, family, responsibilities of all kinds. We could simply be who we were, safely distanced from anything that might really bother us. Nature was our boss. If the fish didn't bite or nothing turned up hunting, it was maybe a little disappointing. Compared to the disappointments of the outside world, these were joys by comparison. None of us even brought a cell phone. I had had one, but my doctor told me to get rid of it when he told me to sell my business, since the threat of impending disaster with every ring did a number on my nerves. We were in a world of our own, rumbling down the road as it ran parallel to the river and sloped gently downward. At 2:30, we emerged from the woods onto a sunny clearing beside the Cape Fear River and got our tackle boxes and poles from the truck bed.

∞

Under a corridor of the dry, gray-brown branches of deciduous trees, the river meandered by. It was still-seeming, deep water the color of strong sweet tea. With the largest river basin in all of North Carolina, it was rich water flowing through fertile land on its way south toward Wilmington. The amount of land whose waters flowed into it also meant it was fairly polluted with mercury, chromium, and other chemicals. Officially, people are warned to only eat the smaller, younger fish that aren't bottom-feeders or apex predators; but the guys weren't going to let that stop them from doing what they wanted.

After the guys got set up at the riverside I decided to go on a walk in the woods to the south. It was a relief to be alone. I felt okay about the fact that there were at least four people I hadn't let down, that at least this job had gone off without a hitch. I walked along the river looking for the birds and wildlife that had captivated me as a child hunting with my father. I came to an old oak tree beside a gully I remembered from when I was a kid, sat with my back against its trunk and watched the water ease by.

The angle of the sun that time of year was such that it had to fight through branches earlier in the day to reach the ground. Sunset that day was 5:18 p.m., but where I was it was starting to get dark by 4:00. I decided to walk back and check on the guys and Junior. They were there in the clearing chatting while they fished. There was more sunlight there as it wasn't so enclosed by old tall trees. Instead of holding their fishing poles, they had staked tree branches into the ground to prop them up out over the water. From these four rods extended fishing lines and lures drifting in the current. Attending to the rods and the project of fishing was the lightest of burdens. They were on the clock, but just barely. It was happy work.

"It's fixing to get dark here in a bit. How long do y'all think you wanna stay?" I asked.

"We're just getting started!" one of the guys said.

"Yeah we might build a fire," Junior said.

"Yeah why don't we get started on that," another said.

The five of us went into the surrounding forest and gathered sticks and logs of all sizes. Pretty quickly, we had assembled a large pile of fuel near the cooler and the fishing rods. It wasn't dark yet, but it was getting cold quickly, so the accomplishment of summoning warmth from the environment was already rewarding. It was work, survival, and leisure all in one. The stakes were trivial but the fire's comfort was real.

After they had got the fire going, I decided to go on another walk. Part of having been so depressed for so long was I got into the habit of leaving happy situations before they could turn bad, or my stomach acted up, or I was reminded of money problems. I left the guys to their business and immediately I was immersed in a much deeper darkness than on the riverside under the oak tree. There, I realized, I'd had at least some exposure to the clearing in the canopy made by the river. Here, I was fairly sealed in. At least the clearing lay ahead in about 200 yards. I did not know why I couldn't simply allow myself to enjoy one afternoon with my son. He left school to come to work with me and took care of me when I would get sick at the job site. He defended me to our friends and neighbors. He had seen the most of our old, easier life and bore the brunt of our family's material losses. He was the son to whom I'd given my own name. I wanted to have a good time with him, but I didn't want to ruin his time either. I kept walking away through the dry winter air.

As I walked, I heard a rustling in the brush to my left. These woods were as much my home as the bedroom I shared with Yvonne. I had probably spent months' worth of time there over the course of my life. Probably, it was some curious deer accompanying me on my lonely walk. I wanted to see whether it was a doe or a buck, and stopped walking. Then, the rustling stopped with me. Strange, I thought. I kept walking and the rustling began again, the same kind of stepping and branch displacement that a deer would cause if it were nudging its way through dense brush. It sounded close enough that if I peeked through at the right moment, I might meet its wide black eyes. I stopped, and the rustling stopped. I moved aside as much of the brush as I could with my arm, and saw nothing. I got down on my hands and knees to try to look underneath the brush. No sound of running away. Just silence and open forest beyond the brush. I kept walking, and again the rustling started beside me, this time sounding like it was a two-footed creature instead of four. I had hunted around there since I was five years old and never had cause to fear anything in those woods apart from bears and snakes, but an intense fear came over me. I walked faster to get to the clearing.

When I got to the open field, it seemed like the sun had set to the west behind the hill, though there was still enough light that I felt safe there. It was a massive relief to be able to see my surroundings. Whatever had been walking with me I had left behind in the woods.

I walked up the road to the west, dodging mud puddles, hopping from clump of grass to clump of grass in my tennis shoes, which I didn't want soaked for the rest of the evening. There was an open gate at the crest of the hill that we had driven in on. As I walked up the gentle slope of the hill, I was mainly keeping an eye on the dry patches on the road, and would look up occasionally toward the gate. About twenty yards away from it, I saw over the crest of the hill what looked like the top of the setting sun peaking out. A reddish-orange sliver sitting on the horizon, glowing.

I thought nothing of it and continued a couple more steps hopscotching my way along. This time I looked up and saw the entire sun. This was strange because I hadn't traveled far enough or gained enough height in those few steps to have had such a drastic change in my vantage point. The angle I had on it was pretty much the same, and yet instead of a sliver disappearing behind the curve of the spinning earth, it was the whole thing. It shone brilliantly, and yet it was still dark out in the field. I arrived at the crest of the hill a few steps afterward and from there could see the whole field, from forest edge to forest edge.

As I climbed the hill I saw a second sun, the same size and color as the first.

I was stunned. It took my breath away. I dropped to my knees in awe of what I was looking at. Not only was it strange that these sun-like objects did not light up the sun as suns would, but also that they were close, barely farther than the far side of the field two hundred yards away. Two flaming spheres hovering in the distance in perfect silence, each about forty-five feet in diameter, as big as houses. Having spent so many years flying, I knew that these were not any kind of aircraft I had ever heard of. After dropping to my knees I scrambled back down the hill to where I came from to hide in a reedy ditch. Terror, dread, and curiosity rushed through my head as water from the cold mud seeped through my sleeves and pants.

Should I stay? Should I go? What on earth could those things be?

I thought of Junior and the other guys down on the river. Junior and I had always been close to each other. Just like my dad and me, everything I did, Junior did too. I worried for him and wanted to get back to him, not knowing what was going on or how I could help, but at least we would be together. Before I went back to them though, I wanted to get a better look so I wouldn't make them panic for no reason. Slowly I edged my way out of the reeds, staying low, toward the crest of the hill where I had seen them. As I crept up, I saw them again, exactly where they had been before, swirling red-orange flames like the sun when it is about to set but is dimmed enough by the atmosphere that you can look directly at it for a few moments without hurting your eyes.

Awestruck, mesmerized, I watched them hover.

I remembered Junior and decided I had to run back to be with him. This was too strange. It was a long dark quarter mile back to the clearing, and a million thoughts raced through my head. As soon as I prepared myself to make the run down to the river, at that very moment I decided to run, I looked back one last time. A third one suddenly appeared high above and dropped down instantly alongside the other two. It was as though this one was in charge. It knew my fear. This all happened in the split second I decided to run and this sudden realization shook me to the core. It was as though it had been watching me lie low in the reeds, trying to process what I had seen and what I should do. The three of them sat there over the tree-line now, unmoving but swirling with their red-orange flames.

I felt an intense connection with them. They watched me watch them. My hair stood on end in the realization that I was being looked at by these things. Again, I tried to hide from them, lowering myself into the reeds.

The next thing I remember, I was fifty yards from the fire, running toward it. I was terrified but relieved to be back in the clearing and away from the field. The guys were going to lose it when I told them what I had just seen. Hopefully they all could get in the truck and come see them too. Out of the dark I ran into the small circle of visibility around the fire, and I noticed a couple of odd things. My truck had been moved and was now pointed toward where I had just run from. I remembered it being pointed toward the river. The large pile of sticks and logs we had gathered was now gone, and the fire itself had dwindled to a few ankle-high licks of flame.

"Where in the world have you been?" one of them asked.

"What do you mean? I was just up the road in the field."

"No you weren't. We've been up there all night looking for you. You see your truck moved? We've looked everywhere in that field."

"What are you talking about? I was just gone a few minutes... Wait, where's Junior?"

"He went back to where you first went walking. Two of us took the truck and drove everywhere up and down that road looking for you while the third stayed and tended the fire."

I panicked. The only thought in my head, repeating itself louder and louder: *Where is my child? Where is my child? Where is my child? Where is my seventeen year-old baby?* Junior. Gone. Alone on a cold night into a head of woods about fifty-miles long. Looking for me, who yet again had arrived at some dire circumstance and needed saving.

Immediately I started jogging south to look for him. I could not have cared less about whatever it was I had seen. I ran faster, shouting after him in the trees with no flashlight. I ran faster, hearing nothing in response. I broke through the brush, briars and thorns lashing my face. I kept pushing through, trying to get past the thickets.

"Da…"

"Daa…"

Just to my side, I saw a figure trying to stand up in the thick interweaving of branches. Something grabbed my arm.

"Dad!!"

"DAD! WHY DID YOU LEAVE ME? WHERE DID YOU GO? THERE WERE THESE CREATURES I WAS PARALYZED I COULDN'T MOVE!"

"Junior, I've only been gone twenty minutes."

"No Dad, you've been gone all night!!"

I led him back to the fire and he was fiercely mad at me for abandoning them all. I could not wrap my head around why they were saying that I had been gone all night. I wasn't drinking anything. I hadn't eaten anything unusual that day. I wasn't on any medication. There was the strange gap in my memory between cowering in the field and arriving back at the campfire, but that could have been because of a spike in adrenaline or merely a product of acute panic. It made no sense that more than four hours had passed.

Walking back to the fire, Junior started to describe how he had gotten so deep in those thickets. He had been the first to worry about where I was, leaving the others to fish while he went off looking for me. It had been two hours, it was dark and getting colder. No matter how depressed I was, I wouldn't have left them for more than an hour. At first, Junior started down the pitch-black path toward the field where I had walked two hours earlier. It was a fairly straight shot down the eighth of a mile toward the field, so you could see a long way within the enclosed tunnel of growth. As he was walking and his eyes were adjusting, he saw deep in the woods two deep red spheres drifting from the left side of the path (where the field was) to the right (where the river ran parallel to the path). They seemed to him about the size of bowling balls. It spooked him because he knew I didn't have any kind of light on me, or why someone with that kind of light would cross over from one side of the path to the other with no regard for the difficulty of traveling through the undergrowth.

Junior turned back from the path toward the fire again and told the guys what he had seen. He told them about a red light moving through the woods, and the guys told him to stop joking around and trying to scare them. At this point, the guys had gotten a little worried for me, and didn't want to deal with a seventeen-year-old's pranks.

Fed up and scared, Junior turned back around toward the road and again walked to the point in the path where you can see a long way until it turns west toward the field. He was starting to call out for me, getting no response. Again down the path, Junior saw the two red orbs float across, this time from right to left toward the field. Except this time, they stopped in the middle of the path and came toward him. They approached so quickly that he didn't have time to get back to the fire. He dove deep into the brush, backing up as he went, to hide from them.

He lay stock-still watching the lights approach in the overgrowth. They stopped fifteen feet away from him, hovering close to the ground blocking his path back to the fire. He described them as two little entities, glowing softly with red fiery eyes. The eyes were mechanical in nature, about an inch and a half round, opening and closing like shutters, straight up and straight down. The little translucent beings walked around playing with stuff. They would pick up sticks and pieces of trash and look at them curiously, then throw them back on the ground. One of them was always watching him, guarding him, like they had a job to do. He couldn't scream and he found that he was paralyzed, unable to yell or move.

For two hours, my son lay in the brush in abject terror, trying to scream for help, trying to move back to the fire. When

I went looking for him, he could hear me calling out to him but wasn't able to respond. It was sheer luck that I entered the forest near enough to him to hear his efforts at saying "Dad."

∞

We arrived back at what was left of the fire. The three men had heard me talking about lights hovering in the air and now heard Junior weeping, upset, talking about these red-eyed creatures that had paralyzed him. These were rough, tough men who'd worked construction all their lives. They had been in plenty of dangerous situations and were by no means quick to scare. But these hardened guys were starting to act spooked too.

The sky was dazzlingly clear. Something about winter air brings a clarity to the night sky, and it seemed like a sea of stars hung over us. Frost had fallen on the grass, which troubled me, making me question how sure I was about only having been gone twenty minutes. Junior was saying he wanted to go home. *Take me home. I wanna go home. Please, please let's go home.* The poles weren't packed up, still resting in their props, lines drifting into the river, but we were ready to go.

"Oh my god," one of the men said, pointing up at the sky.

Nine balls of light, about the size and color of Venus on a clear night, shone from far up in the sky and started to gather into one circle directly above us. The circle began to rotate and then scattered like salt across the sky. As this happened, three of them began to flash and descended into the woods across the river from us. It wasn't a wide river; my daughter had swum across it and back as a six-year-old. These were the same size as the ones I had seen, about forty-five feet across, but pulsating a brilliant white and electric blue light, like the blinding light from a welder's torch. They hovered there silently, blazing stupefyingly bright. It was a brief moment we just watched before all hell broke loose.

CHAPTER 6

His body was like topaz, his face like lightning, his eyes like flaming torches, his arms and legs like the gleam of burnished bronze, and his voice like the sound of a multitude.

—Daniel 10:6

None of us had seen anything like this before. Our fight or flight instincts were confused as our expressions morphed from wonder to terror. We were no more certain we could fight these things than we could outrun them. How does one respond to an event that should not be happening? Education, religion, and culture are aimed at preparing us for what *is* or what *might occur.* There is no set protocol for coming face to face with the impossible. At 11:30 p.m. in early January, a team of framers, friends, a father, and son did the best they could with all the knowledge and courage they had.

"This is it. It's all over! Nice knowing you guys, we had a good run."

"Shut up let's go."

"Let's get in the truck and go right now. Right now!"

"I can't believe it. I can't believe it."

"I want to see my wife again damn it! Get in the truck!"

"Forget about the fishing poles come on!"

"Forget about the cooler."

I got in the driver's seat and the rest of them piled in, screaming at me to floor it, screaming at each other, screaming at the lights, screaming just because adrenaline demanded they do something. If it was the end of the world, if the planet was being invaded, what would we need to do before we died? Who did they know who was a doomsday prepper? Who had guns, if guns could do anything to these red-eyed beings? How quickly would it all be over? We flailed trying to save ourselves, trying to quickly and confidently make life-defining choices. Who mattered to us the most? Should we stay and try to fight? Could we save the world if we did? All these thoughts and hundreds more ran through our minds and in our random frenzied shouts. If there were one guy fewer, we might have been dumbstruck, but somehow we organized ourselves to get out of there. I pressed my foot to the gas as the last of the four doors closed.

I headed toward the road out through the woods. In my sideview mirror I saw the fishing tackle and cooler lit by that flickering blue-white light. The only thing worse than the end of the world was if I got us all killed in a wreck for no reason, so I put my brights on and kept my eyes on the muddy, overgrown road. We made it into the forested section of the road, which was a relief; whatever those orbs were, they allowed us to gain distance from them. Then, when I thought there would only be darkness and branches lit red by the brake lights, one of the orbs appeared, following us down the path. We were far from finished. I kept driving and looked back again. It wasn't there anymore. The volume of the screams and the shouts in the cab was deafening.

We turned and made it to the field, driving up toward the crest of the hill where I had first seen the two red-orange orbs. It seemed we were in the clear and the guys were begging me to floor it out of there. I accelerated toward the top of the hill and the truck went airborne a couple of feet.

The two fiery red-orange orbs were still at their original location. The third one that had appeared when I began to run seemed to be in control and was now down in the middle of the road before us. It changed from a forty-five foot ball of red fire to an egg-shaped dazzling array of light that appeared like crystals, spikes, revolving around and around.

Immediately I slammed on the brakes and the five of us crashed forward against our seatbelts, sliding ten uneasy feet closer to it on the greasy mud. Blocking our path was the same third orb that had appeared over my head, watching me watch the other two. Forty-five feet wide, it had an oblong shape like a tic-tac lying on its side. It hovered about five feet off the ground. This time it was the same brilliant, electric white light of the orbs back by the river. Dazzlingly brilliant rays spun around its surface, flaring off in spiked blazing bolts as if it were so charged with energy it couldn't help but emit this luminousness. The ditches and mud on either side of the road were too impassible to try to get around it. We were trapped. Obstinate, the radiant egg-shaped object simply sat there, sparking its otherworldly beams.

One of the guys said he knew of a family that lived in a trailer at the far edge of the field. I turned the truck to the right and crossed a ditch and headed straight for the mobile home. We were hoping to use a phone at the very least, and to see if the people there were seeing what we were seeing. As we looped around to the trailer, we could see its windows were lit up. I drove straight up to their small porch and the glass-paned storm door. Their main door had been left wide open. Their TV was on, but no one was on the couch. One of the guys jumped out and knocked and knocked on the storm door. Banging and pounding on it while he called out yelling if anyone was home. No one came to the door.

I looked at the guys in the back seat and could see through the back window that the orb had come within 150 yards of us and was hovering 5 feet over the road blocking our only exit. With the screams and shouts coming from everyone looking back, I started blaring the horn to get the attention of my friend standing on the porch steps and anyone inside the trailer.

Still no one came to the door.

Back the way we came was still the only exit from the field. After so many years hunting on this land, we were the quarry.

Like a fox on the run from dogs, we were running out of options and time: each turn could be our last. There was no way of knowing if we were being herded toward a barrage of gunfire. On the other hand, we figured that if these things wanted us dead, they'd already had plenty of opportunities to do so.

We drove back and were again confronted by the same ball of fire. Trying to get a better look this time, I eased the truck up thirty feet closer than our previous stopping point. It blazed there as it had before, hovering just off the ground. We stopped, mesmerized, watching. What was it? How was it? Why us?

Out of nowhere, we heard a gunshot. The report of the gun slowly faded under the sound of the idling engine. Despite having been shot, I was comfortable with the sounds of gunshots as long as the gun wasn't in the hands of an eight-year-old. No one in the truck could tell which direction the gun had fired from. No one could tell what the gun was aiming at: us, the lights, or if it was just some trigger-happy drunk that happened to be roving through that field.

There was another gunshot a few seconds later, sending us looking out the cab windows and the sunroof in every direction. At the third gunshot, the egg-shape began to rotate, pivoting what appeared to be its nose directly at our truck. It seemed to be *aiming*. Soundlessly, it approached us. Gathering speed. As it got closer it became no less decipherable. There were no gaps or consistent variations to the pattern of its general brilliance. Like watching the flames of a campfire, no two moments watching it were the same.

Just when we thought we were about to get rammed head-on or vaporized by this blazing tic-tac, it started to gain altitude. It cleared a twenty-foot-tall roadside tree in front of us, then slowly moved over the roof of the truck. A buzzing static fell over the truck as though we had been charged by collateral energy the object was emitting. We looked up through the open sunroof as it passed slowly and quietly directly overhead climbing toward the tree-line. It paused there, just above the tops of the trees, and rotated itself again, pointing upward north. Suddenly it shot up into the sky like it was fired out of a cannon. In a moment, it had disappeared into the night sky.

The show seemed to be over. The guys thought they might have a chance to see their wives before the full-on invasion took place and made it clear to me that was their intention. I had been their boss, but now, first and foremost, we were all one thing: prey. With a chance to escape—whether it be some fluke of a mistake or our hunter had lost interest—I floored it out of that field, flinging mud behind us as we went. When we got to the paved road, we saw another orb keeping pace with us over the trees to our right. The show was not over.

I ran stop signs, but the way the guys were yelling at me to drive, I couldn't have run them fast enough. With Junior in the car, I refused to drive any more dangerously than I was. If these things were going to get us, let them: I wouldn't be the one who killed us. There was a beauty to the orbs that calmed me, and I found I was curiously immune to the men's chaos, rage, and fear.

"Faster!!" They screamed. The orb above the trees did not seem to have a problem with the speed I was going. It seemed laughable that a truck could outrun this thing, but I understand these guys wanting to try to get away at all costs. We made it about a mile down the road and came alongside about two hundred acres that had recently been timbered. This was all still part of the same land that my dad's hunting club had used, so everyone in the truck had been back there and knew there was nothing but woods back there. A whole city skyline's worth of lights blared at us, just above the stumps of the clear-cut land. It looked like hundreds of these lights pulsated near the ground, sending the men into yet another level of frenzy while I kept calm. One eye on the road and one on the lights.

We drove south past the Cape Fear River Baptist church. Thirty-six years earlier, in that same churchyard, I had been surprised and mesmerized by the yellow saucer-sized eyes of an owl before getting shot a week later. Twenty-five years earlier, I had pulled over there to reconsider my jealous feelings and turn back to a cookout.

We came to a curve and saw yet another orb hovering over a powerline. Defying the men's urgings, I slowed the truck down to the speed limit: thirty-five. In an overwhelming surge of emotions, every detail of that night twenty-five years ago came back to me at once. This was the dead man's curve where my first wife died in my arms. I would not let this same curve make an end to me or my son too. I slowed down to fifteen miles an hour.

I could not say why, but this orb's presence above the site of the most traumatic moment of my life filled me with a sense of peace. It was an immersion in supreme grace. Time seemed to slow down. For the first time, I truly believed that what had happened to her was not my fault. For the first time, I truly believed that being able to hold her in my arms as she died was a gift to both of us. My jealousy had not ruined our lives. I could almost see us there in the grass. Two bloody twenty-year-old kids holding onto each other and, what little remained of their shared life.

The men were pounding on my seat, howling like hell at me to put my foot on the gas. I wanted desperately to get out of the truck and watch this huge black rectangular shaped silhouette hovering just above the high voltage power lines. There appeared to be a row of square glowing lights, like windows, down the side facing us. The enormity of it took my breath away. I wanted to receive all of its message. I wanted to stay with these feelings. I wanted to hold onto this guiltless peace forever being in the very spot I was twenty-five years earlier.

"CHRIS! GO!"

"DAMMIT CHRIS LET'S GET OUT OF HERE!!!"

The moment ended and time sped up again. The men had decided that the guy who lived the farthest away, who was also the biggest, could go home first. We went and dropped him off, then headed back toward the powerline. The other two happened to live near the dead man's curve, so as we approached it we could see the same huge rectangular craft still hovering over the powerline. The two men's wives had been terribly worried and came out in their front yards to meet us. After we dropped those two off, Junior begged me to not go back by that curve, and I listened to him. We took the long way home, stunned by the sudden silence in the truck as much as what we had just seen. On the highway we saw eight cars pulled over as if they were looking back toward the powerline. It was an eerie drive. Despite my positive experience, I couldn't help but feel we were just biding time and waiting for the other shoe to drop.

Yvonne and the other three children were away visiting family, so I could only hope they were okay. When we got back home, Junior was still in a state of panic. He went around the house turning on every exterior and interior light, closing all the blinds, locking every door, including the bathroom that had no window, where he hunkered down. I went straight to the TV to turn on the news. Surely this was a world-wide invasion. Surely there was some breaking report that could explain what had just happened to us. There was nothing on but a rerun of an Elvis special.

Over the sound of the TV I heard the whomp-whomp-whomp of what I thought was a big helicopter heading in the direction of the river. Something *had* happened there. We had not totally lost our minds. Then I heard the dog kennel erupt barking and wailing. Having spent most of my life around hunting dogs, I could hear fear in their voices. There were about fifteen in the kennel at the time, and it must have been all of them barking with all their might. Every breath, fierce with terror, it was as though they were fighting for their lives. I had only heard this kind of barking when they came across the scent of a bear.

Junior came out of the bathroom and I told him we better check on the dogs and my dad's garage in case it was getting broken into. My dad had kept it as a workshop for his boats and hunting and fishing gear. *Please Daddy please no don't go out there please Daddy please.* He was vehemently opposed to the idea. Eventually I convinced him to come with me and not bring a flashlight, and use the darkness to our advantage to take a look in the garage from far away. I said our hundred-and-ten pound Chesapeake Bay retriever, Rosie, would come with us to protect us. I had hunted with Rosie too, and she knew how to flush what we hunted out of the woods. We had our plan and we hoped we could put an end to this for the night.

The kennel was fifty yards back in the woods next to the garage. The kennel was a fairly large structure with a roof and lights and had a full view of the garage. Rosie was on the back porch barking along with the dogs in the kennel, the hair on the back of her neck standing on end. I opened the porch door and Rosie leapt off the steps straight toward the kennel. She got forty feet away and stopped to look back at us, wanting to know if we were coming too. We moved to go down the steps and she took off sprinting into the trees.

Junior had agreed to come but he was still terrified, holding a fistful of the back of my shirt, refusing to let me get out of arm's reach of him.

We sneak around on a path that loops through the woods around the side, hoping we could surprise whoever it was in the garage. We got close to the kennel, which was submerged in the darkness of a heavy forest, the din of the dogs growing louder and louder as we approached. I noticed the dogs weren't barking toward the garage, which was toward the houses, but back behind the kennel, where there was nothing but woods. This was strange to me. If somebody had come to rob the garage, they would have come from the road and then would have run back toward the road to get away. Rosie was a good bird dog, and had waited for us by the kennel, growling and barking with the rest of the dogs. She too was pointing toward the back of the woods. Having hunted with Rosie and other dogs my whole life, we both knew what to do. I would send Rosie after whoever was back there, and I would run back toward the clearing to watch what got flushed out. It was a basic hunting tactic I had done hundreds of times.

I tapped Rosie on the rear and she dashed away in long bounding strides into the thickets. Junior and I turned back to the clearing to keep up with Rosie and whatever she was chasing. We ran down the path and got to the grass, which was slick with frost. I slipped as I turned to look where I thought Rosie might emerge. I was so focused on watching that strip of tree-line that I didn't realize that Junior let go of my shirt.

I figured he was still behind me, but he had sprinted back to the house instead. I ran as hard as I could to the back of the clearing where I heard Rosie barking and stopped myself against an oak tree at the edge of the woods. The way she was barking, I could tell that whatever was in the woods wasn't going to stay in there for very long.

Rosie was still in the thickets somewhere barking. Panting, leaning against the tree, I was trying to catch my breath and figure out what to do next. I looked over my shoulder expecting to see Junior behind me. I felt terrible for allowing us to get separated when he was so scared. I turned fully around.

"Oh my god."

Standing four feet in front of me was a three-and-a-half foot tall being, gently glowing the color of the moon. Two red eyes. A glassy translucent triangle was fixed on its chest. Again I shook with terror.

"I'm sorry. You got me. I'm sorry for running. I surrender."

As I said this, the being was responding: "You don't understand. We are not here to hurt you. We are here to help you."

A few seconds passed. Still on the being's trail, Rosie came closer, barking through the thicket. She leapt out from the bushes and in that same instant the being disappeared. Unfazed, Rosie kept sprinting in a straight line a quarter mile away, leaving me shocked and befuddled in the backyard. What had happened?

I thought of Junior back in the house, where I hoped he was safe. I jogged back over the frosty grass and was relieved to see him waiting for me staring out the back door. I did not know how I was going to tell him what had happened. My nerves were shot, so once I knew he was safe, all I could think about was having a cigarette. He was asking me question after question, but all I could do was ignore him and collect my thoughts. In my study, I lit a Marlboro and planned to crack the window since Junior wouldn't let me go outside. Junior begged me to not even open the blinds.

I opened the blinds enough to open the window. The backyard floodlights were still on. On the grass fifty feet behind the house was another being. This one much larger and taller than the first. Patiently, deliberately, it walked toward the house.

I slammed down the blinds.

"Junior we got to get out of here right now."

We ran out the front door to the truck and were able to get away. We drove to a hayfield five miles away and parked right in the middle of it. If anything came toward us, it would have to travel a long way over land we had a panoramic view of. The stars were out. The waning gibbous moon cast a blue light over the dry, brittle field. We watched around the truck in every direction until our exhaustion took over and we slept.

CHAPTER 7

In the cold cab, I woke to the empty field. Junior was still sleeping curled up on the back seat. Mist rolled across the brittle grass. Condensation from our breath fogged the corners of the windshields.

Morning. *Why did my son and I sleep in this field?* I knew the answer and I didn't. My head flooded with the events from the day before, apart from the four hours I was gone. The world hadn't ended while we slept. The same winter sun sent its rays splintering through the treetops to the east. The sky hadn't fallen: would it even feel like anything to have the sky fall on you? Or was it always falling? Dark blue wisps of clouds slipped by as the last of the visible stars winked away.

The field was like any hay field and I marveled at how normal it appeared. Just a winter morning in the south, the vague hues of night giving way to daylight. Exactly like the many dawns I'd spent on hunting trips with nothing to do but wait in silence. Baffled, ashamed, I was not even sure my son and I were safe. My mind raced as I tried to reckon with what had happened and what I should do next. These are the same questions I still wake to every day.

When I don't know what to do, I return to the familiar. I checked in with Junior and drove us home. All the lights were on and the shades all closed as we had left them. The yard, my dad's house, the kennel, all unchanged. Birds were singing and Junior and I were hungry for breakfast, having not eaten the night before. Seconds ticked indifferently on.

I called the three subcontractors to check in. They told me they were going to get all the fishing gear we had left on the riverbank. In meek disbelief they rambled down to the site we had run screaming from the night before. They hurried to get in and out of there, but there was no sign that any of it had happened apart from our footprints and a black pile of ash where the fire had been.

They decided on their way out to pay a visit to the people who lived in the mobile home at the edge of the field. They asked them if they had seen or heard anything unusual the night before. The answer was no. They asked about lights in the sky, if they had heard the knocking at the door or the truck honking, and they shrugged saying they had been home all night. No one had gone out shooting, nor had they heard the three shots that sent the egg-shaped orb flying toward us then away into the night sky. With both their cars in the driveway, their main door wide open, lights on, and close 10:00 p.m., how could they not hear our frantic screams, the pounding on the glass storm door, or the blaring horn of the truck?

It can be very hard to predict how someone will react to news that runs contrary to their understanding of what is possible. It challenges a person to reconsider what they know, which can be anything and everything between frightening, angering, and thrilling. The subcontractors, Junior, and I went through all these intense emotions that day and afterward. When we told the people in the mobile home what we had seen, their disbelief came with judgment: of our character, sanity, and reputation. Telling them what we had seen marked us as different from them. Overnight, we were forced outside the community of what is acceptable to discuss and assert. A breach of trustworthiness in this respect undermines an entire social existence. We could see on their faces that we had no common ground. It wasn't that we disagreed on the basic terms of reality, but that we had had an experience that caused us to question what they were. We all realized then that this would have to be handled carefully, for my own good and for my family's reputation, which had already fallen so far because of the troubles with my business. Trying to figure out how to live with this experience was almost more confounding than the experience itself. We had no answers, but we had each other. That has always been enough to keep going.

∞

That Tuesday night passed quietly without event, as exhausted and overwhelmed we were by what we had witnessed. Such extended periods of extreme fear and adrenaline had taken their toll on us. Junior walked over to tell my dad what had happened, and before he could finish was laughed at and turned away. Dad had just chalked it up to him being a crazy kid on drugs. Unfortunately, I would come to learn that my dad's responses were quite generous compared to most of the reactions our telling has garnered. Yvonne and the kids were out of town till Friday, so I had some time to try to account for what had happened and figure out how to parent Junior through the most traumatic night of his life. I felt rotten for having abandoned him for so long, that his sense of safety at home was forever compromised, that his conceptions of reality were so dramatically challenged at such a young age. At seventeen, he had barely begun to develop a conception of reality.

That Wednesday night, Junior and I were watching TV at home when the dogs started barking again. We were filled with dread. *Not now, not at home, not to scare my son again.* Dread turned to anger and I grabbed my rifle and went out back to the tree farm against Junior's pleas.

"Junior, I have to see what this is. I have to finish this."

The night air was thickened with the dog's baying. This time they were pointed toward a neighbor's plot of land that was a Christmas tree farm. The thick fir trees in that direction made an impenetrable wall. Whatever was in there would be well hidden. Whatever was in there would have to deal with me and my gun.

I crossed over a broken fence and began to see a brilliant light through the evergreen branches. From playing on that land as a boy, I knew that the only way to see or travel through there was to army crawl on hands and knees underneath. The trees were mainly quite tall and had a few feet of clearance from the needle-strewn ground to their lowest branches. As I got down, I again saw the brilliant light, this time directly. It blinded me. I felt a powerful humming static reverberating around my body. It was as though a tremor ran through me, intensifying as I crawled closer, rifle cradled in my arms. It quickly became too intense to continue approaching it. The sensation was close to the resistance met by trying to touch opposing ends of magnets together. A painful, prolonged zap ran through me. The light, or the force of it, drove me to crawl backward the way I had come. Whatever was there would not let me approach, rifle or not, no matter how determined I was to protect Junior.

When I got far enough out of the trees to stand up, I came to the same broken fence I had entered by. In front of me, flickering from total invisibility into a translucent, moon-like glow, stood two of the beings I had seen two nights before. They were short, with red eyes and the same elongated upward-pointing triangle on their chests.

As we stood there looking at each other, an overpowering emotional understanding crashed over me. They communicated to me this obliterating epiphany: the singular, ultimate importance of all living beings. It was a thought and a philosophy as much as it was sweeping emotion. All my memories, all my thoughts, all my emotions were changed. My whole worldview reorganized itself around this foundational priority. A scope of meaning, grander and nobler than anything I had ever felt, bloomed around every lifeform. We living things shared this meaning that summoned in me the utmost care, respect, and, above all, love.

As this happened, shame and disgust arrived, sickening my heart. *What was this murdering tool in my hand? How could I undo the harm I had done to these innocent creatures my whole life?* The beings stared blankly back at me as I processed all of this. I sank into a profound state of mourning and regret for having killed.

Poof, they flickered invisible again. I gasped in the dark. Suddenly alone, or so it appeared, I felt my sadness turn to relief. Finally, it seemed I had been given a clue as to what this all was about. A problem existed that might be fixed. A sickness that could be healed. The terror and trauma of the past days were pointed toward some benevolent end. This was to become my work, whenever and however that work appeared to me. This was the message that the beings had gone to such extraordinary ends to convey. This understanding remains at the core of who I am. I never squash a bug, I never fish or hunt. Through all my trials since, this belief has guided me, giving me the hope and courage I have needed to carry on. Friday, Yvonne and the kids would come back to a changed father and son.

CHAPTER 8

The experience wrought a change in Junior and me that everybody had to reckon with in their own way: my relatives, co-workers, our church, even other grocery shoppers browsing the produce section. Most often, when their eyes met mine (if they even risked looking directly at me) there was nothing recognizable in them but pity or scorn. I had lost my company, and now appeared to have lost my mind clinging to what they could only understand as a desperate man's unlikely fantasy. Rumors about me spread like wildfire. There is no nobler beginning to gossip than a guise of concern or of warning.

"That poor family, after all they've been through."

"I wouldn't let that guy operate a hammer, much less a forklift."

"The devil is at work in that man."

Yvonne and the kids came back from their trip. With Junior being so shaken and me being so profoundly changed, there was no hiding what had happened. Yvonne met the news with some generosity and a lot of skepticism. She thought I had had a relapse from the medication the quack doctor had put me on two years before. I might have considered this explanation if it weren't for the fact that four other people saw what I saw. No aftershocks from the lithium toxicity resulted in anything but depression in me. We loved each other and our children first and foremost, so we navigated our domestic life around the event as best we could. There were school lunches to buy, homework to do, dinner to cook, sports practices to drive to, stomach aches to soothe. The other children believed their oldest brother and father and listened to us with great excitement and curiosity.

It quickly became clear that Yvonne would not tolerate talk of what had happened in the house. No mother as fiercely devoted to her children would have. Even if she had been there that night, she understood the social cost of attesting to such an event in such a religious community. The Pentecostal church sees Halloween as a pagan ritual used by Satan to encourage demonic worship; if the holy book did not account for its presence in our world, then it was necessarily either a sinful folly or the work of the devil. Yvonne knew that the rumor would spread, and she knew that Junior needed to be believed, so it was a difficult position for her to be in. She could neither affirm or deny what had happened to her friends, family, and fellow congregants. The church her great grandfather had helped create was too ingrained in our lives to turn our backs on. I remain so grateful to her for managing to strike this balance and keep our family together. Her patience and grace in the face of this still amazes me.

Everybody around me faced terrible consequences for not flat-out denying what had happened to me. Yvonne, the children, and my parents all did the best they could to laugh it off or change subjects. The pity and scorn I faced was passed on to my family. Every time we left the house, we risked terrible treatment. Almost no one defended us precisely because of how laughable the rumors were or how I had earned this by somehow going against God. The worst of all was that my kids were mocked at school, either for what they asserted or for having a crazy dad. I still regret the shame and ridicule I caused them to suffer.

In the weeks following January 8th, 2007, all my Crohn's symptoms disappeared. I stopped taking my medication. Possibilities opened up before me. I didn't have to stay close to my bathroom all day and could find steady work again. Unfortunately as rumors spread, it became harder and harder to find anyone who would risk hiring me. To relatives, people I had formerly employed, people who didn't know me but had heard a story somewhere, I was persona non grata. Unfortunately, this happened as soon as I gained freedom from that debilitating illness.

Stuck at home, unable to talk about what had happened, I retreated into myself. The memory of those nights had an irresistible pull on me. Every day, the mystery of what had happened vexed me. I wondered and wondered why I had felt no fear, where I had been those four hours, what it meant that this bath of peace and compassion came along with such unforgiving social exile. In particular, I wondered about the many times I had approached total ruin. God put me through the wringer, bringing me within inches of my life on several occasions only to bring me back, allowing me to build a successful business only to slip back into poverty.

Locked in my study, where I would often sleep alone, I would attempt to remember what had happened on that second walk of mine. The astonishment of seeing a second sun in the distance, then a third directly above me, watching me. I could retrace those moments, footstep by footstep, as I went to hide in the reeds. The blazing swirls of brilliant tangerine flames in the twilight. Then, nothing. Next thing I know, I'm running, forty feet from the smoldering remains of the campfire. If I set my mind on the time between, an intensely nauseating headache settled over me. I had never had a headache that was overwhelmingly painful. There was no way out of this labyrinth of questions. I got quiet and spent as much time alone as I could. If everyone turned their back on me, turning my back on them was the only thing I could do to stave off my misery.

∞

One night in the stuffy air of that sad study, after a family dinner at which I'd said nothing but the perfunctory necessities of fatherhood, I heard an odd sound. *Hoot hoot... hooo hoot*

hoot... hoot hoo... Loud, urgent, insistent in some kind of communication, a great-horned owl bellowed over the house's tinny roof. It was January, just a week after Yvonne and the kids had come home, when I was only beginning to realize the extent of my second ostracism. Yvonne and I stopped talking, passing each other wordlessly in the hall.

Hoothoot... hoot hooooot...

It seemed my isolation was not total, though I wanted it to be. All night long, it sounded like a few different owls were hashing out some territorial dispute directly over my family's heads. The hickory tree dropped some of its nuts on the roof, which was nothing unusual. No one slept well that night. All night long they bellowed, cooed, and screeched over us. The next day, I looked in the trees nearest the house, and saw no owls. They would come back almost every night and stayed all winter. Sometimes the kids would get fed up and go outside to yell at them to be quiet. When all I wanted to do was lock myself away, those owls reminded me there was a world that had not rejected me, where I was not a failure or a father, where I was simply one vulnerable living thing among others trying to survive.

These owls' reminders of the peacefully indifferent natural world were persuasive. I went to the outdoor store and bought a sleeping bag, a backpack, and a small gas stove. I had never camped before apart from fishing with my dad at the beach, but the wilderness called out to me and I had no choice but to answer it.

I sold what few toys and tools I had remaining to try to keep us afloat. I couldn't keep up with the payments on my truck and lost it. Yvonne had to live a double life, continuing to be part of a church that saw me as troubled and demonically possessed, while also tolerating and supporting me as best she could. The kids had to endure the sight of church leaders sprinkling me with holy water as though I were a monster. The standard-bearers of goodness we had raised them to respect cast me out of their ranks as insane, sinful, untouchable. They even came unbidden to our property to sprinkle holy water as if the ground itself needed to be purged of some Satanic curse I had brought into my family. There was no fixing these things; they would simply have to be lived with.

To stay alive in this circumstance, and to not run away from my family and community forever, I either holed up in my study or went to the woods. That winter, and all through that year, I went on trips to the Appalachian trail. Sometimes I would stay for over a week, sometimes I would visit for few days to volunteer maintaining the trail. I would sleep out as often as I could, lying on my back in my sleeping bag looking up at the stars. There were certain bald mountaintops I particularly loved, where there were no sounds of highways and little light pollution. Families of black bears, deer, hawks, and squirrels roved harmlessly around me. Their company soothed me, and I was treated with something like dignity.

When I was looking for more things I could sell, I came across an old CB radio and it occurred to me I might find a friend who didn't know or care about who I was. I remembered the Caterpillar rental facility had a hundred-and-thirty-one-foot-tall antenna that they no longer needed and I could have it if I could take it down. Since I had so much experience repairing electronics and appliances as a boy, it was easy to get the whole set-up rigged up at home. When I had used the radio as a kid forty years before, I had used Hunter or Hound Dog as my callsign or handle. I turned it on for the first night, not knowing what to expect from such an outdated technology.

"Hello this is Hunter."

"Hello Hunter this is Seven-Seven," came booming deafeningly loud through the speakers. One aspect of CB radios is that the volume is partly a product of proximity between conversant parties. I hadn't realized that since my antenna was so tall I could talk to people within a huge radius. It was rare to get such a quick and clear response, and it was fun to remember and use the lingo I hadn't used for so long.

"Hunter, let me introduce you to my friend E.T."

When he told me that I almost fell out of my chair. I came to learn that the majority of the remaining CB radio community is either the disabled or elderly, and this was true of E.T., who couldn't walk and had undergone almost fifty surgeries. When I got on the radio at night, we would have long conversations about everything from the weather to the news. I never told them who I was or anything that could lead them to discover it, but I built a deeply comforting connection I felt with people who were similarly stuck and in need of friendship. The idle chatter and lingo we slung across the airwaves probably was not what one might call fun, but it was an abiding comfort. Picking up the receiver, we couldn't give each other what we wanted, but we could give each other a part of what we needed.

Having hunted, killed, and dismantled the relatives of almost every animal and bird around me, I was attuned to their ways: when foxes were mating, where dove nests could be found, how many deer had left tracks through the mud. The shame I felt at having killed so many of them indiscriminately was crushing. In 2001 on a hunting trip, I killed a black bear weighing over six hundred and sixty pounds, making it the record for the largest in the state that year. Seeing bears, especially moms with young cubs, filled me with sadness, but it also filled me with tenderness. I was constantly reminded of the second night I saw the beings. Their message of compassion toward all life was resoundingly compelling. The valleys and forests I watched soften into spring harmonized with and deepened that message. Solace came when I least expected it.

Having never been to college, I became something like a student of nature. Yvonne brought me a sketchpad, some pencils and brushes, and a set of acrylic paints from the arts and crafts store since I feared every venture into town. I would pass the time on my camping trips drawing and painting what was around me. Flowers, birds, animals—I wanted to capture them all in every detail. The grace of a doe bending its neck down to a creek would stun me into a profound humility. The hours I passed until dark considering how I might portray that neck were some of the happiest of my life. The short tawny fur, how her tongue met the water. I hadn't failed life. Life wouldn't fail me.

CHAPTER 9

The wilderness was a good friend, but it was quiet. The peace I found there lacked staying power. After a trip I might feel good for a couple of days, but my all-encompassing exile ground me down quickly. I would sink deep into sorrowful shame every time I left the house. At the house, Yvonne and the kids exercised heroic levels of patience with our changed circumstances. Fall and another school year arrived with all of the strife that a family with four young children undergoes. There was less time for me to go camping, and the coming winter promised less pleasant excursions. I would have to insulate myself against the chill of the stars, hiding in a tent. I needed other answers.

The kids had asked for the internet for ages and all their friends had it already, so Yvonne and I budgeted the thirty dollars a month to bring broadband to the house. The kids could use it for homework, and I could look for answers. I had never spent much time in a library, so it hadn't occurred to me that there were ways for me to learn about what had happened. Even if it had, I had no reason to suspect the local library would offer any kind of insight or sympathy. I would have dreaded the face on the librarian as I checked out a book on UFOs.

The internet was different though, and one night in October when Yvonne and the kids were asleep, I found out about a show called "The UFO Files." We hadn't had TV since we lost our old house so I looked up a clip from one of the shows. At the end of it, Stanton Friedman appeared on screen with message: "If you have seen a UFO, be sure to contact MUFON, the Mutual UFO Network, on their website." I looked up this man's name and saw he was a nuclear physicist and the first civilian on the scene at the Roswell crash.

My first feeling was relief. He was a professional and trustworthy man, offering a path forward for me. For the first time apart from my time with Junior and the guys, I believed in the possibility that someone out there would believe us. That was enough. I didn't need or want some vindication that would usher me back into the good graces of my community. The simple fact that there was a protocol for what had happened to me was reassuring. After almost a year of being locked away inside the mystery, a key was offered. Maybe the key didn't work, or only led to another mystery, but it was something in which I could place hope. My self-entombment might somehow, someday end.

I typed everything out as fast as I could, sparing no detail. The series of events was seared into my memory, and it was deeply cathartic to feel like I could confess all of it without any self-censoring to protect me or my family's reputation. Once I had typed it all out on their online form, I was ready to press send. I paused. My heart sunk. Of course, they would want to send an investigator. If an investigator came, Yvonne would want to know why a stranger was lurking around the yard. If they called and Yvonne answered the phone, it would be a major breach of trust between us, since we had agreed to keep our children's upbringing as untouched by this ostracism as possible. The kids and neighbors would find out too. There was never a chance of really hiding anything among us and the people we knew. Then there was the question of what the consequences of such an investigation would be. I didn't know which outcome would be more disastrous, whether our experience was somehow proven or debunked. Maybe worst of all would be an ambiguous outcome, extending this purgatory that was only pushing me farther away from my family and everyone we knew. Would it prove controversial enough that investigators would continue to harass us for the rest of our lives? Would our small patch of woods become the next Roswell? I thought of the shanty towns of touristy gift shops that would spring up around us. If that happened, all the Bledsoes would have no choice but to move far away. I wouldn't risk it.

∞

But I didn't delete what I had written either. For two weeks I wrestled with what to do, torn between an intense need to have my story heard and my deep-rooted instincts to protect my family from further embarrassment and pain. My curiosity kept me from deleting my account. Even the smallest chance of winning back my reputation was irresistible. I wanted so badly to be seen as human again in the eyes of my friends, relatives, and coworkers. I knew it was unlikely that such an investigation would lead to that result, but the rigid protocol of their process, the fact that their investigators were trained, had an air of legitimacy that I so direly lacked. Even the term "investigator" had a respectability to it that made me hope others would agree with whatever outcome the process led to. No matter what was discovered, a rational, facts-based investigation might put all of this to bed. We could move on. No matter the risk, the allure of ending my family's lonely torment was deeply compelling.

Turning it over in my mind those two weeks, I kept thinking of my account. I went back and edited it for clarity. I added details I'd left out earlier and drew a map of where all this had taken place. Junior and I had an agreement to talk about it when no one else was around, and I brought it up to him. He was as curious as I was and drew a picture of the beings he saw. We compared our memories of what happened, minute by minute, hour by hour, and found no discrepancy. Going through this together for the first time since it happened, we found our own personal shame and loneliness were lessened. This was no longer a freak incident to suppress and move on from. It was our story, our vexing problem. We came to the conclusion that the problems it had caused for us weren't going to go away unless we took action.

Like that second night we heard the dogs howling, the dread I felt was matched by a fearless curiosity that made me grab my rifle and set off into the dark. After two weeks lingering on the MUFON website, I pressed send.

A day later they emailed back from their headquarters in California. A nauseating mix of relief and dread swirled in me. Of course, they wanted to send investigators to my house. I knew that was the protocol but I hoped they could bypass that step for the sake of my family. I emailed back.

"No, absolutely not. Do not come here."

They started to call, and I would run to our phone and hang up before anyone else could answer it. They were persistent but stayed away for the time being. Still, what I had done was irreversible: I had opened Pandora's box. Havoc was coming one way or another.

A few days after this exchange, in the third week of October, Yvonne and the kids were on their way back from a day spent with Yvonne's mother and the church I no longer dared to attend. They had eaten dinner at her mother's house and had a twenty-minute drive back home. It was getting dark out. They had made that drive hundreds of times, Yvonne and Junior up front and the three younger children in the back seat.

About halfway home, they saw what they described as an ice cream cone shining and hovering through the air in front of them. It shifted through all possible colors, this iridescent shimmering elongated triangle. Their eyes were glued to the windshield, and they were amazed at this cone that seemed to be intent on ushering them home, just over the treetops. All of them sat in shocked disbelief at what was happening. After a few miles, just before they arrived home, the cone disappeared as though it had gone through some hole in the fabric of the night air.

From my study I heard the trampling and shouts of the kids.

"Daddy! Daddy!"

"Daddy you won't believe what just happened!"

"There was this ice cream cone hovering in front of us as we drove home!"

"I've never seen anything like it before! It had the most beautiful colors to it, they were always changing!"

Yvonne walked in, eyes big as pie plates, and said yes, that's what happened. After such a long and heavy silence in my study, it was shocking to have my small room suddenly filled with my family. Even more shocking was what the content of what they were saying. The shape of what they had seen sounded exactly like the glassy shape I had seen on the chests of the beings. Yvonne had the sense to call the federal air traffic controllers and ask if their radar had picked anything up in the area. They hadn't detected anything. Hearing that news, Yvonne relaxed into the same helpless acceptance I had.

I was overcome with gratitude. To see their faces look at me in solidarity and recognition instead of sympathetic concern almost made me weep. I had felt little else but the deep ache of my depression the past ten months. For the first time in ages, something like happiness arrived in me. Junior was elated too. The isolation and trauma he had from the night his dad disappeared, abandoning him paralyzed in the brush, had left a profound wound on his psyche. His school friends lent no more credence to his story than the adults in my life, which made it difficult for him to talk about and process. The children of the subcontractors went to school with my children, but there was little to no comfort and reassurance they could offer each other. There were no therapists around, nor would we have had the money or inclination to use them. He had nightmares constantly that whole year. Sleeping on the couch in my study, I would hear him screaming out in the middle of the night at some sound he'd heard, a *whoompwhoompwhoomp* almost like the sound of a helicopter's rotors. He said he saw shadowy figures in his bedroom watching him. At seventeen years old, he would come sprinting down the hall in sheer terror in the middle of the night to be with his mom.

The whole family now shared the same problem. As parents, we confronted the fact that we could not protect our children from whatever was out there. The kids confronted the fact that adults barely knew more than they did. All of us had been knocked off the axis of what we understood the world to be. On this new, shaky ground, we clung tightly to each other.

∞

As fall turned to winter, we all felt the presence of the phenomena come closer to us. Junior's bad dreams never

Sketch by Emily at ten years old

relented, and I started to have some myself. Apocalyptic visions caused me to wake from sleep shouting. The air in the house became tense with these eruptions of terror in the middle of the night. Darkness fell earlier and earlier every day, and the stability we had uneasily established for most of the year became more and more difficult to maintain. Pressure built. It was horrifying as a parent to see your child quake in fear over something you yourself didn't understand. All I could tell Junior when he came to me saying he was afraid to sleep was to call out to God, say his name, and the shadows he saw would back off. The rest of the kids wanted more and more to talk about what they had seen and what Junior and I had seen, and Yvonne wanted more and more to keep our family within the bounds of sanity. Despite them all having seen it, Yvonne still did not want us to talk about, and understandably so. Our youngest, Emily, was just ten at the time, which made discussing all of this very difficult while preserving a safe and nurturing home life for her. These conflicting impulses challenged all of us, and despite our newfound closeness made home life hard.

By December, I knew I had to take some kind of action, this time for all my family instead of just Junior and me. The only thing I could think to do was call MUFON again to see if they could give us any answers. They had kept calling and writing me that whole fall, but I ignored them, fearing their involvement would be the final straw that ended my marriage. Maybe an official process would allow us to come to terms with what had happened. Maybe if all of us were on board, an investigation could be carried out discreetly, without the community finding out. In early December I relented and started a correspondence with a local MUFON investigator in Raleigh.

Steve was interested in UFOs and had become an investigator to learn about them. He and I became friends talking that winter while I spent the loneliest holiday of my life. My whole extended family spent Christmas next door at my dad's house while I was holed up in my study. We decided it would be best if I stayed away from the people I loved most in the world, the people to whom I had devoted my entire life, whom I'd employed and provided for in times of need. I might have borne their rejection alright if I had gone alone, but I would not allow my children to see me treated that way by their own family. So, I stayed home.

MUFON investigators don't get paid for their work, so it wasn't until February that Steve's job allowed him to make it down to Fayetteville to conduct interviews. I was thrilled to finally have him come, for something about our family dynamic to change, since it couldn't get much worse without totally falling apart. He sat me down and I rehashed the story as Junior and I remembered it with Yvonne sitting in the room with us. It was the first time she heard the entire story from start to finish, and it was kind of her to listen so closely. Steve meanwhile took notes, only asking a few clarifying questions as I went along. I finished the story and felt a closeness with Yvonne that I had greatly missed the whole past year.

When I thought we were finished with the interview, I was surprised to hear Yvonne pipe up for the first time from her chair in the corner.

"Have you ever heard of shadow people?" she asked.

I looked at her in total bewilderment. I had never heard of anything like "shadow people" apart from Junior's reports of his nightmares. She launched into a story about how in the weeks before Christmas she had been sitting in the living room, when all of a sudden there was a quick double flash of bright, blinding light, one right after the other. She described the flashes as coming from orbs, after which out of both of them, two dim, translucent beings stepped out and into the living room. She stood up and followed them as they walked down the hallway toward the kitchen. They rounded the corner and she saw them again, just as they disappeared walking straight through a wall. She rushed around to check the bathroom on the other side of the wall, but they were nowhere to be found.

Two of the children had been sitting with her and had decided to keep it a secret among them lest Junior or I get even more nightmares. Having never heard any of this before, a wave of joy and gratitude crashed over me. The whole previous year I had wanted nothing more than for Yvonne to believe me and trust in my account of what had happened. Her silent tolerance pained me more than any other rejection, and now my prayers that she experience it too had been answered. I told her this and she told me to never pray for such a thing again. After seeing the ice cream cone, she had tried to sweep it under the rug, but this event she could not bring herself to deny. She wanted the same answers I did. As parents, we wanted peace at home and good lives for our children. From then on, we would be able to work together toward these ends.

CHAPTER 10

Enemies disguise themselves with their lips, but in their hearts they harbor deceit.

—Proverbs 26:24

After Steve submitted his report that February, we kept in touch. It became clear that MUFON was interested in a more comprehensive investigation. As Steve was a lower-level volunteer overseeing North Carolina and Virginia, the top brass decided to get personally involved. It turned out that MUFON had recently gotten a greenlight from the Discovery Channel to make a three-episode series on the investigations they were most interested in pursuing. MUFON suddenly had far greater resources at their disposal than usual. They also had a deadline to deliver the episodes and were actively looking for reports to film.

My report had gotten attention from the get-go. After my months-long resistance and Steve sending back a detailed, credible report, MUFON began to push harder and harder to direct their newfound resources toward my case. In messages from MUFON and Steve that winter, they told me that I would make a great witness as a family man, that my son and other witnesses lent credibility to the account, that this was my best chance at actually finding out what had happened.

Despite wanting answers for her own experiences, Yvonne was still against the idea. There was no way of knowing whether a higher-level and better-funded investigation would give us more definitive answers. Even then, it remained a question whether or not those answers would give us the stable family life and reputation we had gone without for so long. Now that the whole family could talk more freely about what had happened, the kids' curiosity grew. The thoughts and opinions of our churchgoing world began to wane as we began to share our thoughts and opinions with each other. Each of us had been isolated, and these conversations were a balm. It became clear we all had a desire to find out what happened and what was still happening.

At first, Steve mentioned the possibility that we would be filmed anonymously. No names, blurred faces, distorted voices. Yvonne was almost happy with this, though she knew that the news would eventually come home to roost. What made us finally agree was the kids. Who were we to deny them some kind of public vindication for all they had suffered? There had been so much public ridicule, it seemed unlikely that it would increase in any meaningful manner. Also, they had just gotten the internet and were learning a great deal about the world outside Fayetteville for the first time. They were excited at the prospect of being on TV. It may not have been ideal, but it was something unique and positive that we could give them, after having felt we deprived them of so much. As the kids' excitement grew, Yvonne's protests lost steam. The show became an inevitability. It would come to be one of the worst decisions of my life.

A few things were promising about this show. For one, our story was slated to be the series premiere. This seemed like a serious amount of buy-in to our story, us, and the quality of the episode itself. It also lent an aura of Hollywood glamor to the idea that had an intoxicating allure for the kids, who had barely even traveled in their lives since money had been so tight. It seemed like a good indicator that the episode was hour-length rather than half-hour, since some of the other programs I had seen came off as unserious or scandalous bids at TV-making rather than serious investigations. It seemed like if there was going to be a TV investigation, this would be the best possible one apart from a *60 Minutes* report. Steve was a good man who was kind to my family and me. We had no reason to think the other MUFON members would act any differently toward us. Steve said that they would portray me as a respected member of my community, though that had not been the case since 2001. Yvonne stipulated that the shooting on our property be as discreet and quick as possible, and MUFON and the producers promised that it would be.

But just as when I had sold my company to people I thought were good-faith buyers, my inherent trust in people came back to bite me. In the South, reputation is everything, so one cannot get far in life here with sharkish, manipulative, or cruel business practices. People talk. Always. What this meant is that I rarely had to resort to thinking the worst of people before making a deal. I trusted Steve's word and MUFON's mission, though I had not yet met the leaders of the organization who would be the primary hosts of the show. Yvonne and I agreed and signed a few forms. Production was to begin late that spring, with the premiere of our show in late October, 2008.

Once we told the kids, their expectations soared. They would talk to each other about things like who would get the most camera time, who was going to get noticed by some executive and become a star, and whose encounter would be the one to break open the case and explain everything. Even Yvonne and I, swept up in this tide of optimism, that maybe we could somehow turn this into some kind of healing opportunity for the children, agreed to allow the cameras to briefly show our names, faces, and voices. We wanted so badly for our community to look at us again as human beings, and everything about the show seemed to indicate our being taken seriously by respectable people.

∞

A couple of days before production was set to begin, we hadn't heard anything from Discovery or MUFON. We did not know anything about how a TV show was really made and what was normal for people in our position. We were simply excited that the time had finally come. The Sunday night before we were first supposed to meet, a producer called and asked for hotel recommendations, telling us they would meet us at our house at 8:30 the following morning.

We all scrambled around the house making it spit-shine clean. We got our best Sunday clothes out and got up early the next morning to make sure our life looked presentable and respectable. Friends, neighbors, and relatives would eventually see this was a perfectly normal home, not the radioactive demonic cesspool they treated it as. It was July, and the kids had spent the whole summer waiting for this day. Even in anticipation of their arrival, a relief set in between us that morning that we hadn't felt in a long time. We looked at each other, our home. Finally, we were going to be seen, we were going to be believed.

8:30 rolled around and there was still no word. We figured they were Hollywood professionals and some minor mishap had kept them from maintaining their strict schedule. The phone rang.

"Hi Chris. We're actually going to need you and Yvonne to come by our hotel to sign some more documents. We're staying at Wyndham Hotel. Can't do anything until after we've taken care of this. Then half the crew will film at your house and the other half will film at the river. We'll break for lunch, so tell your family to think about their orders from Applebee's restaurant."

It was the voice of a young woman, exasperated and urgent. The hotel wasn't the one I recommended, but I didn't think that was too strange. The kids were disappointed to not see any of the action until lunchtime, but eating out was a rarity for us and they were excited about that.

Yvonne said, "Junior, you're the oldest, you babysit. We'll be back in an hour after we sign some forms at their hotel." We drove over, parked, and went to the lobby. We hadn't taken a number we could call and didn't know whom to ask for at the front desk. I waited in the lobby for ten minutes, looking for Steve's familiar face or anybody with a camera. I thought to myself, maybe there were a lot of moving pieces, and since the show was new, they were still smoothing out some kinks in their shooting process.

A man came up to me. "You must be Chris. Come with me." Then he walked off down a hallway. Leaving Yvonne behind, I followed him down the stylish corporate carpet to a pair of double doors. Three black cameras were rolling. A wall of people behind them standing against a wall watching me. There was total silence in the room.

"We're going to have you take a lie detector, Chris. This is Bob Durdak, your polygrapher. He's worked with the FBI and is among the best at what he does," one of the voices said. I got very worried. I didn't see Steve. I didn't know who was with MUFON and who was with Discovery. Only a couple of people had been introduced to me apart from the man whose job it was to judge, debatably scientifically, whether or not I could be trusted. It was a total shock to be treated with more mistrust and scrutiny than even my own neighbors had. Anxious thoughts raced through my mind. *Was this what this all hinged on? If I mess this up, will they just move onto another case? How could I tell my kids that even MUFON thought I was crazy?*

Men and women holding various pieces of audiovisual equipment—lighting, microphones, cameras, clipboards—stood in silence as I tried to process what was happening. I felt betrayed by this ambush, that they would begin filming a polygraph examination the first day before asking me about any aspect of my story or the physical evidence that had been compiled. Instead, it was a direct inquisition of my character and honesty. Without knowing what they were going to ask or who I was in the room with, I gritted my teeth and took a sharp breath. There was no backing out now. I took a seat at the conference table. They got the cameras rolling and strapped me into the various belts and sensors of the machine.

It became clear that one of the cameras was pointed at MUFON leaders. They glared at me with a severe and concerned curiosity. Clearly, they took their jobs very seriously. No talk about the weather or how their trip down was. No smiles. Their priority seemed to be to get a sense of me and my honesty before anything else happened. I thought maybe it was part of the objectivity of such a high-level scientific investigation. Maybe afterward they would loosen up a bit and we could get to know each other. For being stared down by what felt like a firing squad, I decided to engage as amicably as I could.

Two miserable, nervous hours passed as they grilled me with the same thirty-four questions. I had thought I was coming to sign documents and would be back home in an hour. Junior and the kids were alone. Not knowing how polygraph tests were supposed to work, it felt like a punishing and cruel ordeal to sit through. I did not know why they kept asking me the same barrage of questions when I couldn't answer them any differently than I had the first time. The worst of all was that every time I tried to recall that four-hour stretch of missing time, the same headache pounded in my brain as it always had.

But the show wasn't about my story, it was about ratings. The intrigue of UFOs was a thin veil for the show's actual focus: Is the seemingly honorable man hiding a dark secret, hoaxing the world for attention or out of genuine delusions? This was by no means clear during the shooting, but every shot in the editing process is geared toward this central tension in the plot. In the final cut, every dramatic moment and every pre-commercial break cliffhanger is another insinuation of how or why I might be a liar. Every other aspect of what actually happened was glanced over. At its core the episode is nothing but an effort at a scintillating exploitation.

"Okay I think we have enough here," another anonymous voice said. Without any indication regarding the results of the test, they started packing up their equipment. I drove back home with Yvonne rattled and confused, hoping the children wouldn't be treated like the zoo animal I had been.

We arrived back at the house and shortly after vans began to park all over the yard, and inside twelve or so crew members started rearranging our furniture. The kids sat meekly in a corner, watching all the strangers at work at their mysterious tasks. A woman with a clipboard came around asking everyone for their lunch orders. The kids presented theirs and seemed happy. Maybe things would turn around.

The crew went about their business and next thing I knew I was due for a meeting with a psychiatrist. I had stipulated that the show include this test because I wanted, at the very least, to have the show prove that I was not an unstable madman. The test went well and I was able to answer her questions with less anxiety than in the polygraph test. Unlike with the polygraph, she did me the kindness of telling me my results. Not crazy. Not narcissistic personality disorder, or anything else.

By the end of that, it was time for lunch. Again, my family was bossed around like livestock. Time to eat. The crew assistant who had taken lunch orders came through the door with armfuls of bags for everyone, except for me and my family. When everyone began to prepare their meals, we waited for her to go back to the van to get ours, but she sat down and began to eat. Being polite southerners, we sat patiently in the corner of *our* house, watching everyone else eat. I asked the woman if we should go get our lunch from the van.

"Oh sorry. Actually, you weren't in the budget for lunches. Hope that's okay."

This may have seemed like a trivial disappointment for a TV producer. It was probably a trivial disappointment for everyone the producer interacted with. But my kids had dealt with hunger. On several occasions they had gone without to support the family in times of need. At their first brush with fame and Hollywood, as a better life they'd dreamed of for months was condescendingly dangled in front of them, I saw their hearts break. Ignored, they looked hungrily on. Yvonne and I scrambled to throw together some leftovers in the kitchen.

The filming continued at a brisk and unpredictable pace. We went to the backyard, the river, the field. In the final cut of the show, they spend about five minutes recounting only a sparse smattering of the details we told them. The head investigators from MUFON were oddly uncurious about what had happened. Clearly, they had agreed to a certain script from Discovery that they couldn't diverge from. They interviewed the three subcontractors that were with us that night, only to use a handful of their soundbites. They interviewed Junior, a traumatized teenager, only to speculate accusingly about his extreme "angst." Our long story, with all the painstaking detail with which I had reported it, was reduced to brief clips of language and a rudimentary 3-D rendering of the orbs we saw. Of the whole show, those are the only frames worth watching. Of the whole experience, the only worthwhile ordeal was the regression therapy, which over the next year slowly unlocked my blocked memories. Beyond these two things, it is merely one professional-seeming person after another staring at us with a studied concern.

They had offered trauma counseling for all of us, but never followed through. We called, but they had other shoots to get to. They had gotten all they needed and we never heard from them again. We dreaded the premier. There was nothing we could do to stop it so we just hoped that they would refrain from the obviously damning portrait they had been painting. Of course, it was worse than we had feared. Our family was left in late October of that year not with vindication, celebrity, or revelation, but a nationally televised interrogation of our character with inconclusive results. Now, there was nowhere we could run away to. The episode would follow us the rest of our lives.

CHAPTER 11

I built a garden in the backyard, hand-tilling row after row in the rich soil I'd grown up playing on. Centipedes and worms emerged from the ridges of furrows then tunneled back into the earth. I bought all kinds of seeds: vegetables, greens, fruit, anything there might be need of. It was large enough that there was always another task waiting for me. Every season and each day's weather asked new things of me. I held a conversation between the earth and sky, fertilizing the soil for the following spring, covering beds during a late-spring frost, and always watering and weeding. The garden and I needed each other. Its mysteries—why a certain row of beets grew smaller, why the aphids were worse one year—were familiar and comforting compared to what we had experienced. Like everyone else, I did not know how to raise children or find work in a community that mistrusted me, but I knew there was one thing I could do: provide. There were no definitive answers, so I stuck to what I knew.

The garden yielded far more than we could use or preserve, so I gave it away to neighbors, strangers, and the elderly. There was no winning my reputation back, but it comforted me to be seen as a positive contributor to the community rather than malicious and insane. The kids could interact with a community that at least thought their father was well-intentioned. Though the garden saved us a great deal of money, we still needed income, so Yvonne went back to work as a home inspector for a bank. I kept selling various boats, model toys, and other things lying around that had accumulated over the years. With a little help from my parents and Yvonne's mother, we found ways to make ends meet.

I had a growing sense of dread in the weeks before the premiere of the Discovery episode. An invitation to the Virginia MUFON conference arrived and I accepted it against my better judgment. One night's keynote event was to be about my case and presented by Rich Lang, one of the hosts of my episode. He called me one night a couple of weeks before the conference trying to convince me to come.

My wariness was due as much to how poorly the shooting went as to how we were treated in the aftermath. We as a family had accepted the deal in the first place because they promised us special trauma counseling for the children, especially Junior whose nightmares hadn't abated, as well as control during the editing process. The counseling never came, with MUFON and Discovery assigning blame to the other party, and no one taking responsibility as Discovery had already pulled the plug on the series. The cheaply made, exploitative, sensationalist series remains one of the biggest debacles in the entire genre. Naturally, both MUFON and Discovery wanted nothing but to wash their hands of it. The MUFON conference ended up being just as condescending as the shoot had been, and I drove back home thinking of how to prepare my family for yet another disappointment. The producers of the show ignored all my requests to at least see, much less influence the editing of the episode before it premiered.

The storm of ridicule and judgment that fell on my family was beyond anything we had imagined. Emily, just ten years old, would come home crying because of what other children had said about her and her dad. Ryan, then thirteen, faced similar treatment. Jeremy, fifteen, already having to face the daily cruelties and indignities of being a freshman in high school, turned his back on all of us in embarrassment. Dealing with a widespread public rebuke of their family on top of trying to grow up made a deep and abiding wound in all of them. Junior had it worst of all as the only one filmed. At seventeen, my oldest child was the most traumatized, both from the unexplainable terror he had undergone (and continued to feel most nights in nightmares) as well as from the ridicule he met everywhere he went. He did not go back to school. He became afraid to sleep in his own room and would go to my study. Some nights he would not come home at all. If the gossip of churchgoers and businessmen was so damaging to me, it was nothing compared to what happened to the children. They became known for being the UFO guy's son or daughter, which left little room for themselves. In the hallways they were either ignored or openly mocked. Even their teachers got in on the fun, calling them out in class and joking about the episode. It made no difference to the community, or MUFON, that some neighbors had called me after the episode aired saying they saw the same things that night.

That winter we all battened down the hatches at home, avoiding all possible contact. The kids still had to show their faces at school. Jeremy and Junior were at the most vulnerable ages, trying to go on dates or to high school football games with this black cloud looming over them. These things are hard enough without the whole school having seen you on TV attesting to having seen a red-eyed alien. Opportunities and invitations they would otherwise have gotten didn't come. The family they had been raised to love and trust above all else was now the source of their misery. Being at home hurt, but being out in the world hurt more. A somber Christmas came and went, and day by day the storm worsened.

∞

Junior ran away from home. He was eighteen. We had no idea where he had gone, and could only guess that he had gotten fed up with everything. Despite my efforts to convince him that the orbs were benevolent and well-intentioned, his nightmares and screams shook the house several nights a week. Beyond that, living in a place where he felt so deeply judged was a waking nightmare. Months passed without a word, giving all of us a sustained low-grade panic. Again, rumors spread about my sanity: that I had driven him away, that all my kids were losing their minds too.

Since I had to do something, I readied the soil in December and planted onions and potatoes in January. That feeling by the campfire that the world was coming to an end returned, and I started gardening with a fervor. I added more rows and bought more seeds, teaching myself everything I could about how to grow as much food as possible. I refused to use unnatural pesticides and fertilizers, wanting to be in harmony with the land. As part of this, I built a chicken coop and bought forty Rhode Island Red hens, raising them from when they were chicks. They would eventually all lay about an egg a day while producing enough manure to fertilize the garden. I spent our precious little money on a hundred gallons of oil for lamps. If the world were on its way toward ending, at least we could live out our days in relative comfort and our nights would not be dark.

Having lost a son, it felt as though the world had already ended. I had failed as a father in a final, decisive way. Junior did not finish school and home was intolerable, so he left. Jeremy too was pained to acknowledge my existence, and would eventually leave for college and barely ever visited. Facing these facts has been one of the most difficult parts of my life. To stay sane, I gardened. I gave food to strangers. In the depths of my failure, I found a way to succeed as a provider.

Ryan was young enough to take an interest in what had happened. Others' judgments didn't faze him. Luckily, seventh grade is a natural time to take an interest in the final frontier. Having the internet also connected him to a world of people who were far more sympathetic than our neighbors. He grew up in a meaningfully different environment from his older brothers because of his access to the internet. This validation protected him to some extent from the real life judgment he faced at school. He was motivated to learn about the history of UFOs and convinced me to attend some conferences together. He was a smart young man with a great memory, and much of what I learned about astronomy in the early days I learned from him. I loved these trips: no one knew who we were, and if they did, they received us with much more kindness than back at home. I was glad to be able to offer him some solidarity during an experience that was so profoundly isolating.

Part of Ryan's excitement had to do with his first encounter with Hal Povenmire, a six-foot-five man who showed up at our doorstep just before Christmas in 2008. The rest of the family was sitting at the dinner table when the doorbell rang. Ryan went and came back, saying there was a big man outside looking for a Chris Bledsoe. When I got home, I introduced myself and he explained that he was with NASA. He must have been 240lbs sitting on our living room sofa explaining that he had seen the episode and was simply curious about the case. He told us his credentials: a graduate of Ohio State in astrophysics at the age of seventeen, he was immediately recruited at the beginning of NASA in 1958. We sat visiting for about an hour as he asked us oblique questions about ourselves and the case, and then he left.

No doubt, as much of a blessing the visit was for Ryan, who longed for the kind of validation a NASA official could bring, it made the rest of the family all the more anxious. It seemed the world's microscope would stay aimed at our family, with all the suffering that came with it. Another concern was that the government's attention meant that our livelihoods were now in the hands of a vastly more powerful and dangerous entity than MUFON and The Discovery Channel. The thought crossed all our minds that one agency or another would come one night and disappear us all, sweeping the whole thing under the rug forever. There was no shortage of movies or references on TV to men dressed in black who did the disappearing. We were hopelessly lost and afraid. Every group that was supposed to help us ended up embroiling us further into a state of confusion and anxiety.

As I gardened that winter, I noticed the usual aches and pains I had were worsening. Work had always been synonymous with pain, but this felt like something new. Digging open the hard cold dirt, I would have to grit my teeth to stand the ache in my knees and keep a firm grip on my trowel. Also unusual was the pain's persistence: every day it was the same unignorable and constant hurting. Since it had come on without warning, I hoped that it would go away on its own eventually. It wasn't as inconvenient as Crohn's, and since I'd been through so many painful things in life, I wouldn't allow myself to give up on providing for my family in the only manner I had left. I took an Advil and suffered through it.

One night after hobbling around the garden all day, the torture was unbearable. Yvonne drove me to the emergency room where the doctors diagnosed me with Rheumatoid Arthritis, an autoimmune disease that inflames the connective tissues that surround joints. The body's immune system mistakenly attacks itself, resulting in inflammation and swelling. This explained why my knees were swollen, why it felt like I was sticking my hand in a deep fryer every time I pulled a weed out of the ground. The causes of RA are poorly understood, so I felt as though divine punishment were being handed down to me again. Eventually a doctor would suggest that Crohn's can sometimes transition into RA, but I lacked the genetic marker that indicated this was the case. It was a separate onset: I was just unlucky.

The medication I was offered took enough of the edge off that I could keep up with the garden, but there was now this deep underlying sorrow. My body was rebelling against me for reasons I didn't understand. Why, on top of all the heartache my family and I were going through, should I also have to suffer extreme physical pain? Zaps would shoot up from my joints at seemingly random intervals, blinding me for a moment while I twisted open a doorknob or picked up a pencil. It's the kind of pain that overtakes your entire consciousness. Nothing exists but agony.

Winter turned to spring as we endured day after day of ostracism and fear for our missing son. The garden exploded with vegetables and fruit as I planted and harvested everything the weather would allow. Most nights I spent alone in my study chatting to my CB radio friends, asking if they knew of people who needed food since I could hardly give enough of it away before it went bad.

One morning in June I got up at sunrise to beat the heat. I opened the back door as the first light coaxed my yard out of the dark. A heavy fog dragged slowly across the grass and through tree branches. I walked to the garden amazed by the eerie cloud engulfing the property. I looked back at the house and noticed the CB radio antenna pointed skyward from atop my study. The thin post of metal was still as the fog draped itself around it, exposing different sections here and there. Three very long guide wires extended up to it from different directions, shifting in and out of view. There was a break in the fog. A huge great horned owl perched on top of the hundred-and-thirty-one-foot tower. It hunched down as if to get a better look at me. I shuddered with fear, remembering the owl I had seen before getting shot and the owls that kept us awake in the months after the incident. I stood there locked in its gaze for minutes. Fear started to overwhelm me so I hurried back into the house to shake off that feeling. When I came back out, it was gone.

That evening before dinner I was talking to my radio friends as Emily played piano. She sang and practiced for hours every day on a keyboard that was just outside my office, and it was a great joy and comfort to me to listen to her. Every now and then she would stop and we would talk about the music or whatever else. Over the sound of her playing I heard some thunder rumbling in the distance. I thought to myself that I ought to turn off the radio. Emily stopped playing to check on her mother, who was sitting working on her computer on the front porch. It was Yvonne's spot. Emily comes back quickly.

"Mom says she needs you for something," she said and turned away.

I got up out of my chair and walked the fifty feet to the front of the house.

"Whatcha need?"

CRACKBOOM

A shockwave shook the house, taking the breath out of us. Terrified, Emily ran back into the house. Yvonne and I looked at each other. I had never seen her eyes so wide open.

"That was close," I said. She just looked at me.

Then from inside we heard Emily's voice, calm, matter-of-fact, "Hey dad, the house is on fire."

I saw the glow of flames coming out of my study and sprinted to the back of the house. I grabbed a glass of water on the kitchen counter and threw it on the flames. All the radio equipment, my easy chair, the carpet, and the floor were ablaze. There was no time to think.

"Call 911!"

I ran to the back of the house and desperately worked to untangle a hose and turn the spigot on as fast as I could. It was pouring rain. As I fought with the hose, I was certain that I would be struck next. Deafeningly loud thunder crashed over me. Once I got the hose untangled I sprinted back to the house with it and pointed it at the burning cradle of flames in the exact spot I was sitting in a minute beforehand. Water from the hose disappeared into the wall of fire radiating a heat that was difficult to face head-on. In the distance I heard sirens over the crackling roar of the fire.

CHAPTER 12

The fire caused thirty-five-thousand dollars' worth of damage, handing our family another insurmountable burden. When the fire department arrived they directed their hose at the flaming underside of the house. Having avoided being fried by a mere twenty seconds cast a new kind of fear into the family. We added acts of God to the list of things that were out to get us: men in black, MUFON, Discovery Channel, the community, the church.

This called into doubt my insistence that these were benevolent beings sent to help us. Like all my previous near-death experiences, I was amazed by the fact that I was still breathing. It horrified me that the danger that followed me threatened my family too. Any of us might have been in the room at that particular moment. It was impossible to tell in which direction the cosmic bounty on my head was tending: life, death, something in between? If some battle was being played out for my life, who was keeping me alive? Who was trying to kill me?

This wasn't my first brush with lightning. In June of 1987, I was in the garage working on the 1940s airplane I had been restoring. I took a break from what I was doing to watch a storm roll in. It was a two-car detached garage close to the house with both doors up. Leaning against the garage door frame, I saw the clouds gather and darken as the tree branches swayed in the rain and wind. An ear-splitting crack, a sudden charge in the air, and the color green fell on me. The next thing I knew I was on my back, stunned. Mere feet away, the bolt had branched from the corner of the house up to an oak tree that hung over it. Both were on fire. If I had been holding a wrench or leaning on the opposite side of the doorway, I may not have stood up again.

Like everything else unexplainable we had experienced, all we could do was put our heads down and survive. So many factors had to go right, it was clear that something was protecting me. It just so happened that Emily had come to a stopping point in her playing, that she decided to check on her mother on the front porch, that her mother had something she wanted to tell me, that instead of waiting, I got up out of the chair immediately. I became more and more certain that the sight of the owl on the antenna that morning had warned me on some level to get away from the radio. To this day I feel protected by owls. We found a way to proceed with life walking on this razor's edge, grateful to have survived for as long as we had. Months passed as I did my best to repair the fire damage and be the good father I so desperately wanted to be.

One evening in the fall, the phone rang. The feeble, trembling voice was Junior's. He was homeless on the street in California with no money. My heart sank hearing his unfamiliar voice: sad, rough, thinned by hunger. Luckily, he was alive, and Yvonne and I managed to scrape together enough money for plane tickets to fetch him. Again we had narrowly avoided tragedy.

Back at home, Yvonne and I did the best we could to get him back on his feet. Still, he was afraid of sleeping at home and his nightmares returned. The lightning strike was yet another reminder of our powerlessness. I slowly repaired the room in the back corner of the house, but the rest of the family avoided it. Now and then in different parts of the house, you could smell a trace of burnt plastic. Once that much smoke gets into a house, no amount of wall-scrubbing and carpet cleaning ever totally eradicates it. Ridicule of our family slowly waned, becoming less of a line of attack and more a part of our identities. The community gradually moved onto other rumors about other people, but still I could not find a job, which was worsened by the financial crisis. At that point I was grateful to be out of the construction business.

My RA continued to make gardening miserable. At night I would search the classifieds for equipment that could make it easier for me. Most of all I needed a tiller: breaking up the soil by hand was terribly painful. I had been praying every night for the money to buy a cheap one. That September, I happened to get a call from an old friend that I had been giving vegetables to for a while. He was in his eighties and needed help moving stuff out of his garage in Tennessee. As we talked it came up that he had a twelve-hundred-dollar tiller that he couldn't use anymore, and he said that if we came and helped, he'd give it to me. It was a great stroke of luck. Yvonne, Emily, and I were ready to take a small vacation for the weekend and the boys had arranged to stay at friends' houses. It would be a beautiful drive over the Blue Ridge mountains. We packed, locked up the house, and left on Friday afternoon with plans to get back Monday.

When we returned I noticed my laptop was missing. I had set it on the counter next to Emily's and Yvonne's, both of which were much newer and nicer than mine. The boys hadn't seen it. No one we knew would have borrowed it. I went around checking all the doors and windows for signs of a break-in. Everything else was locked and secure the way we had left it on Friday. We were glad it was just the single, cheapest laptop taken, but the professional nature of the theft was terribly worrying. Whoever it was—a government agent, a MUFON member, a curious neighbor—that took it was very good at what they did. As with the lightning strike, we were all reminded that our house offered us little protection from whoever was out there. This sickened me as a father, but I was relieved the focus was on me and not the kids. All my correspondence and files pertaining to our experiences disappeared. Photos, stories, details, testimony. Everything was gone.

On New Year's Eve in 2009, Yvonne was driving Junior back from a routine outpatient surgery. The procedure had gone smoothly, and he lay reclined in the passenger seat still dazed by anesthesia. Yvonne drove down the highway as the weather worsened to a steady downpour. Traffic picked up and they were stuck behind a white semi-truck, its small circular brake lights hovering opaque and red into the car.

"Oh my god the EYES!!!"

Junior recoiled toward the back of the car as quickly as his groggy senses allowed him. Yvonne tried to console him as he shook in terror, wincing at the red circles blaring into the car. She waved her hand over his eyes trying to snap him out of it, but he was still drugged, confused, unsure of where he was and what was happening. For all he knew, he was back hiding in the bushes along the Cape Fear River paralyzed as the eyes approached him. It was another nightmare he couldn't wake up from.

Powerless, Yvonne kept driving. Having seen the absolute horror on her son's face, something shifted in her on the drive home. She had seen Junior come crying to her bed after a nightmare many times. She was of the opinion that every attempt at maintaining a normal home life should be made. Nightmares and the unexplainable things he had seen were just that. This time however, there was no comfort she could offer. Something in his face beyond fear and dread struck her: recognition.

Her stomach dropped. No longer would she be able to afford herself the comforts of partial denials or religious explanations for the things we had seen. She was flooded with guilt over the years she subtly ignored the cause of his suffering, realizing this underlying disbelief only served to put distance between them. As a result, Junior himself rarely brought up the root cause of his suffering and why he ran away. She had never wholly given him the comfort he so desperately needed. All her consolations were tinged with some doubt. He had run away to the opposite side of the country trying to find consolation and was forced to return without it. Red light on their faces, she sat with him in his terror for the first time. A new year was coming, but they were driving home, the very place Junior feared most in the world.

The North Carolina MUFON chapter had been emailing us all year asking us to speak at one of their meetings. That winter, Doctor Michael O'Connell emailed us with a message that convinced us to give it a try. His regression hypnosis represented the only positive outcome from the entire filming process, so we trusted him. Evidently, the Discovery series had caused a huge amount of upheaval in the community, and MUFON membership locally and across the country was dropping. The local chapter was outraged at the show's methods and focus: all the resources that could have been used for an actual investigation were instead used to pathologize me and question my credibility. It seemed that by going and talking, we would receive some of the vindication we had hoped to get from the episode.

Yvonne and I drove to the Unity Church where the meeting was to be held. It was almost two years to the day after the initial encounter. The weather was about the same too, which made those nights feel eerily close. We were relieved to find that this MUFON chapter had turned on the national organization and was intent on repairing some of the damage the show had done. Doctor O'Connell, Yvonne, and I sat side-by-side on the stage. It was the first time I was able to tell my whole story to a group. They were a receptive audience and asked all their questions in good faith. Doctor O'Connell took it upon himself to point out the many deceptions and hypocrisies that had occurred during the filming. The surprise polygraph test in particular had been a farce. After our talk, Yvonne and I met dozens of people who wanted to know more and keep in touch. I was surprised to see Yvonne engage so openly and directly with these questions given all her past resistance. She acknowledged what she had seen—the flashes and shadows in the house, the orb that followed them driving home the previous fall—to perfect strangers. Part of it was that she felt Charlotte was far enough away from her fellow Pentecostal Holiness members, but the bigger reason was that she was looking for answers for Junior as much as for herself now. She needed her son's condition to improve, and she would do anything to help reduce his isolation. The silence about these phenomena in the house had caused their own issues. Now it was our turn as parents to undo it.

Another reason I trusted Dr. O'Connell was that his regression hypnosis had lingering positive effects. During the session I was able to remember the events of January 8th and 11th, 2007 more clearly than I had been able to before. The panic the others had felt about the world ending and my guilt over Junior's paralyzed terror subsided, and I was able to focus on what had happened. His greatest gift had to do with the biggest missing piece in my memory of that night: where I had been the four hours I was gone. He told me my brain was protecting itself and wouldn't allow me to remember what happened all at once. If I did, it would overload my brain and I'd go insane. Over the next year, he said that the hypnosis had programmed my mind to allow bits and pieces of that time to slowly emerge. This way the memories wouldn't break me.

Flashes of this knowledge had begun to arrive since the previous fall, just as he said it would. Most often these memories came in dreams that rocked me awake in a sweat, yelling, screaming, and crying. They were the most intense dreams I ever had. Once every few weeks, my shouts and cries would wake up the whole house. When I shouted in my dream but didn't wake up, my kids would bring out an iPad and start filming what I was saying. I told them not to wake me up no matter how upset I seemed because I wanted to know what had happened those hours. Junior's shaking voice -*where did you go Daddy you abandoned me*—still haunted me. His pain drove me to find out all I could.

There were two kinds of these dreams. The kind I most often received were visions of apocalypse: famine, plague, widespread destruction and suffering. I did my best to keep what I saw to myself so I wouldn't worry my family, but I was deeply troubled. All I could do those years was keep gardening and preparing for what I was seemingly warned about by the beings. They were profoundly strange visions as well. I saw the Egyptian pyramids. It was unclear whether I had visited these places and times or whether they were images the beings had projected into my mind.

The second kind of dream came far less often. They were memories of my actual physical circumstances during those hours. One of the orbs had taken me up into it. At first it was a spherical ball of swirling fire, but as it came closer to me it appeared more like an oblong tic-tac shape, not unlike if you were to press down on a rubber kickball. Inside it was a total, unrelenting darkness like I had never seen before. It was four hours I spent inside the craft. I could hear my own breathing. It sounded as though it were echoing around the walls of a round room. I tried to move but couldn't.

No doubt these dreams unsettled everyone else's sleep in the house. Junior continued to scream himself awake from time to time. I began to dream of being pulled upward through the rafters of the attic and flying around the property. It was as though I wanted to understand what had happened from the orbs' perspective. I figured maybe if I could see

143

the yard from their point of view, their intentions might become clearer.

Early one morning I dreamed again of being pulled up out of the house. As usual, once I got to a certain height over the roof, which was curiously intact, I was able to choose more or less where I flew. There was a thick fog rolling over the neighborhood in my dream, and I decided to not fly too far away in case I got lost. Immediately, everything below me was the same indistinguishable gray sheet. I began to panic: it seemed to me that I would disappear forever if I didn't find a way back to my family. I hovered, trying to peer through what few gaps there were in the fog. Always, it was some unremarkable treetop or patch of grass. Getting more and more worried, I decided to plunge downward through the fog and get home on foot if I had to. I flew down, this time accelerating uncontrollably as if gravity were starting to affect me again. Formless white engulfed me. I saw nothing. The next thing I knew was a violent crash breaking through the leaves and branches of an oak tree, a violent pain screaming in my neck.

I woke up and the pain was still there. Five years earlier, I had dropped a heavy TV on my neck and back, blowing out three discs. It had slowly healed over the years, and I had almost been able to forget about it. That morning though, it hurt as much as when it had happened. I got up, confused and scared that a dream had hurt me. I went to the kitchen to try to start my day gardening. In addition to RA, I now had to deal with a neck that flared with pain every time I tried to look in any direction but straight ahead. Junior came into the kitchen, waiting to go to work with a friend he carpooled with, and we talked about my dream. His friend came in complaining about how it was so foggy he could hardly make the drive to our house. All Junior and I could do was look at each other, stunned.

∞

That spring, members of the North Carolina MUFON chapter continued to email me begging to come visit the property. They wanted to know if everything I said checked out as much as to experience the phenomena itself. There was a deep need in them to do this, and they had treated me well at their meeting, so I had a hard time saying no. The first time they came there were about twenty of them. Many of them were older and very kind to us. They would bring food and clean up after their visits out of courtesy to Yvonne. Still, it was a lot of people inside a small house, and all my kids were being asked god knows what by these strangers. It was nice to have some sympathetic attention on us for once, but the chaos of the visits rubbed Yvonne the wrong way. More often than not, I would find ways to sneak especially desperate people on our land without her finding out and getting upset.

It had been a few months since they had come when Yvonne decided to make a trip to the beach with her mother one weekend. I emailed the group saying they could come spend the night in the yard if they wanted. That was what they wanted more than anything, but Yvonne wouldn't allow it. That Saturday afternoon, fifteen or so cars came in and parked all over the yard. Some of them had come as far as 350 miles away with just a day's notice.

They got out their mattress pads and sleeping bags and arranged them all over the back yard. Twenty people were lying on their backs watching the sky all night long. I watched for a time with them, happy to talk and pass the time. At a distance, orbs came. A hushed reverence fell over the field. I believe it was a collective good will that caused them to reveal themselves. The kids came out and saw them too. They tried to take pictures but none of their cameras could capture it.

I got carried away by this visit and the excitement of what we saw. I forgot that Yvonne and her mother would want to make it back for their morning church service. When she got back early that morning, she arrived at a house that looked like it had been colonized by an invading force. Fifteen unfamiliar cars parked all over the yard. Twenty groggy people laid out on blankets and mattress pads, most of whom had given up on watching and were curled up asleep. She stomped into our bedroom and glared at me. It was the last time I would ever pull a stunt like that.

CHAPTER 13

You may understand my knowledge in the mystery.

—Ephesians 3:4

Without notice Junior ran away again. We figured he had earned enough money to be alright for a few months. Our worrying didn't take over our lives like before. Still, it was crushing to see him gone with no explanation. Once again, we had failed to provide him a home he could feel safe and comfortable in. The other kids were growing up quickly, the garden was getting bigger now that I had a tiller, and Yvonne continued to work for the bank as an inspector. Every now and then one of the North Carolina MUFON people would come by to watch the sky. The phenomena remained a subtle presence in our lives, coming and going as they wished, either as shadow beings or as orbs in the trees over our house. We held it together, Junior returned, and life went on.

The more phenomena we experienced, the more we wanted to document what was going on. Ryan took a particular interest in this and helped me research how this could be done. From the pictures we had tried to take with phones and regular cameras, we found that the orbs had a way of either disappearing as the shutter closed or frying the camera. I struggled with this. It made no sense that they would give me a profound sense of well-being and compassion toward all life, while at the same time instilling so much fear in others and traumatizing Junior. It made no sense that they would cure my Crohn's overnight, only to replace it with RA. I had been so devoted to the church, but here was a spiritual experience as powerful as any I had ever felt at church. I served as a deacon for a congregation that turned me into a pariah. I had depended on the church in facing the big questions in life, and when I needed them most they accused me of courting demons. The comfort I felt from prayer in church was the same as when I prayed looking up at the night sky, with only my soul and whatever was out there for company. It seemed that the orbs appeared in the night sky most often when I was praying. Just as in church, I thought about the well-being of all those nearest and dearest to me, those facing hardships and challenges. In the void left by the church, I made an exercise of this kind of prayer most nights. If the orbs and beings were sent from heaven, as some at the North Carolina MUFON meeting had said, I couldn't square that with the fact their eyes appeared to be mechanical.

I wanted desperately to prove what I was seeing and share this with the world. I had already faced so much shame and disappointment from my business failures, from the death of my first wife, from the ridicule my entire family received, and now I faced the embarrassing problem of even capturing what I and others asserted was happening. Was I the butt of some interdimensional joke? There was an emotional component that I could never quite put into words. These beings and their orbs seemed to respond to feeling in a way that no photograph or video could capture. During these years, both on my own and with North Carolina MUFON members, I found they communicated most directly to those who were at the deepest depths of their despair. Just as I had been stricken with an overwhelming depression in early 2007—poorer than broke, with no job prospects and a son who wouldn't be finishing high school in large part because of me—those in the worst condition found they were the ones to whom the beings were most willing to reveal themselves. I was torn between these contradictions, alternating between extremities of hope and despair. My only consistent hope was the well-being of my family and a sense that the story wasn't over yet. It would have to be seen through to the very end, whatever that might be, no matter how much suffering lay ahead.

Just as when I was growing up, someone had to mow the grass every two weeks. The rich soil made it grow faster than we could keep up with, and there was always another portion of the five acres that needed attention. Though the riding lawn mower made it go faster, it still took the better part of two days to get to all of it. After that it had to be edged and trimmed with a weed whacker. Yvonne loved riding around the yard in the lawnmower, visiting every corner of the yard. I was usually busy all day with the garden so her help was much needed.

Every now and then she'd run over something that stopped the mower and she'd come looking for me to fix it. A log or a hose hidden under the grass would be too much for the blades to handle, and I'd walk over with her and do my best to get it unstuck from the blades. I had been fixing lawn mowers since I was a kid so it usually went pretty quickly. She liked mowing at the end of the day when it was cooler out, often turning its headlights on and going well after nightfall.

One night that fall Yvonne was out riding the lawnmower a little later than usual. The rest of the family was inside the house doing homework or other chores. From my study I could see the backyard. Around 9:30 p.m. I saw her headlights come around for the last section of the back yard. It was about four hundred feet from the house to the tree-line, and she started by going around the edge and then making parallel rows back and forth from the tree-line. The mower was fairly old and small, only covering forty inches across. I was working on my computer, occasionally looking up to watch her as the whirr of the mower slowly grew louder and faded. She worked her way from the right side to the left, at the back corner of which stood a towering old oak tree. My dad's dog kennel was back there too. Yvonne was always afraid of going back there at night because it was where I had seen the red-eyed being, just four feet away.

Eventually I noticed the sound of the mower was neither growing nor fading. I looked up and the mower was stopped idling halfway between the house and the tree-line, and from the glow of the headlights I saw the chair was empty. I heard a violent crash on the back porch. The heavy wrought-iron furniture sounded like it had all been overturned at once. I went to the back door and saw Yvonne on the ground, both legs bleeding, gasping for breath. I asked her what happened several times over, but she couldn't move air in and out of her lungs fast enough to speak. Afraid of what was still out there, I helped her inside.

Blood dripping to her socks, she explained what happened. She said she had been getting an eerie feeling in the last section of the yard. Going back and forth she wouldn't let herself look over to where the oak tree and the dog kennel were. She made about six turns and was heading back to the house when the mower got stuck on a grapevine. Then, she gave in and looked over. In the dark shadow of the brush she saw two red eyes. Three feet off the ground, looking straight at her. Without thinking she leapt off her seat and ran for her life to the back door, crashing through the furniture.

Part of me hurt with her as bruises began to darken down her legs, and another part was thinking about what this meant. Two things had begun to happen in these years: the beings had started to appear more often, and it seemed they were becoming more and more sensitive to our behavior. A more or less consistent call-and-response was beginning to form between us and them. As Yvonne explained what happened, I saw more than fear and pain in her eyes. There was also recognition. I left her with the children and went out to the yard to turn off the mower and see if it was still there. Nothing.

$$\infty$$

The children faced new challenges in high school. The Discovery Channel kept playing our episode as a rerun every two weeks, so there was always one person or another watching it for the first time. Money was tight and nothing came easy.

In August 2009 the family was hanging around the living room talking about what we wanted to do the last Saturday before school started. We decided we'd all go have a day on the river knee-boarding before everyone got busy. I had a little aluminum boat with an outboard motor. There was a boat launch about nine miles upstream from where we had gone fishing January 8th, 2007. Naturally, we would avoid that area. Emily, Ryan, and I were sitting on a wide leather sofa, with Jeremy opposite us on a loveseat and Yvonne to our left in a wingback chair. It was a beautiful morning and I was looking forward to a day with the family. Sunlight poured into the room from three big open windows directly behind Emily, Ryan, and me. It wasn't too hot out. Yvonne was sitting sideways in the chair facing the three of us on the couch.

We were talking about plans for the day when all of a sudden Yvonne leapt up out of her chair, her face white as a sheet. She was looking right past me, pointing at the window directly behind my head. Her mouth was wide open in shock.

"Did you see that?!?" she asked, half whimpering, half screaming.

"I saw it," Jeremy muttered from the loveseat across from us the moment she asked.

"Oh lord you will not believe what I just saw. Quickly! Go outside. Someone just walked up to the window," she said.

Emily, Ryan, and I whipped our heads around and saw the same old back yard we'd always seen.

"There was a man behind you," Yvonne said, trembling with fear.

"A big one," Jeremy said.

Ryan and Jeremy shot up and went running around both sides of the house looking for who was in our yard. Yvonne said he must have been eight feet tall, which made me worried for Ryan and Jeremy so I went out with them. We didn't see anyone or anything else unusual. Back in the house, Yvonne described what she had seen: a dark figure the shape of a man with no distinguishing features but a pair of eyes had drifted up directly behind my head. The house had been converted from a modular home and was lifted three feet off the ground, so by the shape of its shoulders it must have been a giant to occlude the entire window behind me. Its eyes looked directly at Yvonne. Stunned with fear, she could hardly move until it was already gliding away, in the same manner it had come, from right to left behind the other two windows and Emily and Ryan's heads. She said there was no walking motion or turning as it went. It simply whisked itself away. It was more solid than the shadowy beings she had followed down the hallway a couple of years beforehand. It was physically imposing, looming over us. She was deeply shaken. We were all too scared to go to the river. The beings had never appeared in broad daylight, and they had never appeared so solid. If they weren't just shadowy ghosts or made of light, but physically material, we were horrified to realize they could touch us.

The following spring I had plans to meet up with an old friend. His lawnmower had broken down and I had just finished fixing it. I also wanted to spend time with one of the few people in town who had stuck with me through all this. He called me the Friday night beforehand saying he might just come to my place and save me the trip of driving his mower out to his house. He said he'd let me know in the morning.

Yvonne's car had been in the shop, so it was just my truck at the house that Saturday morning. She was on the front porch at half past eight, talking on the phone with her mother. I was back in my study when she came in asking if I would stay around the house that day because her mother wanted to get lunch. Her mother lived twenty-five minutes away and Yvonne didn't want her to drive all the way out to the country where we lived. I told her I was waiting on a call from my friend to see what he wanted to do. Twenty minutes went by and Yvonne came back asking if I had heard yet. I told her not yet but I'd let her know when I did.

By quarter to ten I still hadn't heard from my friend. Emily had been on the front porch with her mom and came back to tell me mom needed me. Since avoiding getting struck by lightning, I was in the habit of responding promptly to requests like this. I got up and went to the front porch. Yvonne was in her chair still talking to her mother.

She covered the receiver with her hand and said, "Your friend's here. He just went around back."

"Oh cool," I said, and turned to walk to the back porch. We had a noisy gravel driveway that stretched about a hundred yards from the road to our front door, then looped around the side toward the back where it dead-ended by my shed and the chicken coop. Standing at the back porch I looked around. Nothing there. I thought he must have driven back around to the front to park for some reason. I walked down the back porch steps hoping I'd catch him on his way to the front of the house. I looped around the side of the house to the front expecting to see him talking to Yvonne.

No one was there, just Yvonne talking on the phone. No car parked in the yard either. Yvonne watched me come around and I just threw up my hands in a shrug.

"Nobody's here," I said. She shrugged back at me.

"You know what was weird? He was in a blue truck but it was old and shiny. Didn't know he had a car like that."

I thought somehow I'd missed him back there and went back the way I'd come. I saw the grass was still covered in morning dew. If someone had walked or driven on it, they would have left a markedly visible set of tracks. The only tracks I could see were the ones I had just made. I thought about how noisy the gravel was and how I couldn't possibly have missed the sound of a car coming around by my study. Again, nothing and no one in the backyard.

On the front porch, Yvonne ended her phone call as I sat down across from her. She realized I hadn't seen anything but didn't want her mother to hear about it. After hanging up she told me what she'd seen: a gleaming, polished, sixties-style light blue truck had turned into our driveway from the road and stopped by our mailbox. She thought it was odd my friend was driving such a well-restored old model. He did drive a blue truck, but it was beat up and dirty because he worked out of it, and it was decades newer than the truck she saw. Keeping an eye on it as she talked, she saw it suddenly accelerate down the driveway to the back of the house. As she told me what had happened, she remembered that the truck didn't make any sound on the gravel. Either she was focused on listening to what her mother was saying, or she figured at the time that the speed of the vehicle somehow made it quieter.

We sat looking at each other, alarmed at the confusion in the other's eyes. When these things happened, our first thought was always the safety of the children. While events like this were usually quick and over before we really knew what was happening, there was no way of knowing how long they would go. We made sure the kids were okay. Nothing unusual had happened with them, so Yvonne and I went back to the front porch. We couldn't stay there trying to understand what had happened: there was a day ahead of us we had to tackle. We had to accept the supernatural drive-by as though it were an everyday event. Just as we reckoned with bee stings and rainbows, this gleaming truck was another passing miracle, out of our grasp before we knew what it was. The only dots to connect were that of the orbs from the river incident, the giant being that stared at Yvonne the previous August, and this truck made similar departures. None of these things were burdened by the drag of any kind of conventional propulsion. Instantaneous acceleration: here one second, zipping miles away the next. They simply went, as smoothly and quickly as they pleased.

CHAPTER 14

Beloved, do not be surprised at the fiery trial when it comes upon you to test you, as though something strange were happening to you.

—1 Peter 4:12

The Saturday before Easter, Ryan and Jeremy had some of their friends over to spend the night. They were close enough in age that they were all friends with each other. One by one they filtered into the house with TVs and monitors so they could play video games side by side. Yvonne was watching a movie with Emily in her room, as much to scare away the rowdy boys as to enjoy some time together.

Weeks were hard, with gardening and everything else I did to scrape together a living for us, but weekends I would fall into a deep, futile sadness. With no work to do, I had to confront our family life. All the difficulties these phenomena and their consequences had wrought on us weighed heavily on nights like these. In some ways we had been brought closer together by adversity, but it would have been far better to have been brought closer together by good times. Jeremy in particular faced far more cruelty from his peers than was his due. Every once in a while Emily would come home from school crying about what another student or a teacher had said. The two-week rerun cycle of our episode on Discovery Channel was a relentless source of ridicule. None of it was letting up: nightmares and the voice in the back of our heads that feared anything out of the ordinary were two of the worst consequences of the phenomena. Any situation could slip from mundane to unsettling. Fear can act like a contagion in close quarters between people who know each other well. We would run to each other for refuge only to find ourselves the next day washing dishes, spooked by some dark motion out of the corner of our eye. Even if we kept them to ourselves, these brief moments of terror insinuated themselves into our daily life, affecting all of us. Worst of all was the thought of the cumulative effect of all this on my children's lives: the friends they otherwise might have made, the social and academic risks they otherwise might have taken, all the nights they were thirsty but too afraid to go to the kitchen sink to get water. I was sad and so angry with myself that I had allowed this to happen.

I couldn't help but feel these conditions were my fault. I had been the first of us to see something unexplainable. As glad as I was to see my children happy with friends and doing well in school, my guilt followed hard after thinking how much of a rarity this evening was. I spent nights in my study, checking in with the family, but always siloing myself off as much as I could. If they were happy, I didn't want to ruin it by reminding their friends they were in an exile's house. I never understood the games they played—different permutations of soldiers, cartoons, and aliens fighting each other—but I loved that they had found themselves a small pocket of happiness and friends who were kind to them. After dinner I went back to my study.

It felt like nothing would ever change. It seemed my bad luck and selfish choices had marked us forever. Everything henceforth would be an uphill battle because of me. Around 9:30 I got up and went to the back porch steps. The same trees and bushes now waking up after winter, getting ready to grow a little taller, a little fuller. Soft rectangles of light pooled on the grass. I heard crickets and muffled punches from the video games inside. The night was calm. I felt a bit of peace in giving up this torturous fool's errand. If these phenomena wanted to come to me in a manner that yielded proof of their existence, fine. If they wanted to continue this subtle game of winking away at the most frustrating moment, fine.

I wanted nothing more than to show the world what we saw, that their message was one of peace, compassion, and support for humanity. But looking at my garden and the trees reaching above it, I told myself this world is more than enough. When I planted a row of zucchini or squash, they either grew or didn't for reasons I couldn't understand. When my family and I were sitting together planning the last Saturday of summer break, there was no understanding why a tall dark man would loom over me like that then suddenly glide off. How could the appearance of a stalker-like figure square with a compassionate mission? Had I failed to put the puzzle pieces together? Was there some pattern I was missing that, interpreted correctly, would give us an explanation? Was our fear, confusion, and ridicule the point of all this?

I looked up from the yard I understood to the sky and vowed never to speak of them again. It had to be finished for good if my family was going to live any kind of life worth living. I told them I was grateful they cured my Crohn's, but I wouldn't let my family hurt anymore by talking about it. No more conferences, no more visitors, not a single mention ever again. For a moment after, I kept looking up. The stars shone as indifferently as the blinking lights of a plane passing thirty-thousand feet in the air. I went back to my study to sleep on the couch I'd put there, exhausted and heartbroken. The boys were playing their games more quietly now. A small part of me felt better hoping this vow might spare my family from further harm. I drifted off to sleep with this thought.

∞

"ARISE!"

A roaring thunderous command shook me from sleep. I gasped as the word's second syllable was coming to a close, realizing some man must be in my room. The volume was unbelievably loud, like a sonic boom. Immediately I felt a chill. I shot up from lying down to sitting up in bed, looking around for him. I saw 3:00 a.m. glowing from my alarm clock then looked toward the foot of the bed. Goosebumps formed over my whole body. Movement. The hallmark dim holographic outlines of the shadow beings. I couldn't tell how many there were.

I found I couldn't move on my own anymore as I stood up to get dressed. It occurred to me they were willing me to dress, as impossible for me to resist as waking up when someone shouts in your ear. Pants, shoes, shirt: nothing entered my mind but fear and a sense that I was going to an appointment. The house was dark when they led me out the back door. I walked at a steady pace, locked on three shimmering shadows gliding into the woods toward the dog kennel. When we approached the edge of the forest, about ten feet from the dog kennel, they stopped and I kept walking. One of them turned around and extended its arms toward me. I stopped and looked at what it was holding.

"Take this. It is yours. You must keep it."

In the dark, I hadn't been able to take a good look at what was being offered, but it felt dangerous to decline, as if I even had the power to say no. I reached out and accepted what was dropped into my hands. About the shape a small chihuahua dog without a head or tail, it had rough prickling fur. It squirmed slightly. It was alive. There were no discernible limbs. Then the fur sharpened, as if into the spiked quills of a hedgehog. I dropped the creature out of surprise. It writhed and twitched helplessly at my feet.

"No. Pick it up. Keep it."

I bent down, thinking for the first time how this story would sound to the outside world. It demoralized me to think of the response—"so they gave you a headless limbless tailless chihuahua?"—but there was no time to linger on the thought. I lifted it up and saw the beings were gone. My only thought then was that I could not hold this thing. It hurt my hands and I didn't know if it was going to bite or sting me. Since they told me to keep it, I decided that instead of holding it I would put it in the dog kennel. I realized the beings had relinquished their control over me as I walked over, set it down, and closed the door so it couldn't get out.

I might have run straight back to the house with my newfound freewill. Before I could think of running, I started walking. I took a few steps when a powerful blast of air hit me. On this calm, clear night, the almost hurricane-force gust made me stagger backward. My eyes had adjusted, having been in the dark for enough time, so it was only detail and not substance that escaped my sight. I looked up to where I thought the gust was coming from, and saw in the trees that a hole had opened up several feet off the ground. A zone about the size of the car was suddenly a complete blackness, with nothing discernible within it. The second I felt the blast of air and saw the void, out of it came charging a fifteen-hundred-pound black bull with horns. Growing up next to cows, I knew what this meant. An angry charging bull does not give up, just like in a bullfight, but I was not a matador. My whole inner being screamed with terror as it ran full speed at me. It galloped as if it were itself an aspect of the wind. Just when I thought I was about to meet my end, it went over me, knocking me on my back. I saw the underside of its head, its powerful shoulders and haunches. Like the shadow beings, I was surprised to find that it wasn't entirely solid. I saw stars and branches beyond its translucent body as I fell backward. I was stricken and dazed, having narrowly missed getting trampled to death.

I rolled over to my stomach so I could try to stand up and run. If that bull was turning around to come charging back, or if something else was going to come out of that void in the night, I wanted to be out of its way. I pushed myself up from the ground to my hands and knees.

Before me, a woman floated in a circle of light. Poised still and silent, she gazed down at me. Her beauty tranquilized me and my fear vanished. I thought no more of the bull. I rose to my knees and spent a minute trying to take in what I was seeing.

I was kneeling within the circle of light emanating from her. Everything else in the woods dimmed in comparison. I felt gently cradled by the soft light of her presence. At about the height of my chin, her feet were bare and pointed downward as she hovered. The gleaming robe she wore hung down to her ankles. The garment was simple and featureless apart from the evenly spaced rolls that formed from the bunching of the fabric. They seemed to be some ancient priestess's robes, with long sleeves drooping past her wrists and an unadorned collar. It reminded me of goddesses' robes from Roman sculptures and mosaics. She had blonde hair and the most dazzling blue eyes I had ever seen. I realized she only seemed tall because of the angle I saw her from: she must have been four and a half or five feet tall at the most. My sense of calm deepened as I looked into her eyes.

"You know why I'm here."

Her lips hadn't moved as she spoke in a high, clear voice. I knew what she meant, and a wave of embarrassment, remorse, and sorrow overtook me. I had vowed to abandon whatever path she had set me on just five hours beforehand. No matter how much pain my family and I had already been through, I could no longer allow them to suffer for a cause I couldn't even trust was leading anywhere. It devastated me to turn my back on all of it, after so many dreams and experiences had compelled me to tell the world, but I reached my breaking point: I would not allow the house full of laughter behind me to return to ostracism, fear, and misery. Now, looking at her, I regretted it with every cell in my body. However, within that mysteriously placid expression on her face, I knew my error was not final.

She had appeared to offer me a way forward, to show me that these tribulations had not been in vain. There was a subtle dance of meaning that had been playing out over the years that led to this night. I had to trust that revelations like these could not be delivered all at once in blinding clarity, otherwise they would be rejected or ignored.

"You cannot quit now. You made an agreement that must be kept."

I was in total awe of her: it was clear she was director of all that had happened. In a trance-like state, I could not move and didn't want to. She communicated to me that the orbs, the beings, the missing time, were all tools she had been using. She talked of the beings as guardians she sent to do her bidding, of my apocalyptic visions as a possible future for earth, of our agreement requiring absolute trust in her. She vowed that if I continued in this mission, she would protect my family and me, she would allow the orbs to be photographed, and she would allow me to show these phenomena to witnesses outside of my family. If I continued to talk about what I saw, she said that she would never leave my side. I was overwhelmed with gratitude for this protection and assurance. For long portions of her disclosure, she raised her pointer finger up to her lips as though she were telling me to keep a secret or be quiet, and I could not understand what she was saying. Afterward she said that I would be able to understand what she had said when the time came. I asked her what the lump of living fur was that I had been given. She said it was an icon of humanity: directionless, senseless, without head or tail, in dire need of protection and guidance.

Toward the end, she conveyed the importance of my visitations. She warned that there were forces at work to cast phenomena like this in a negative light, and that if this view won out, humanity would be set on a path to ruin. She said that my work was to prevent this dangerous deception from taking root. She did not tell me why, but I had been chosen to tell humanity of the phenomena's benevolence. The first step in this work was the simple acknowledgment of what I saw.

"A new knowledge must arrive. Mankind must awaken to it."

After twenty or thirty minutes on my knees listening to her, I was disoriented and totally drained of energy. When she finished talking, her halo of light drew back into her and she vanished. Forgetting to check on the prickling creature in the kennel, I scrambled back to the house, wobbling and deliriously tired. I got in the back door and passed out on the hallway carpet, covered in dirt and forgetting the boys had friends over. As I fell asleep, I remembered her words.

"This is your burden. You must bear it."

CHAPTER 15

First light shone through the back door that Easter morning on a new father, husband, gardener, and friend. Everything the lady said was pulsing through my head. Stiff from lying on the carpet, I got up and went to the back porch to brush off the dirt and leaves stuck on my clothes. I looked around. Another morning, my garden readying to burst open and my family safe inside, I felt a profound sense of acceptance. Our world was not imploding. With the lady on our side, we would see better days. All I had to do was keep speaking out. There would be no way out but through.

I went back to sleep trying to think how I could break the news. It scared me to risk another round of public shaming, but it felt right. The lady said it was my burden to share my story, but she hadn't told me how to share it. By this point, I was far more at home telling the truth than suppressing my thoughts and feelings, but it had to be handled delicately. It seemed like the damage had already been done the past several years, but I refused to risk it. Every time in the past I thought things couldn't get any worse, I ended up wrong.

Only a few days after my encounter with the lady, I received a call from the North Carolina MUFON chapter asking me to speak at a conference in Asheville. They wanted me to talk about the river incident, but I knew I owed it to the lady to talk about her. It was too much of a coincidence that I received their invitation so quickly after the encounter. After four years, my story continued to garner attention. Because the Discovery channel episode kept running every couple of weeks, there was always a new group of people asking me to come and talk about everything that didn't make it in the final cut. Maybe they wanted to hear about a cover-up, or maybe they just wanted to meet me, but for one reason or another I always drew a crowd. Ryan was always excited about these conferences and events, so we planned a trip together up to the mountains.

On the drive up, I told Ryan about the lady for the first time. In those two weeks I never found a good time to tell the family, so I put it off until after our trip. Again, it seemed the lady had given me some flexibility in terms of how and when to share what I had seen, so I didn't feel I was being dishonest. Ryan responded well to the whole account. I knew without a doubt that we were on the right path. It had been years since going to something like this, so we were both a bit nervous. I could hardly believe where I was headed, given that just two weeks before I was swearing on my life never to speak about UFOs again.

∞

The small room in the Ashville library was packed. For the time being I was just another face in the crowd. There were about seventy people in the room. For as much ridicule as people interested in UFOs garner, there was nothing unusual that separated us from the rest of the world. We had jobs and families, drove cars and dressed like everyone else. I looked around: no tinfoil hats were poking out. I saw a couple of familiar faces, but not enough concerning ones to make me worried about how we would be treated.

When the MUFON official started introducing me, I was still waffling over which story to tell. I had discussed the night on the river dozens of times over the previous four-and-a-half years, and each time was as agonizing as the last. There was no divorcing the emotions I felt that night from retelling what happened. Along with the nuts and bolts of what happened came the same shame over Junior's sense of abandonment, the fear and confusion, the absolute certainty that the world was ending, and even a lingering sense of being unsafe at home. Add to that the feeling that every sentence I uttered was subject to interrogation and mockery, and you can imagine the fraught state speaking publicly put me in. My introduction finished and I walked up to the stage still undecided.

I owed it to the audience to tell them the story they came to hear, but I felt I owed the lady even more for bringing me there. I started with the river incident, leaving out most of the context I usually include. It felt wrong. Every second that passed was a missed opportunity. I had to carry out the task the lady had entrusted me with. What if time got away from me and I forgot to talk about her? What if someone pulled the fire alarm?

Just a few minutes after beginning the river story, I started to explain why I had chosen to come speak again after ignoring their invitations for so long. I heard hushed murmurs and anxious creaking seats as the audience stirred. I said that two weeks ago, I had vowed to abandon everything related to the phenomena because of the misery that had fallen on my family. I told them about falling asleep and being woken by the voice and the beings. The murmurs grew louder. People leaned over to tell their neighbors jokes. Their neighbors laughed. I told them about the gust of wind, the bull, and the lady. I didn't want to look at Ryan or for Ryan to look at me. Some women were heckling me, shouting that they wanted to hear about the river.

"This is important. This lady appeared to me. It was real. She told me to tell you what she said."

No response but the impatient rustling of the crowd.

"There will be a 6.8 magnitude earthquake on September 23, 2012 in Baja, California. In New York this fall the elections will be disrupted."

I was breathless. I had no idea why I had said what I'd said. I realized my face was wet with tears. I looked up at a room of wide eyes. The murmurs and laughs stopped. I took a deep breath and found Ryan's eyes. He looked as surprised as I was. I figured I had said as much about the lady as they would let me, so I picked up the river story where I'd left off.

I told them about the orbs, the beings, our fear, pointing out the parts of the encounter the Discovery producers had left out or flat out ignored. The rest of my talk went smoothly.

Some event organizers approached us and told us that they were going to have a sky watch afterward on a lake forty minutes away. The crowd had warmed up to me somewhat so I felt okay about going. I preferred to talk in smaller groups and we'd made the four-hour drive, so I figured Ryan and I might end up having a good trip after all.

Down at the lake there was very little light pollution and it was a beautiful clear night. About half the people who were at the talk gathered at the shore in small groups, talking and looking up. When word got around that I had showed, several people came up to meet me and ask questions. One man shook my hand, saying he and his wife had come all the way from Wilmington to hear me speak. His name was Dan. We talked off and on the whole night. Several others approached me asking about the lady as often as they asked about the river incident. I felt better; what's laughable in a conference room isn't so funny when you're huddled together gazing across incomprehensible distances at old specks of light. Just as we stood at the edge of the lake, we stood at the outer edge of earth confronting what we hardly knew.

∞

A few weeks later MUFON called me again, asking if I would go down to Wilmington to meet a scholar named Diana. Apparently she was Dan's wife from the sky watch in

Asheville who hadn't spoken to me. They didn't want me to give a talk or do anything other than meet Diana. She was a religious studies professor at the University of North Carolina at Wilmington and wanted to get to know me and my story. They dropped hints about us collaborating on some project, and I am always eager to learn more, so I was excited to go. After the talk, there would be a dinner and a sky watch on the beach where we could get acquainted.

Junior was curious about college so I brought him with me down to Wrightsville Beach. We would also get to see my second-eldest son Jeremy who went to school there. Driving down, we remembered the months we had lived together in the area, framing a house with the same guys we had gone fishing with on the Cape Fear River. The route we took followed that same river through Fayetteville down to Wilmington. It was a clear Saturday morning, and it seemed like we were finally taking care of some unfinished business. Before that day, he had never wanted to talk about what happened or even listen to other people discussing it. It was too raw of a wound for him to tolerate its reopening. However there was something about Diana's reputation that made him willing to explore the subject. She had a master's from Berkley and a PhD from Stanford, I thought she might offer him some validation. Having a legitimate and academically respected person on his side to vouch for him would make a huge difference. It wouldn't silence his critics and detractors, but it might make their voices a little quieter.

We arrived at the lecture hall a half hour early, but Diana was there waiting and getting ready to give her introduction to the speaker. She waved us over and gave us a friendly welcome. I remembered her from Asheville and thought it was curious she hadn't talked to me if she was so friendly. We listened to a colleague of hers give a talk while we sat together toward the back of the room whispering quietly to each other. It turned out she had been contacted by MUFON the previous winter. They had sent her a stack of around two thousand reports of UFO sightings that included descriptions of angels and other religious aspects. When I confirmed with MUFON that I would speak at the Asheville conference, they sent word to her that I lived nearby and our experiences would make an ideal subject for her research. I was impressed that the MUFON administration was running smoothly enough to organize our meeting, but I was shocked that the lady had appeared when she did. If she hadn't, there was absolutely no chance that I would have accepted an offer to drive six hours to talk to them in Asheville. Realizing this alignment humbled me. It wasn't the first such alignment and it would be far from the last.

That evening a large group of colleagues and her students came along with us to do a sky watch. Diana was kind to Junior and talked to him about college and what it was like to start a little later than most. Jeremy had brought some of his college friends to meet Junior and we all had a nice time. After dinner the kids and students went farther down the beach with their telescopes and cameras. I was glad Junior was having an experience with people his age who didn't write him off. A ways off from the others, Diana and I sat together in beach chairs looking up as the waves came in.

She said that in all her years studying the bible, she knew that the popular image of angels was completely at odds with the texts in which they appeared. Of the many descriptions of angels in the bible, virtually none of them are the typical children's illustration of a human with wings on their back. Rosy-cheeked babies are not crawling around in mid-air in the Book of Revelations. Of all the modern accounts of these encounters, she said mine, down to every last detail, felt closest to what she believed was the truth. It was a turning point for her. A few days later she emailed to say she was changed by our talk together, that she believed the beings I saw were angels and not aliens from distant planets.

The next day, Junior and I talked the whole drive back. He was thrilled to have found people who didn't judge him for his experiences. Diana's students and Jeremy's friends asked the same questions he had never felt permitted to ask, making it a liberating and healing day for him. I had only ever heard the occasional report that deemed unexplained phenomena angels, so I was amazed and relieved to have met anyone, much less a tenured professor, who stood with me in that belief. From the very first night I saw the orbs over the field, when I called out to God to protect me, I knew I was looking at something divine. Most everything about MUFON's sci-fi theatrics had always rubbed me the wrong way. Their theories and approaches were full of fear-mongering and egotistical pseudo-philosophies. These experiences were not hobbies or thought experiments for my family and me, they were a challenging, almost daily confrontation with forces beyond our understanding. On a deeply intuitive level, all of it felt sent from God: the lady's words, the beings' (or guardians as the lady called them) directive of non-violence and compassion, the otherworldly appearance of the orbs themselves, with all their contradictions to physics as it now is understood. Even before the river incident, something about the course of my life was too fated to be merely the meddling of some little green men. All my near-death experiences, losing my first wife in my arms, gaining and losing a fortune, going from being a respected member of my community to an outcast: all of it brought me a more complete appreciation of life itself. If I had felt rich beforehand, with two planes and a big house, I felt just as rich arriving back at the house to my wife and children. The lady had set me back on this path, and I was determined to stay on it this time.

Diana and I continued to talk for the next few months. The demands of her academic research led our conversations as often as her own personal interest. She immediately began writing my story in the hopes of getting a book out. We talked about the finer points of what I had seen and felt. I also learned a great deal from her about the various religious contexts in which experiences like mine figured. It blew me away how often experiences like mine appeared in the bible and in religious texts broadly. She was extremely well-versed in world religions, often comparing one element of my story to that of some medieval saint or mystic. I had read all the bible passages before, but it never occurred to me to read them in this light.

It just so happened that she had recently acted as chief religious consultant for a pair of Hollywood screenwriters, twin brothers Chad and Carey Hayes. They wrote a horror movie that was to come out the following year, and consulted with Diana about the various religious implications involved in a Catholic haunting. Diana had enjoyed the work and maintained a good relationship with the screenwriters, so she decided to pass my story onto them to see if they wanted to make a movie out of it. At first it had seemed like an idea worth exploring, but I was wary because of all that had happened with the Discovery episode. I would not allow my family to get dragged through the mud again, and there was virtually no way of guaranteeing that in the making of a feature film. Still, Diana was adamant about me at least giving the Hayes brothers a chance by meeting them in October when they were in town. She said she felt that the four of us were meant to make this movie about UFOs and how UFOs are major factors in the world's religions. She continued to work on the book about me, which I preferred mainly because I would be able to arrange my approval before it was published. She wanted the title to be *Seraphim*, an ancient term for angels and other celestial beings used in ancient Judaism, Christianity, and Islam. Her husband Dan and their children came to visit a few times, and we all became friends.

The brothers were to be in Wilmington for about a week. Diana was still hoping that I would agree to meet with them, and I might have agreed if the story were mine alone to tell, but the family's well-being was something I couldn't risk again. I told her the Monday beforehand I would go out and pray for a sign every night. If the beings wanted me to meet with the screenwriters, I had a feeling they would let me know.

I didn't see anything the first few nights, and it had been raining all Tuesday and Wednesday. She emailed me Thursday and I had to politely respond that I was sorry but I hadn't seen anything like a sign. I felt good about this. I'd gotten tired of getting my hopes up, and Yvonne was relieved when she heard the news too. I went out to the back porch around nine o'clock that night, it had finally stopped raining, but everything was still wet in the backyard. I was thinking about checking on the vegetables when Yvonne opened the back door and said, "Look Chris. What is wrong with that tree?"

About seventy-five yards behind us I saw a tree erupting in flames. We yelled for the kids to come out and look. It was an old northern catalpa tree toward the back of the yard. The top twenty feet of it had fallen away a year before, leaving a twenty-five-foot trunk about the width of a basketball. As we got closer, we realized it wasn't some errant firework, but a full top-to-bottom blaze all through the interior of the tree. We stood around it, confused, astounded. None of us had been outside beforehand, there had been no lightning or thunder that day, and the grass was still wet from the rain under our shoes. Through openings in the trunk we saw the ravenous flames spiral and chimney upward. Emily drove down the driveway while Ryan was filming the trunk with an iPad. Her headlights showed the top of the tree expelling a rapid stream of smoke. That video shows her asking from a distance, "Why is that tree on fire?!?" We stood around it, mystified.

After it began to die out, I went inside to write to Diana that I had gotten my sign and that I'd see her and the screenwriters Monday morning. Yvonne made the drive down to Wilmington with me. If we were going to put our family in jeopardy again, we had decided that we would at least take equal responsibility this time around. We met Diana and the brothers at a dinner. First thing they wanted to know was the sign that brought me there. I showed them the video Ryan had taken and they were all taken aback. The brothers were kind to Yvonne and me, and I got enough of a good feeling from them that I was willing to let them work on a proposal. Diana mentioned the pages she had written for *Seraphim* could serve as a launchpad for them. They made it clear that as screenwriters they could not guarantee any kind of control over the final product. Still, Yvonne and I were curious enough to see where it went, so we agreed verbally to the idea of a movie option for *Seraphim*. Later I received an email from Diana about changing the name to *Cape Fear Prophecies*. The beings seemed to be making themselves more and more visible. That fiery gash in the wood on an otherwise normal night was unforgettable. It was as plainly urgent as any of the other phenomena I had experienced. I had my instructions from the lady: I had to keep speaking out.

Meeting with Lue Elizondo and Tom DeLonge

*Chris Junior standing in our backyard
where a UFO traveled*

Brandon sitting on the President's desk in the Oval Office

Timothy Taylor, PhD (NASA) traveled from Huntsville, AL to attend Emily's High School Homecoming Pageant.

Honored to meet Dr. Harold Puthoff, Physicist

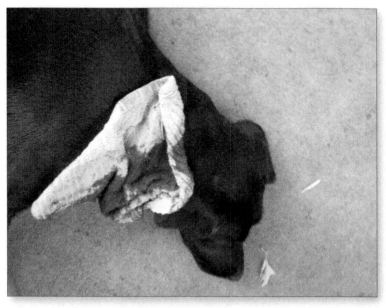

Nellie bleeding from mysterious neck wound

Orb with what appears to be a baby inside

With my good friend Colonel John B. Alexander

*Jim Semivan and his wife Deborah
visiting Emily at NYU*

*David Broadwell helping me with a field EEG
experiment using ZETO Active Electrode Technology*

The Broadwell family witnessing the phenomena during a quantum entanglement experiment David and I were conducting from Fayetteville NC and Bluemont VA

Double-blind experiment with metamaterial at the Monroe Institute

The Burning Tree

Chris Jr., Ryan, Yvonne, myself, Emily, Jeremy, and Biscuit

CHAPTER 16

The electoral disruptions I had predicted at the Asheville MUFON conference ended up happening. Diana emailed saying that I was correct about this disruption and that the storm had caused a lot of problems. It delayed a conference Yvonne and I had been invited to a few months beforehand. The invitation, which came entirely out of the blue, was for an event called the Gathering. It came from a businessman named Larry Frascella. They wanted to fly us up to Philadelphia for the weekend and sent us a booklet detailing some of the events and attendees. One dinner would be held in a government centrifuge facility formerly used to train astronauts and pilots. The attendees featured in the booklet were physicists, Egyptologists, and all manner of government officials. I arranged to have Diana invited along with us, and it seemed legitimate enough, so we weren't too worried about getting disappeared by men in black. We figured the worst-case scenario was we would have a small vacation.

On November 16th, Yvonne and I headed to the airport not knowing what we were getting ourselves into. As usual, the birdshot in my chest set off the metal detectors, but other than that it was a smooth trip. We walked out of the terminal in Philadelphia and were met by a driver in a suit with 'The Gathering' typed out on an iPad. He drove us to the hotel in a limousine-style bus. The rest of the weekend we were treated like celebrities. No expense was spared. Limousines brought us to an exquisite dinner at the vineyard. I had heard of several of the guests in my own research of UFOs, but Diana and Yvonne were the only ones I had met before.

There were ice sculptures, linen tablecloths, and candles strewn around a room set for two hundred people. All the fanfare made me a bit nervous, but Yvonne was always the life of the party, so we ended up making some important friends. We had on our best clothes and got all dolled up in the hotel. The second night we went to the centrifuge, which was an even more extravagant party. A huge industrial concrete room was decked out for a banquet. It was the kind of place you wouldn't be surprised to see James Bond sleuthing around in. The centrifuge itself was a long arm made of latticed steel that extended to a mock cockpit the shape of an M&M standing up on its side. Partygoers could climb into it for fun the whole evening, putting themselves in the same position as the astronauts who tested their mettle there, resisting passing out for as long as possible trying to earn a spot on a crew. Yvonne and I got to sit in the same seat as Neil Armstrong.

The various speakers and materials directed us to talk to each other as much as possible about our work and experiences with what they called phenomena. I was singled out as only one of two direct experiencers in the audience. The number of serious people there who were serious about finding answers almost moved me to tears. Here were the best and the brightest, the top brass, the people who were supposed to know what was going on in the world, and they seemed as uncertain as I was. Part of me envied that their status as agents, officials, and scientists legitimized their questions in ways that being a builder in Fayetteville never afforded, but I was glad to be there regardless.

I mainly stayed at our table with Kathleen Marden and Linda Moulton Howe, two of the best-known writers and journalists on UFOs and abductions, Stanton Friedman, a nuclear physicist who was first on the scene at Roswell, and Diana. Yvonne went all around the room meeting as many people as possible. Larry Frascella, the man supposedly behind the curtain for the whole event, noticed Yvonne from a distance and left the group of people he was talking with. Apparently remembering everything about us, he came up to her and jokingly gave her a hard time about not supporting me at first.

Yvonne just laughed it off and said, "Well I'm here now!"

Eventually his family and ours would become friends, but at the time it came as a bit of a shock. We had a great time the rest of the weekend and ended up meeting many incredible people, several of whom we have kept up with since.

Colonel John Alexander was there though we did not get the chance to meet then, but we would become close friends and collaborators in the coming years. Many of the people whose paths I crossed that weekend I would meet again. Three years later Larry was driving me and John Alexander through the streets of Philadelphia trying to gather information on a future assassination attempt on the pope.

Yvonne and I had a flight back early Sunday morning. The kids had a million questions about the weekend and we were happy to answer them. That evening I walked next door to my parents' house to fill them in as well. They lived so close to us, there was usually something going on. The kids loved to go over there to have their grandma's cooking. I went over when it got dark around five o'clock and visited with them for a few hours. I was tired from getting up so early and all the excitement of the weekend, so I wanted to go home around eight and get to bed early. I started the short walk back and saw it was a clear, cold night. When I was almost to the backdoor, an orb appeared just as it had many times before, this time directly over the house. It was a beautiful sphere of pure light. This one was a bit closer and larger than usual, so I figured I would try to take a video of it.

I took out my phone and pressed record. I was shocked. This time it didn't blink away, fade out, or zip away from the camera. I pointed the phone camera and watched it with my eyes as I usually did. I risked taking my eyes off it to see if it appeared on the screen of the phone. It was there, a little duller and smaller-seeming, but it was there. For almost six years I had tried to capture the orbs and beings to no avail. It was one of the most frustrating aspects of my life those years. It almost felt cruel of the beings to appear so readily to me and the people around me, but then refuse to be recorded. I had tried 35mm film, digital cameras, phones, and iPads, and none of them worked. I could hardly believe that it was still there in front of me and on the phone screen at the same time.

When it did make its exit, I was overjoyed to see the recording had successfully saved to my phone. Whatever energy or radiation the orb emitted hadn't fried the device, and I was able to send the video to Yvonne. I went inside the house and showed it to the kids too: it was beautiful and humbling to finally have what I was seeing be backed up and thought of as 'real.' It was a breakthrough, and further confirmation that the lady was supporting me on my mission to tell the world. I believed then that nothing happened by coincidence with the orbs. If they allowed themselves to be filmed, they would be filmed. Ever since this night they have become more and more willing to be recorded. I could only guess that the lady was pleased that I had gone to the Gathering and so rewarded me with the ability to capture orbs on video. All around me, everywhere I went, a whole unseen world was beginning to reveal itself. She was fulfilling her promise.

That winter my arthritis became unbearable. Often the hardest physical labor of gardening came in the colder months when it was time to prepare the soil for spring. I was committed to using fertilizer from the manure of my forty hens, since I wanted to be able to provide for my family and neighbors in the event that my apocalyptic visions came true. There would be no hardware stores or Miracle-Gro to go out and buy in that kind of world. Making fertilizer the old-fashioned way posed the risk of contaminating the crop with botulism, so it had to undergo a fairly complicated aging process before it could be used. All of this required heavy lifting and shoveling. My joints were so swollen and painful I could hardly carry out the most basic tasks without blinding myself with pain. The cold weather in January and February made all of it even worse: stiffer joints, harder soil, fewer people willing to come out in the cold and lend me a hand.

January was slipping away and there was still a great deal I had to get done before February, when potatoes, cabbages, onions, and turnips had to go in. I called my old friend of more than forty years, Bobby Blue, and he came by to help. He was always there for me when I needed him. Slowly, the sun stayed out longer and longer, easing open the earth as the first shoots emerged. All that spring, I kept capturing videos and images of the orbs and sharing them with those I trusted.

∞

That Easter in 2013, I met the lady for a second time. This time, she brought me to her. Part of it felt dreamlike, and part of it felt as real as what I ate for lunch yesterday. My arthritis had gotten so bad it started to disrupt my sleep.

When it flared up, there was hardly a position I could find that didn't hurt, whether standing, sitting, or lying down. Even the pressure of a mattress on my joints caused discomfort. I slept in my study then to not keep Yvonne awake with my tossing and turning.

In the early morning hours of March 31st, I was gently awakened by a subtle departure of pressure underneath me. It wasn't so much that the ache had dissipated, but that gravity itself had let go of its grip on me. I was floating. Opening my eyes, I saw I was rising up through the top of the house, alert but entirely relaxed. Usually when I woke up in these months, the first thing I felt was a severe pain from moving after a long time being still, yet now I moved freely and painlessly. Some giant hand was lifting me upward seamlessly through an opening that had appeared in the ceiling, past the boxes and rafters in the attic, through the roof. There was no tractor beam or jerking, just a steady rise. I saw I was being drawn into a brilliant bluish-white light hovering about a hundred feet over the house. At this point I was no longer surprised and felt no fear about what was happening. A part of me remembered what had happened the previous Easter and being taken at the river: nothing that happened was a coincidence. If they hadn't harmed me yet, there was no reason for them to do so now. I felt deep down that they were doing all of this to prepare me to tell the world. This was just another step in the process of molding me into the kind of witness they needed. I rose into the light and became enveloped by it.

Its brightness became so intense it seemed to invert itself into a familiar dark room. It was the exact same space I was in during the missing time at the river incident. I was standing upright in total darkness and could hear my breath echo around the walls. Just as before, the total silence of the space gave me the impression that the echoing of my breath demarcated a round room. I noticed the walls were no longer the electric bluish-white of the orb, but transparent. I found I had the ability to walk, and went forward toward the wall, placing my hands against an invisible boundary that held me inside. In front of me I saw we had risen far outside of earth's atmosphere and were moving past an endless expanse of stars. I had no idea where I was going, but I knew I had traveled unimaginable distances when suddenly I was lowering through the atmosphere toward a surface. It was either a very dim daylight where we were descending or a pale evening. I looked downward and saw no lights, houses, or roads where we were headed. There was only what looked like an endless expanse of desert floor. It could have been Egypt or any other desert on earth, but for some reason I got the sense that it was Utah. As the orb lowered me down, I realized our descent was aimed at a canyon carved deep into the land. Before I knew it, the surface of the orb was replaced with the feeling of warm, desert-yellow sand under my feet. I was shoeless and still in my pajamas, looking up at hundreds of feet of jagged canyon walls on either side of me. When I landed, the orb opened its walls, almost popping like a bubble, revealing three beings the same size and shape as had led me to the lady the previous Easter. Their bodies glowed ivory-yellow like the moon, and it occurred to me that they must wear a kind of cloak to protect my eyes from their brightness. They must have been inside the orb with me the whole time, escorting me to wherever place we were.

All at once the three of them glided past me down the canyon. Utterly bewildered, I could hardly get myself to move, but they stopped and made a motion for me to follow them. Curious and afraid to be left alone, I began to walk in their tow. Ahead of us, the canyon walls seemed to wind on and on forever. I walked behind them for a long time, what felt like the distance of a mile. As on the orb, it was totally silent in the canyon. I didn't try to speak and don't know if I could have if I tried.

I was walking behind them at a steady pace when suddenly out of the gloomy darkness of the canyon I saw the wall of a canyon ahead awash in brilliant light. The light came from behind a left-hand corner in the canyon's winding. Seeing the canyon wall so clearly shocked me. It looked so much like canyons on earth. As we approached I grew more and more impatient to discover what the light source could be in such a strange, desolate place. The beings continued ahead of me at the same patient pace.

Finally we rounded the corner. The lady was there, beaming. She was the light and the light source. The canyon gleamed around her the same color as her bluish-white aura, and her dress was such a bright white I could hardly look at it. She was seated on a massive stone-carved throne in a recess in the canyon wall. As the beings led me to her, I watched her, unmoving, powerful, unspeakably beautiful. When we approached the front of the throne, the beings gave her a slight bow and turned to walk away, leaving me alone looking up at her. She stood up from the massive throne and hovered over the carved-out floor beneath it, never touching the ground. Just forty feet away and twenty feet above me, she spoke a parable that took a long time for me to process.

"When the red star of Regulus aligns just before dawn in the gaze of the Sphinx, a new knowledge shall come into the world." I was not sure what that meant. I have come to understand that around Easter 2026 there will be the end of an old way and the beginning of a new.

I felt overcome with a newfound ability to feel others' pain as well as an impulse to help them through it. The thoughts and emotions of others seemed vitally, extraordinarily connected to me. She communicated to me that she could now trust that I was forever committed to sharing what I knew with the world, whatever the cost. She wanted the world to know and trusted me to deliver as much of this knowledge as I was meant to. They would help me in the journey and were grateful that I was willing to take on this burden. She said they would not interfere with our free will, which was why it mattered that I had chosen, and continued to choose, to take this path.

I woke back up in my bed that Sunday morning remembering everything that had transpired. Her beauty, above all else, was burned in my mind. I wanted so badly to know how they had made it happen. Put simply, I was blown away. After going on for so long with only the slightest bit of proof, if you could call it that, I now had almost a full year of support, acknowledgment, and approval from some of the most respected people on the planet. Everything my family and I had sacrificed to simply tell the truth of what I had seen was now turning out to be worth something. Gifts of compassion, understanding, and even material gifts like dinners and parties were flowing to us after years of deprivation, isolation, and misery. Only a few days later I found out the lady had given me my most important gift yet.

CHAPTER 17

And the prayer of faith will save the one who is sick, and the Lord will raise him up.

—James 5:15

One of the friends I made at the Gathering was Grant Cameron, a writer and researcher who has studied UFOs for decades. He sat in front of Yvonne and me on one of the charter buses to the hotel, and we hit it off. At the end of the weekend we exchanged phone numbers and agreed to keep in touch. A couple of weeks after Easter he sent me a message saying he would be driving near us traveling between conferences in Washington and Miami. He asked if he could stay with us on his way down. It was exactly the sort of opportunity I knew the lady wanted me to take. There was always more to learn about the history of unexplained phenomena, and he knew as much as anyone in the world.

He had a few extra days to spare between his events so he ended up staying with us a couple of nights. The whole family had a great time picking his brain and he had a million stories. The second night one of the kids brought home some takeout for dinner. I let the dogs outside beforehand so they wouldn't bother us eating. There was Nelly, our beautiful three-year-old black lab, and Bell, Emily's long-haired chihuahua. While everyone else was gathered around the table making their plates, I walked the dogs down the hall through the front door. They were good dogs and went out into the yard without protest. I closed the door and turned back toward the kitchen.

As soon as I had made my plate and sat down, I noticed Nelly and Bell were there staring at me with big hungry eyes. I asked if anybody had seen what just happened. Everyone shrugged it off. I got back up and led them back outside. This time I made sure the door was latched closed. A few moments passed as we ate together when I looked up and there they were, Nelly and Bell again, looking up at me for food. None of the other doors were open, or even openable to anything without opposable thumbs. Yvonne, the kids, and I glanced at each other, smiling. I brought the dogs outside again. Somehow, they found their way inside again. Grant didn't recognize what was going on, but we knew something fishy was going with the beings. This time we decided to just let them stay inside.

Grant left the next morning for Miami, then called us a few days later asking to stay with us again on his way back to Canada. It turned out our house was only a few minutes off the interstate he was using. He wanted to take some photographs of the burnt tree and other parts of the yard where some orbs had scorched the grass.

That Sunday afternoon he called saying he was close. I told him to park at the back of the house and I would be out there to meet him. It was a beautiful late spring evening, about seventy degrees and not a cloud in the sky. The bugs weren't out yet, so we liked to open the doors and windows to let some fresh air circulate and save on air conditioning. After so many years of money being tight, Yvonne especially was in the habit of making sure every light was turned off that didn't need to be on. A cool breeze on a good day was more than a small gift to us. I was sitting on the back porch watching Nelly and Bell play in the grass in the shade of an oak tree when I heard the familiar crunch of a car turning onto our gravel driveway.

Grant got out of the car and stretched his legs. Daylight was starting to wane so he asked if he could go ahead and take his pictures of the tree. I told him yes and walked with him seventy-five yards or so back to the tree while he got his camera ready. Like the faithful friend she was, Nelly followed us back to the tree where we stood around talking for about twenty minutes. Grant took close-ups from every angle as we shared stories. While we were out back, Ryan and Junior and some of their friends had gathered on the back patio. Grant finished and we headed back to the house.

When we were almost back to the house, he stopped to ask me a question. Nelly stopped to lie down next to me while I answered. Eventually, having seen all the boys back there, I told Grant that we could help bring his bags to his room if he was planning on spending the night. He said sure and we started back to the house again. Nelly sensed we were starting off and took off to beat us to the back door. She brushed past Grant. She ran past me and I saw it: a steady stream of blood running down in a trail on the grass. Shocked and terrified, I watched the blood spurting from her neck as she trotted to the door.

"Oh my Lord Nelly is hurt!"

I sprinted after her inside and tackled her just inside the front door. My arthritis screamed in pain as I fell to the wood plank floor with her cradled in my arms. Her black hair was slick with blood. It splattered on the floor and steps as I carried her back out to the patio. I was beyond distraught. I loved Nelly so deeply and there was so much blood, I was afraid she was a goner. Kneeling over her I found the wound, a one-and-a-half-inch gash on the side of her neck. Grant wasn't sure what to do so he just started filming us with his camera. My heart was racing. I didn't know what to do.

"Oh Lord what do I do?!"

I put my bare hand on her blood-soaked fur and felt sick to my stomach. It was so dreadful. The blood kept rising between my fingers as I called out to the Lord again asking what to do. I applied pressure trying to slow the bleeding, but it barely helped, so I lifted my hand to take a closer look at the wound. I looked into the dark red opening. I couldn't tell how deep it was, but it was wide enough to put three fingers in.

"Someone get me a towel!"

Junior sprung up and ran back into the house, quickly emerging with his mother's washcloth. I could barely think. I just pressed the folded cloth to her neck, closed my eyes, and prayed. The cloth was beginning to dampen and I knew she was going to die right there. There was no ambulance for dogs. She was bleeding too fast to get her to an animal hospital. Her dark eyes looked scared and confused. I looked up to the early evening sky and kept pressing.

"Oh God what do I do?!"

I closed my eyes. Something deep in me was unlocked. She started to pant more slowly. She relaxed. I pressed more gently. I lifted the damp cloth wondering what had caused the change. No blood shot out. There wasn't even a gash anymore. I looked over at the blood on the steps and in the house. I saw the blood on my hands and clothes wondering how on earth this had happened. I fell back sitting on the ground, dumbstruck, baffled, relieved. Grant continued to take pictures of Nelly and me as she walked off wagging her tail like nothing happened.

All I could think of was that I felt the presence of the lady with me. I had called out and she was there, her familiar energy had somehow flowed through me. I watched Nelly prance around the yard, overcome with gratitude. However she had gotten cut, she had been healed just as mysteriously. Whatever the lady's reasons, she had allowed Grant to witness and record all of this. In part because of this day, I still have a close friendship with Grant. Somehow, the lady had used me as a conduit of healing. From that day on, I knew she might choose to act through me to relieve people of their illnesses and injuries. Something about a desperate, honest cry for help brought her to us that day. I recognized her power, asked for her, and she closed the wound.

One of the many invitations and requests I received in the wake of the Gathering involved another free trip to Pennsylvania. A publisher there had invited me to spend a weekend in June 2013 with a few of his authors and wealthy friends. He owned a beautiful cabin in the country beside a lake where we could go fishing and, as he described it, "talk about the universe." I was still not exactly sure what they wanted from me, but it seemed like another opportunity the likes of which the lady would have wanted me to take advantage of.

When I landed in Philadelphia, a guy I had met at the Gathering was waiting for me at baggage claim. He drove me an hour outside the city to the country. The scenery around the place was gorgeous and I was really looking forward to the weekend. I was the last to arrive and we all got acquainted in the living room. Fairly quickly we started talking about why the publisher had gathered us all there.

One of the men posed me a question about good and evil: do they exist? How does one know the difference? What is a person's obligation to the good? I felt cornered. I believed that good and evil existed, that like dark and light every person had a duty to pursue the good and the light. One of the men asserted that there was no evil, that the universe and life itself was random chaos. Some of them chimed in, agreeing. At that point I wanted to go home. I could hardly tolerate such a pessimistic, lonely philosophy. It went against everything I knew about life: that nature orders chaos, that nothing happens by accident, that the miracle of a tomato ripening on the vine is no less amazing than a fleet of UFOs dancing in the sky. The lady had left her mark on me, and I knew without a doubt that she was goodness, that she was light.

They kept asking me how I knew that evil existed, so I brought up the case of Jeffrey Dahmer. Surely if there were evil in the world, it could be found in the soul and actions of a man who committed murder, rape, cannibalism, and necrophilia. These were not crimes of passion, but planned and repeated over many years. His victims in no way deserved what happened to them; there was no justice in his actions, and there certainly was no empathizing with him. Everything about his actions went against nature. Every basic instinct about right and wrong within me knew without a doubt that he constituted evil.

Like the sophists they were, they had a canned response in defense of the assertion that evil did not exist. They said that Dahmer's victims had in fact chosen to be eaten in their previous lives. Not only was I confused about why they cared about this topic or what it had to do with me or UFOs, but I was also deeply creeped out. If these guys were willing to defend Jeffrey Dahmer, however indirectly, what else were they prepared to defend in the interest of some half-baked moral philosophy? Such topics were not games for me. The lady had given me a mission to act in compassion and love toward all living beings. I myself had been close enough to the brink of death so many times that cherished life in a way these men did not. I did my best to ignore everything they said the rest of the afternoon.

Eventually a surprise guest showed up named Timothy E. Taylor. I had been told it was just the five of us that weekend, but apparently he had got wind of my being there at the last minute and decided to come. He had heard about me a few months before at a conference in Arizona and had been planning on meeting me. He was on his way home to Alabama from Los Angeles when he got the call, and decided to make a one-day detour to meet me at the cabin. We sat around talking for a while and I noticed that his attention was fixed squarely on me though I was hardly participating in the discussion at that point.

Toward dusk we decided to take a break from talking. I went outside to call Diana for advice on what to do. I didn't know how I could stand to spend an entire weekend with these men, much less the basis of their interest in denying the existence of evil. She and I had continued to try to work on a book together, and in the process she taught me a great deal about the history of world religions and various celestial phenomena. Standing outside by the lake, I told her I had no idea what I had gotten myself into.

After I hung up, Tim came out. The first thing he told me was to not worry about the guys in there, that they simply could not understand my experiences and where I was coming from. He had heard me struggle to talk about Junior's difficulties in coming to terms with what he had seen, as well as the ostracism and rejection he experienced in the aftermath. A part of me still felt like all of his suffering was my fault.

Out in the yard, Tim said that he had worked for NASA his whole life and was interested in my story. This was why he had come all the way to see me. He asked if he could come visit us at home, and that maybe someone credentialed like him could talk to Junior and help him feel validated in his experiences on the river. He simply wanted to help us. The only other person who had offered such no-strings-attached support was Hal Povenmire, who was also from NASA and had begun to visit us a few times a year just to check in. Hal actually told us that he had been sent to us to debunk the story of the river incident, and that after four years of interviewing our neighbors and researching county records, he wasn't able to. He had spent so long on the case that he eventually became something like a godfather to our children.

My family's saving grace all these years has been our ability to make friends out of strangers. Allies came out of the woodwork when we needed them most, and that remains the case today. Tim would become a close friend to our family, just as Hal had. Something about the lady's energy helped me to form a community of supporters and friends that continues to guide us on this journey. After such a long isolation, it felt like an unbelievable gift to have friends like Diana, Grant, Hal, and Tim come into our lives. I know life always exists on a razor's edge, so I take nothing and no one for granted. I never walked by Nelly again without saying hello or giving her a pet.

CHAPTER 18

Word got around in the MUFON organization about Diana's interest in me and the possibility of a movie. In 2013, Diana offered to purchase my Life Story Rights naming her company in the contract, No Coincidences Management and Research, LLC. One sentence in the contract read, "With full knowledge, I hereby grant to you, perpetually and irrevocably, the unconditional and exclusive right throughout the universe to use, simulate and portray my name, likeness, voice, personality, personal identification, biography, and personal experiences, incidents, anecdotes, situations, and events which heretofore occurred or hereafter occur (in whole or in part) based upon or taken from my life or otherwise in any way related to my life, death and story, in and in connection with books, motion pictures, sound recordings, and any and all other media of any nature whatsoever, whether now known or hereafter devised." I turned it down. The screenwriter brothers were still in touch and taking meetings in Hollywood, though it was still up in the air whether a film would get made. MUFON of course felt that they had a claim on my family's experiences, and reopened my case that summer in the hopes of getting publicity and funding through the movie. This was extremely unwelcome news. Their initial investigation had been so unprofessional that I wanted nothing to do with them. On top of that, they had continued to publish stories about us in their newsletters and publications. Many of the things they wrote about us were ridiculous. One article suggested that Junior had been abducted by Bigfoot. I had finally found a small group of legitimately supportive friends who didn't want to exploit my family for their own benefit. This wasn't 2008: I knew I had legitimate resources available and I wouldn't be taken advantage of again.

A woman named Chase Kloetzke had gotten in touch with me to let me know what was coming. She had long been a MUFON investigator but had recently left because of the sexual discrimination she faced in the organization. The poor treatment my family received in 2008 from both MUFON and Discovery was well-known, so when Chase heard they were reopening my case she got in touch to warn me. She was also still interested in doing investigations independently and asked to come collect samples from the burning tree. I was grateful that she had been looking out for me, and she seemed trustworthy, so I was glad to have her come by.

One day in August she came down the driveway, a tan woman with black hair and a bright smile. She brought plastic bags and took pieces of wood and dirt from in and around the tree, then she labeled them to send to M.I.T. to be chemically analyzed. Afterward, she helped me draft a few cease-and-desist letters that I could send to MUFON if they kept trying to involve themselves in my story or write ridiculous things about us in their newsletters.

A couple of weeks later she called with the lab results. No gasoline or other accelerants were found, nor any signs of a lightning strike. The official report determined the cause of the fire was unknown. The husk of the catalpa tree still stood toward the back of the yard about twenty feet tall. We were all surprised to see small green shoots had begun to spring out from parts we thought had died. It had burned a long while, and even continued to burn after Yvonne extinguished it with water three times in a row. Whatever the cause of the fire, it hadn't killed the tree.

Tim Taylor and I had been talking nonstop that summer. He had planned a visit on September 7th to take a look around the yard and talk with Junior about the legitimacy of his experiences. In our discussions since the weekend together in Pennsylvania, I learned that his training and qualifications were unbelievably broad-ranging. He was a genuine expert on medical, aerospace, military, and intelligence technology. As an inventor and engineer he held thirteen patents. His affiliations with government agencies were an endless trail of alphabet soup, though he was officially employed by the National Reconnaissance Office. The whole family, even Jeremy, who had just started another school year in Wilmington, returned home to meet him that morning.

It just so happened that Chase Kloetzke called that morning saying she happened to be in the area with her husband Pete and that she would love to have me meet him. It was short notice, but I was still grateful for her help with the tree and the cease-and-desist letters. Chase and Pete showed up about an hour after Tim, while we were all sitting in the living room talking.

Tim was taken aback by the two strangers walking in, but he was more than friendly to all of us. Naturally, he was inclined to keep his activities and whereabouts on a strictly need-to-know basis. It created a fairly awkward situation at first. Pete was wearing a U.S. Navy Seal T-shirt, and it was impossible to discern from Tim's stoic face whether that comforted or concerned him. Tim had been planning on briefing us, though none of us knew at the time what his intentions were with his visit. I explained that Chase had worked with MUFON and helped investigate the tree. We talked about surface-level subjects for a few minutes.

Out of the corner of my eye I saw Tim give a bit of a wink and a nod to Ryan, who got up and went to the kitchen. Tim then got up with his backpack and followed him in. He explained to Ryan that he wanted to explain a few things to us one-on-one and give us a little test. Ryan led him back to his small bedroom where Tim opened up his laptop and set it on top of Ryan's dresser.

Several minutes passed as the rest of the family and I sat talking with Chase and Pete in the living room. Suddenly Jeremy stood up and went to Ryan's bedroom. I could only guess that Ryan had texted him or signaled to him from around the corner. Next Emily went back there. One by one, everyone in the family except me disappeared to the other side of the house. Yvonne came back to sit with Chase, Pete, and me, but it was clear none of the kids were coming back. Chase and Pete sensed that maybe it wasn't the best time for a visit, so they decided to go back to their hotel for a while and return later that afternoon.

After they left, I looked at Yvonne, totally baffled about what was going on. I follow her back to Ryan's room and saw everybody there, crammed on a couch and on Ryan's bed. All six of us, plus Ryan's girlfriend Jennifer, sat down looking up at Tim and his laptop. The first slide read *FOR THE BLEDSOE FAMILY ONLY*, and the next was a warning declaring various penalties for sharing this information. Of course, I am not at liberty to share the information in the presentation, but suffice it to say that it most likely contained U.S. Government related information dealing with UFOs, unexplained phenomena, and related subjects. It was extensive and detailed, leaving very little lingering uncertainty.

When he finished, he reached down to his backpack and lifted out a small piece of metal. It was silver-gray, about the size of a postage stamp. He handed it to me and I held it in the palm of my hand, looking at it.

"What do you think about that?" he asked.

"I don't know what this is. It's weird how light it is. Hardly weighs anything. It looks a little like a piece of aluminum," I answered.

Tim reached into his backpack and pulled out another container. He took another piece of metal out of it, this one a similar matte, dark gray, but looked a bit wrinkled like aluminum foil. Then Tim demonstrated that it had an unusual property: it could be wrinkled and creased in the same manner as tin foil, but afterward could be perfectly smoothed out as if it had never been wrinkled in the first place. With the silver-gray piece in my left hand, he placed this second scrap of metal in my right.

Out of nowhere, energy jolted through me. My eyes darkened with tunnel vision as if I had just gone into g-LOC in a fighter jet.

"What is that?!" I managed to say despite my racing heart. I noticed my forearm pulsing.

"Why you? Why you?" Tim asked.

Before I knew it, he had taken it out of my hand, placed it back in its container, and set it in his backpack. I was staring at the ground blinking and trying to get my vision back. Breathless and overwhelmed, I had no way of answering his question. Eventually I looked up and everyone in the room was looking at me.

"Why you?" he asked again.

"What do you mean why me? What just happened to me?" I said.

He indicated that this material had isotopes that came from fifty million light years away. These materials and their composition had yet to be understood: they hadn't been made by human hands and nothing like them occurred naturally on earth. He said that of all the people he had tested with these materials, only two people previously had a reaction, and that this confirmed for him the truth of my experiences. What that meant, I don't know. Beyond this, my biological reaction was the strongest he had seen.

Something had shifted in the air. The faces of my family looked back at me with shock and concern. Whatever had just happened, it seemed even Tim didn't understand its full implications. Yvonne was relieved to see me finally catch my breath again. I left to get a glass of water from the kitchen and Tim went back to his hotel, and that was it for the briefing.

It was a huge day for us to say the least. That night my daughter Emily was crowned homecoming queen at the high school football game. Tim came back that afternoon and joined Chase, Pete, and my family to celebrate Emily's award. We took a picture together by the stands: a homecoming queen, some Bledsoe's, a NASA scientist, and NAVY sub-commander. A night to remember.

∞

Two weeks later, I was out on the back patio sitting by a fire I had made, enjoying a cool autumn evening. I didn't have cable TV and didn't miss it. There was always more for me to think about. I kept up a correspondence with both Tim and Hal Povenmire, and I began an apprenticeship of sorts in astronomy, physics, and whatever else I had questions about. Out in the backyard, I thought about what I had learned from them and how it lined up with what I was seeing. I learned how to predict the moon's phases, rises, sets, and even trajectories, noticing how the time of year affected all of these factors. I memorized the major constellations and nebulas. I developed a sense of where the planets were, how each of them orbited the sun at different paces. The disc of the milky way was a bright scar striping across the sky. Polaris hung still in the north while a vast net of stars spun slowly around it. Every night I was mesmerized by this endlessly complicated, beautiful system over my head. Somehow, across such unimaginably large, cold, and empty distances, the sun's gravity held us to its warmth. A photon, light itself, was privileged to move faster than anything else. This urgency astounded me. Hundreds of millions of years ago, little blips were created that traveled hundreds of millions of lightyears, arriving in a steady, twinkling dance in my pupil. All of them begged my attention at once, and it was all I could do to return the favor.

I was sitting out there tending the fire and thinking when two orbs appeared out of thin air. I was sitting back in my chair when they announced themselves with bright flashes. They were a bright, tangerine orange, hanging still quite a ways above me. As soon as I focused on them, the rate of their flashes accelerated, going from dim to radiant to dim again. It gave me the impression that they wanted to get my attention, just as one might turn a flashlight off and on to signal someone in the dark.

They then plummeted downward, with the same instantaneous acceleration and stopping-on-a-dime that I had seen so many times before. As they descended, the orb on the left changed colors to a gleaming white, then back to orange. As if in response to the left orb, the right orb changed to the same white, then back to the same orange. They arrived about a quarter-mile behind my property, no more than a hundred feet over the tree-line. Relative to the trees, they were perfect spheres about the size of mail trucks. Then they stayed orange, but continued their call-and-response by bobbing up and down a little bit. As one went down, the other went up at seemingly random speeds. There was something so playful about their motion and buoyancy, it was as though they had telegraphed to my brain the image of children playing a game together.

After thirty seconds or so of this duet performance, they came to a stop parallel to each other. Like a bullet out of a gun, they shot off due west, directly away from the back of the house. I sat there amazed as the fire crackled beside me. I checked over my shoulder if anyone had come out to watch without telling me. I was alone with the sky again, but by no means did I feel lonely.

∞

Two nights later I received a phone call from Chase. She asked if I had ever heard about a nearby town called Saint Paul's.

219

There is a cemetery there where many of my ancestors and relatives are buried.

I cut her off and said, "Chase, before you say anything else, let me tell you what happened to me Saturday night."

I told her about the two dancing orbs, their colors, and how they bobbed just over the tree-line. I told her that the orbs had flown off exactly in the direction of Saint Paul's, which is just ten miles as the crow flies from our house. I had a rich familiarity with the area's geography from flying over it countless times in my days as a pilot.

"Chris! You have to be freaking kidding me," she said, shocked.

"No, it's true that really happened!" I replied.

She explained to me that in addition to MUFON, she was part of a network of investigators of the paranormal, and that she had gotten a report about an incident in Saint Paul's. That Saturday night, a group of five people had driven an hour and a half from Wilmington to a farmhouse on a former plantation. Among the group was a former police officer, a nurse, a prison guard, and a father and son. They had guns and a whole array of cameras, mics, EVP meters, and other equipment intended to capture evidence of the paranormal. It was a two-story white clapboard house built in 1840 with a one-hundred-acre field stretching behind it.

The group started in the early evening in the house setting up their equipment and recording themselves explore all the rooms. They called out to spirits and ghosts asking for a response. Nothing too unusual happened to them there, and when they finished they decided to check out the property. They walked the length of the farm, about a hundred yards, to a dense tree-line of mostly pines. Ten feet into the trees was an old, dilapidated cabin that used to be slaves' quarters. It was a one-room, low structure that you couldn't see from the open field. The same process of calling out, listening, and recording yielded no results there either.

They then decided to go farther back into the woods to see what else they could find. Directly behind the house, a six-foot-deep ditch ran parallel to the back wall of the cabin. They scrambled down one side and up the other. The moment they had all traversed the ditch, they saw two brilliant streaks of orange light over their heads. The streaks were bright as lightning, zipping just above the tops of the trees.

The group was mystified and began to get scared. As experienced ghost hunters, they were all used to spending long periods of time in spooky places. Often they investigated locations where horrific, gruesome things had occurred. None of them were quick to scare, and they were prepared for all manner of the unexpected, but they weren't prepared for such a compelling and unusual display.

Then, from behind a tree, they saw something lean out and look at them. It had glowing, unblinking eyes. Immediately, two of them unholstered their guns and started shooting in the direction of the tree. In the flashes and report of the gunfire, whatever had been there disappeared. The group was rattled as it went to look around the tree, but quickly afterward decided to call it a night.

When they got back to their cars, they discovered that two hours had passed that none of them could account for. The clocks and devices they had on them were all functioning perfectly, but it was as though their memory had been wiped as soon as they crossed the ditch. The group was so unsettled by this that they reported it the next day.

Chase, who was living in Georgia at the time, knew I lived nearby and took the assignment to do a follow-up investigation of the site with her husband. She was calling to ask if I would like to go along with them the following Saturday, and I told her sure. I had never been a part of any ghost hunt, so I was interested in learning more about what the process was like. Chase had also mentioned her high tech equipment set-up, and I wanted see how she went about trying to capture what was fleeting and elusive.

The next night on one of our weekly calls, I told Tim Taylor what had been reported and that Chase and I were going to investigate the site. He was curious enough about the event to ask to join us, and I said sure. That night he booked a plane ticket from Huntsville. In just a few days, I would be on the former plantation wading into the dark of the woods with Tim, an agent who didn't officially exist, Chase, a lifelong paranormal investigator, and Pete, a former submarine commander. And we wouldn't be prepared for what was coming either.

CHAPTER 19

Saturday morning I drove to the airport to pick up Tim. He only had time for a day trip, and got an early flight from Alabama and another for that evening. On his last visit he didn't have the chance to see the burnt tree, so we stopped by the house first. The whole family was excited to see Tim again. He wore a tight-fitting black collared shirt and looked like a forty-year-old that could still pass navy SEAL fitness standards.

Out in the backyard it was a beautiful fall day. The garden was thriving and the burnt tree was starting to come back to life. As we walked together, I told him more about the tree, that the lab results were inconclusive, that Yvonne had put the fire out three times and it kept re-igniting. When we arrived at the tree, Tim walked around to the long open gash to look into the hollow trunk.

A silver snake emerged from the opening, extending its body directly at Tim. It was as though the tree itself was offering him a curving, scaly greeting. We watched its black eyes lock onto him for a few moments. It must have been about two feet long and had the color of a dully polished aluminum, a small head, and no other distinguishing features. Tim gasped and staggered a couple steps backward, then slowly, deliberately, the snake withdrew into the shadowy hollow of the trunk. Having grown up on that property, I figured I had seen every kind of plant and animal there was to see, but I had never seen a snake that resembled it, and I still haven't. We walked around the tree, checking out the various places where new green shoots had emerged. Afterward we checked wildlife field guides and the only snake close to what we saw was endemic to the Amazon. Back in the house, Tim told me that his grandmother was a full-blooded native American, and that he had attended college on a full scholarship because of it. Something his grandmother had always told him was that the appearance of a silver snake was always a sign from God.

Later that morning we brought Junior with us and drove to Saint Paul's to meet Chase, Pete, and the original five ghost hunters at the house. Tim had asked me to keep his identity as secret as possible because he needed to keep a low profile, so I just said that he was a friend of mine. We skipped the big house because Tim was only interested in what happened in the woods, and he only had a few hours to spend at the site. We walked together behind the house across about two hundred yards of farmland. It was a bean field that had shot up about eighteen inches tall, so we stepped in the furrows. As we went along, we saw several snakes slithering their way toward the house and the road, away from where we were headed. They weren't silver or unusual in the area, but it was deeply strange that all of them were going in the same direction. When we approached the tree-line, we noticed that several portions of the head of woods had been clear-cut and timbered within the past two weeks. Luckily, the section at the back of the property that included the one-room cabin seemed untouched.

Tim was puzzled at having seen so many snakes in a day. He asked me what I thought about it. I said I believed that it was all related to nature: the phenomena, the beings, the lady were part and parcel of the natural world. The snakes appeared that day to show us this connection, and I believed it was the erasure of their ecosystem that had caused the beings to delete two hours of the ghost hunters' time, as well as to scare them. Environmental distress provoked this intervention on the part of the beings, not as force of violence or protection, but because their connection to the woods called them there. Tim and I talked about all this and more as we walked through the piney woods. I would be going back later that night with the ghost hunters, so it was helpful to get oriented in the daylight. We went to the high-tension power lines and past the stripe of grassy clearing, then found a swamp with a slow creek meandering through it. We spent a long time going up and down the ditch, looking at the tree that the former cop and prison guard had shot. The cabin was empty and broken down. Before we knew it, I had to drive Tim back to the airport.

On the way, he said I needed to know about an important strategy when dealing with the beings. It was crucial that I keep them from getting into my head. They had the ability to read your thoughts and fill you with fear even if nothing scary or unusual was happening. He said I had to find a song that was at least four minutes long and that I knew all the lyrics of. Whenever I thought the beings could be near, I was supposed to sing the song to myself, whether out loud or just in my head. I hadn't been truly afraid for a long time, especially since meeting the lady, but I was grateful for the tactic nonetheless.

On the way back from the airport, I decided to stop by the house and see my mother. I was curious about what she knew about Saint Paul's, so I told her what had happened with the ghost hunters, their missing time, and the glowing eyes. She asked where it was, and I told her it was the big white house where Shaw Mill Road dead-ends at Highway 20.

"Well of course my parents are buried right there on Shaw Mill. Some of your father's relatives are too. You know they go way back. Been here a long time." She said, "But I know the house you're talking about. I used to pass by it all the time on the way to school. In fact, when I was growing up, that place was owned by your kin. They were Bledsoes. One of your grandfather's aunts I believe…"

I'd never known about this house before, so I was taken aback, but not too much. By this point, I had been blindsided by so many impossible coincidences that all I could do was smile when things like this happened. It started to get dark. I was due back in Saint Paul's.

∞

I met Chase, Pete, and the rest of the gang at the big house. The plan for the night was to recreate, in as detailed a manner as possible, the events of two weeks prior. They started timers in their cars and finished prepping all their gear. Three donned helmets with cameras fixed on all sides. They all pressed record and headed into the house one-by-one. I went in last wearing jeans and my coat just hoping I didn't get in their way. I'd hunted just about every kind of North American mammal, but didn't want to presume to know the protocols and etiquette of a ghost hunt. In the dark musty attic where we began, Chase could tell I wasn't quite sure what to do, so she just whispered that I'll be fine and stick by her.

I followed the seven of them from room to room as they called out to whatever ghosts or spirits could be waiting for them. In one of the upstairs bedrooms, I was struck by a sudden dizziness and almost fell down. I told Chase I didn't like the energy there and went outside to wait for them to finish. They eventually came out with nothing too unusual to report, though it often happened with these hunts that discoveries were only made after the recordings were analyzed. The audio, video, infrared, and EVP meter all picked up things we might not have noticed at the time.

Next, we drove around the bean field to the cabin, and parked along the tree-line in a spot where we guessed it lay hidden behind the brush. Again, they checked and reset their equipment and we went back into the woods for the second time that day. The undergrowth was so thick we had to go single-file, and it was so dark we couldn't see but a few feet around us without a flashlight. We got to the cabin fairly quickly, and found the front door to be locked. We found our way around to the back and I saw the ditch again. It seemed deeper at night, more so resembling a trench carved into the land than a result of natural drainage. We reentered the ancient, creaking structure and the team did their ghost hunting again, calling out, following some protocol. They put an EVP box in my hand and we listened to its quiet static drone. Apparently, there was nothing going on in the room, but I did appreciate the empathy and courage involved in these attempts, aimed as they were at resolving historical traumas. Pain may not be fixed by having others listen, but if tormented souls needed a sympathetic ear to move on, I thought the ghost hunt was a kindness outside of time more than the chase of some prey. Finding nothing, we went back outside in about the same direction as the initial visit. As we scrambled one by one down one side of the ditch and up the other, I remembered to start thinking about my song lyrics. I didn't sing out loud for fear of ruining their investigation, and also because there is no imitating the vocal acrobatics and falsettos of Robert Plant and Sandy Denny on "The Battle of Evermore." I chose that song because Led Zeppelin was huge when I was a kid but mainly because it was longer than four minutes and I knew all the words already.

With Chase and me as the last two in the chain, we weaved through the trees. One of the original ghost hunters was at the front with a flashlight. After a while walking, we arrived back at the clearing where the powerlines ran as far as the eye could see in a black canyon of forest. Every now and then a gentle breeze would come by and you could make out the way the towering pines swayed flexibly, almost too flexibly, in the wind. One would think such heavy wood would resist a little wind more stubbornly, but then a lot of things one would think are wrong. The ghost hunters were interested in the effect of electricity on their instruments, and they had spent about an hour here the previous time, so that's how long we spent this night. As we walked around, I watched the slow waltz of the pines, singing to myself, "…With flames from the dragon of darkness. The sunlight blinds his eyes! . . ." (maybe not the best song choice) as I was checking the darkest spaces between the trees for anything unusual. After the right amount of time had passed and there was nothing pressing to report, we gathered back together at about the same place we had arrived at the powerlines.

Pete was a naval sub commander and had a high-tech compass on his watch, so he was the point person when it came to navigating. He said it was only about a hundred yards back due east to our cars, that it should just be a fifteen-minute walk back. Again, we plunged into the dark with Chase and I tailing. After a few minutes of the slow walk through thickets and uneven ground, I felt something in the air shift. I saw one of the men up front start to reach for his gun, hesitate, then reach for it again. They picked up the pace while I kept my focus on my song.

Suddenly over Chase's right shoulder my eyes met a pair of luminous, bright green eyes leaning out from behind a tree. I tapped Chase on the back and pointed at them. She pointed too as her jaw dropped. Evidently no one else had seen them as they kept hurrying on. We didn't want to be left behind so we kept walking. I looked back over where they had been and they were gone. After five minutes all eight of us arrived back at the ditch. We went through the ordeal of climbing down and up and met together at the far side at the back of the cabin.

Except there was no cabin. We were back at the powerline clearing, the same place we had just left. We were freaked out. We were all familiar enough with the area to know that what had just happened wasn't possible. We were all deeply unsettled. Pete had kept his compass on the entire time, and none of us noticed any kind of veering in our path. They were all befuddled and a bit scared. Either the man who navigated nuclear submarines underwater had somehow lost his way across a hundred yards of woods he had already walked that day, or there was another explanation. I knew exactly what had happened, though I kept it to myself for the time being. We went back through the woods the same way we had just come. There was no ditch. It was the same path as our first attempt to walk back, then we came to the same ditch again.

This time, when we arrived at the other side, the cabin was there. We rushed toward our cars.

We spent a few minutes standing in a circle talking about what had just happened. More than anything else, I was relieved Junior hadn't come with us this time. We were all perplexed. Chase, Pete, and the ghost hunters were all well-acquainted with their procedures and methods. Such a slip-up was deeply troubling for the well-oiled machine they intended to operate as. Science and objective verification were at the heart of their approach. After a few minutes we got in our cars, not wanting to get trapped there.

The next day, I got a call from Chase.

"Chris, you will not believe what happened last night! We figured it out," she said.

"I know what happened. We lost fifteen minutes of time," I replied.

"Oh my god!" she said. "How did you know that?"

"Because it took about fifteen minutes to cross that head of woods. We must have had one of those crossings wiped from our memory because that was the same ditch we crossed. I was sure of it."

Chase launched into a technical explanation of how the timers they had set in the car showed a twelve-minute discrepancy from the timers they were wearing, as well as the timestamps on their helmet-mounted cameras. As we talked, we realized that somehow, twelve minutes had passed between when we crossed the ditch and when we came out onto the powerline. Whether we had walked all the way back across the woods and had our memories wiped, or we had been taken and transported, or something else, Chase and I knew that whatever we had seen with green eyes was responsible for it.

CHAPTER 20

So many people were contacting me asking to come see the yard and watch the sky that we practically had to beat them off with a stick. A common occurrence arriving back at the house was finding a note or a letter taped to the door asking to meet me. I didn't like saying no to so many people, but I had a family to protect and kids to raise. Having our house turn into a tourist trap just wasn't feasible.

The summer before this ghost hunt in 2013, a man had gotten in touch with me by the name of Doug Auld. He was a painter living in Hoboken, New Jersey, and found my email by contacting a podcast I had appeared on. He was one of the few people to watch the Discovery channel documentary and realize what an injustice had been done to our story. He seemed sincere enough in his initial email so I figured I'd give him a chance, and we kept talking. In our exchanges over the course of the fall, he told me about the first time he had seen an orb. Because he was a painter, he often had a camera on him to take photos he could later paint from in his studio. It had been eight years since he lost his wife to a long struggle with cancer, while at the same time his mother had been ailing in a nursing home. He was sitting on a church's front steps in New York City, at one of the lowest points of his life, when he looked up and saw it. A tiny white orb hovering way up, still and calm above the noisy city traffic.

He said that he had been interested in UFOs since he was a child, and that this encounter was one of his first successful captures. When he saw the episode and heard my podcast, he was convinced that he had seen the same phenomena and had to meet me. Instead of being afraid and incredulous about what happened to me, he actually said he would have done anything for it to happen to him! He knew I had taken up painting and was more than willing to lend any professional help he could. Thanksgiving was coming up, so I told him to come on down. He wouldn't have to be alone, and we could get to know each other a little better.

I met him the day before Thanksgiving at a restaurant and gave him the whole story. Naturally, I cried for parts of it, but he was supportive and patient. Over the dinner table, we talked and laughed about what few superficial differences existed between us, a family of southerners hosting a Yankee. He sat next to my father, Ted, and they really hit it off talking about the phenomena. Doug was surprised to hear my dad describe his own experiences despite being a skeptic in the past. He and my family gelled, and we had a nice time together, though we didn't experience any phenomena—to his disappointment.

It just so happened that on the first Saturday of December, Emily was performing at a huge Christmas concert at the Crown Coliseum. Since Doug was an artist too, he wanted to come support her and decided to come back down the Friday beforehand. When I picked him up from the airport I noticed he was kind of hobbling around and wincing as he walked, so I asked him what was wrong. He said he had been playing hockey the night before in New York and had gotten a terrible bruise just above the back of his knee on his hamstring. There was a lot he hadn't seen on his first trip, so I took him to the sites on the Cape Fear River where it had all happened. I could see how nasty his injury was when he showed me. Purple, red, and black, it amazed me that he could bear to stand up. After I had pointed out where the various events had occurred, we got back in the truck. I saw his leg again and figured I'd might as well say a prayer for him. I placed my hand on his leg and asked God to heal this wound. We had a great time that night sitting around the fire talking.

Over breakfast, he reported what he called a miracle that happened that morning. That his horrific bruise had all but gone away and stopped causing him pain entirely. That night we went to the Heart of Christmas show and saw Emily perform beautifully, after which we went home and sat by the fire again.

Doug had a flight home Sunday evening. I asked him about whether he could make a painting of the lady, and he said he was afraid he couldn't do it justice, but we would keep talking. Before he left, he wanted to say hi to my parents. We walked over and talked for a few hours. Doug was captivated by the story of my father's life, how hard he worked, how he adapted to the internet era, and how he adapted to acknowledge and believe in his son's experiences. My father told him he'd had out-of-body experiences and visions while in the hospital. As I drove Doug to the airport, he said how happy he was to see our father-son relationship had been mended. The next night, we would learn that besides my mother and myself, Doug was the last person to speak to my father.

My mother came home from work to discover my best friend of fifty-two years dead on the floor from sudden heart failure. I will never forget that call: the panic in her voice, crying like I had never heard her, saying how she had found him. It killed me to hear the news and I started crying uncontrollably. I can hardly remember any of those moments. A blur, an ache all through my body, gasping for breath between sobs.

I had been by my father's side for fifty-two years. Through love and anger, successes and failures, we stuck together and always found a way to talk things through. This was the man who made me. He showed me that with a little bit of grit, nothing could hurt too much to bear, nothing was too difficult to understand, that nothing can be permitted to get between me and the people I love most, my family. He was a mountain of a man, unbelievably strong. It was difficult to even conceive that the man who taught me how to hunt, fish, and survive could be touched by death. We played with each other as fiercely as we loved each other. Even my experiences with the phenomena, the issue that drove the biggest wedge between us, we finally overcame. He went from jokingly accusing me of drug-use to total acceptance, standing beside us, witnessing it.

A few years earlier, in the fall after my first encounter with the lady, I started praying with more focus and intention than ever. My father's health was waning. Every day and night, I prayed. I looked toward the sky and pleaded with her, God, angels, or whoever was out there, to save my father.

He had just undergone major surgery and was now back home recuperating, waiting for the biopsy results. We were all gathered at their house waiting for news from the doctors. It was a Friday afternoon and we were all on the back patio. Yvonne, the kids, my sisters, their families, and my mother and father sat together waiting for a call. It was sunny, but we were in agony. Hardly anyone spoke as the swinging bench my father was in creaked back and forth.

Finally, the phone rang. My mother stood up and reached in the back door to pick it up. Utter terror on her face, she held it to her ear. She smiled. After a minute or two of us watching her smile, nod, and cry, she hung up the phone. She said that Chapel Hill didn't detect any cancer. From their MRI, they only saw one tiny speck of growth, which was completely survivable as long as it was monitored.

I jumped up from my chair and raised both my hands straight to the sky. With a lump in my throat I said, "Thank you Lord!"

Suddenly between my hands with fingers outstretched, I saw a tic-tac shaped orb. I pointed and yelled, "Look!" and we all saw it, bright silver-white, a bit translucent and hovering in the air straight over us. Even my dad summoned the strength to stand up from his swing to look at it. It slowly began to move west and then vanished.

We were all overwhelmed. All I could say was, "Thank you Lord for healing my father." We hugged him. We had him back. He spent his remaining years involved in all his grandchildren's lives. He was a fixture, a solid rock all of us could go to for shelter from whatever storm we faced.

Funeral arrangements were made at the Baptist church just two miles away from where we lived. It rained that whole gloomy, cold winter day. It was like nature itself was weeping for him. After the heart-wrenching services, we drove back in the funeral home limo. Everyone was quiet and sad, looking out the window, commiserating with the weather. We came to a place in the country road where the trees encroached up to either side of the road, their branches hanging over the pavement. In the cold gray light, raindrops speckling the windshield, we saw a giant white owl perched over the middle of the road. From its positioning, as well as its disregard for the rain, it had the unmistakable attitude of a guardian that had been awaiting our funeral procession. It was speckled white and brown like a barred owl, but its dark eyes must have been the size of baseballs.

We passed under the bird, just fifteen feet below it. We couldn't help but have the sense it was a message indicating that my father was okay. The same bird that had appeared before I got shot and before the chair in my study was struck by lightning was the same one watching over us. Now though, the danger had passed, and some natural protective force kept its appointment with us. As with most of the phenomena, a clear meaning and emotion was somehow communicated to all of us. These forces were vigilant and abiding. They might not save us from everything, but there is no doubt in my mind that they have compassion for all life. A couple of years ago, my father's first great-grandson was born. Teddy carries on his name. It's my deepest hope that these forces care for his life as they have mine.

CHAPTER 21

In the weeks and months after my father's death, my arthritis continued to worsen. It was more than stiffness and swelling, it was a constant, debilitating ache. Some days I wished I could amputate my hands and feet they hurt so bad. Yvonne would take me to the emergency room, but their shots and painkillers took mere teaspoons out of the river of pain running through me. The doctors recommended I see a rheumatologist, but the waitlist was six months long, so I carried on the best I could. Often, I would spend nights alone in my study again, simply crying at the hurt I had no way of stopping.

That winter and early spring, Yvonne and I noticed Junior was spending more and more time in his room. He would get home from work, say a word or two, then hole up in there until we saw him the evening of the next day, since he was still working construction and got up earlier than the rest of us. Eventually he stopped even saying anything. We were afraid he was going to disappear again. Each time he left before we were wracked daily with worry, but he was an adult now and we had to respect his choices.

The ridicule he faced from friends and family had lessened over the years. It was not so fresh in peoples' minds. If someone cracked a joke about us behind our back, it wouldn't land like it used to. People he interacted with were getting older and more mature too, which helped. Junior had become more comfortable with talking about his experiences over the years. Tim Taylor and Hal Povenmire's NASA credentials and words of support were unassailable shields he could rely on. When he got afraid at night of being watched, he could resort to strategies they had given him. Our extended family that had judged us so severely at first heard about Tim and Hal's involvement with us, and started to avoid us instead of us having to avoid them.

I did my best to talk to him about the benevolent aura surrounding all my experiences with phenomena, but it was difficult to undo the trauma and fear of that first night. Just a seventeen-year-old kid who'd given up his senior year of high school to earn money for his family, it was no wonder that those hours spent in a cold, paralyzed terror left the mark that they did. Then there was the profoundly isolating aftermath. No one his age could relate to his story and would laugh at it if he told it. It set him apart from the world at an age when he was supposed to be finding his place in it. That kind of wound takes a long time to heal. Yvonne and I didn't want to push him away, so we gave him space. My arthritis made me fatigued too, so it was all I could do to take care of myself some days.

Easter 2014 was coming up, and I was hoping the lady might appear again to offer some relief from my symptoms. The night before, on April 19th, the family was in bed early for a Saturday. All the lights were out by 11:30. Next door, my sister's daughter, Stephanie, and her daughter, Anna, had moved in with my mother so she wouldn't feel alone in her grief. They had always been close to us and visited often. Now that they were next door neighbors, they came and went between the houses as freely as we all did.

That weekend, Stephanie and Anna had been dog sitting another relative's dogs two miles away, and it was half-an-hour after midnight when they finished checking on them and returned home to my mother's house. They had a dog of their own, Scrappy, who needed to be let out before they went to bed. They pulled into the driveway noting that all the windows in both houses were completely dark. They brought out Scrappy on a leash for a midnight stroll on the gentle spring night. He was moseying around in the grass when Stephanie and Anna were stunned by a bright light flashing from the front porch of our house. There she was, right on time.

They described the appearance of a beautiful, luminous woman in a flowing white dress. She emerged through the front door, floating just over the porch, then glided slowly down the steps to the front walkway. She cast a brilliant halo around her entire figure, as though she were made of light itself. Compared to her, all else was inscrutable darkness. After a few moments proceeding down the walkway, the lady stopped and turned toward Stephanie, Anna, and Scrappy. Awestruck, Stephanie and Anna made eye contact with her. Radiant, pure, the furls of her dress rippled slowly even as she was still. The lady came toward them for a moment, then shot off between the houses toward the back of the yard in a blinding streak of light. Right away Stephanie texted me about what she had just seen. She was ecstatic, but I was asleep and wouldn't see the message until morning.

"Mom, I'm so sick. I don't know what's wrong with me." These were the first words Junior spoke on Easter morning. He explained that his lower back had been hurting and now it hurt too bad to ignore. He lifted the back of his shirt to reveal a swelling mass almost the size of a soft ball on his side. Yvonne and I were terrified. Without another word, we raced him to the local hospital. He wasn't there long before they put him in an ambulance to rush him an hour and a half away to the bigger UNC hospital in Chapel Hill. The drive there with Yvonne was one of the torturously anxious times of my life.

He was admitted to the intensive care unit, and we learned he had been suffering in silence from a kidney infection for the past several weeks. The infection had worsened every day, and the doctors told us to be grateful for the fact that we brought him when we did. They said he likely would not have survived if we waited one more day. Junior, usually tan and strong from work, was pale and sallow in his hospital bed. It was heartbreaking. He stayed in the ICU for almost two months with a PICC line injecting powerful antibiotics directly to his heart the entire time. He developed myocarditis during this long, agonizing stay, and towards the end doctors warned us that his course of medical treatment would likely cause him to be sterile. Slowly, too slowly, he began to look and feel better as the infection lost ground.

Deep in my heart, I know that the lady had appeared that night to give Junior the impulse to ask for help. I was thankful she had shown up, but I was equally frustrated. Hadn't I been through a sufficient number of near-death experiences? Why was it necessary to bring my son, who had already been through so much, so close to this brink? Why bring him there only to bring him back from the ledge? To all of these questions, I can only guess and remember what I had been told: have compassion toward all life, speak about what I see, and do not ever give up. She had appeared to Stephanie and Anna for good measure to give Junior more support from his relatives. I believe every witness is another gift from the lady. Stephanie and Anna were with me now in a way I can hardly express, but for which I feel an unending depth of gratitude.

∞

In one of the first emails Tim Taylor ever sent me, he said that he was put on this earth to help cure cancer in children. I didn't think much of it at the time, but it seemed like a more than admirable cause. In our weekly talks in early 2014 I found out what he meant by this mission. He was, in fact, involved in advanced cutting-edge medical research. He would send me academic papers and talk them over with me, occasionally introducing me to members of his team who had contributed to the research. The focus was primarily on stem-cell applications, and over the course of these months he started to ask me more and more questions about stem-cells. My task was to meditate and dream about the science he was passing onto me in the hope that he and his team would have a breakthrough.

Eventually, he revealed why he was asking this of me. He said I had a special relationship to the methodology they were investigating, namely, the novel application of quasi-crystal formations in the medical setting. At the most basic level, quasi-crystals are regular geometric patterns that never repeat themselves. Like the irrational numbers pi or the golden ratio, quasi-crystalline patterns can continue forever and still dodge expectation. Pi, for instance, was sequenced to one hundred trillion digits in 2022, and the job is still far from finished. The Egyptians calculated pi with an accuracy of a handful of digits, Archimedes a few more, and we're facing the same incredible, seemingly eternal, math problem. The golden ratio is another such irrational number that simply does not end in complexity, no matter how powerful our computers get. Quasi-crystalline patterns proceed following this golden ratio, which is significant because of how profoundly tied to nature it is: the flowering of an artichoke, the arrangement of a bee's eye cells, the positioning of leaves on a stem all follow this number as a guide.

In mosques in the middle east, perfect quasi-crystalline patterns were used in brilliantly colorful and complex mosaics. In the 1980s, a scientist had synthesized an arrangement of molecules in a quasi-crystalline pattern: what he saw in his microscope defied all accepted knowledge about what constituted solid matter. It wasn't until 2011 that this scientist, Daniel Schechtman, won the Nobel Prize for his discovery, though it took him a thirty-year battle with the academy to convince them of what he had seen. As Tim explained all of this to me, I could not help but feel that it was deeply related to the phenomena: how no two orbs look entirely the same, how coincidence governed my life in such unpredictable ways, how there was always a subtle difference in one night's sky from the previous one. There is a saying that history doesn't repeat itself, but it often rhymes. If there are patterns in nature that never repeat itself, I believe the appearance of these phenomena to me and others may be just another rhyme.

He told me that during our family's briefing, the metallic-seeming silver things placed in my hands were these very same quasi-crystalline structures. He did not say where they came from, only that they were dated to fifty million years old and did not come from earth. He said that the galaxy was itself arranged in this regular, non-repeating pattern. My reaction indicated to him that I was connected to this formation of matter somehow, and that he needed my guidance even if he didn't completely understand why. He told me that the objects had imprinted this pattern on my mind and body. The metals were too precious to give to me, nor would I want to have that dizzying g-LOC experience on a regular basis, so he asked me to meditate on pictures he sent me to see if they unlocked anything. I found that looking at these images of various quasi-crystalline formations provoked powerful dreams, and I got in the habit of looking at them every night before bed. Like looking at the stars each night, it felt like another way to connect with nature in a deeper way. Sometimes Tim would have a particular kind of experiment the next day, and would task me with something particular to focus on. We did all kinds of exercises with each other on this mission, hoping my connection to the pattern would glean clues to his scientific pursuits. Mornings, I would wake up and draw whatever kind of geometrical pattern appeared to me in my dream. I thought of them as cells, growing one from another from another. I had the sense that cells, stars, orbs, and everything else in nature was integrated by this design.

After Easter when Junior went to the hospital, my efforts in this respect multiplied. I still prayed and asked for his healing, but I also put a huge amount of energy into these projects. The illness of my child summoned something in me. These efforts with Tim gave me hope for Junior, the rest of my kids, and the whole world. Tim's primary concern was his team's first operation. They had finally received approval from the government to attempt their methods and technology. The patient they approved for the surgery was a forty-year-old

Spanish lady with severe bone cancer that most doctors considered inoperable.

∞

While Junior was in the hospital, Yvonne and I received an invitation from some friends of ours to go on a weekend retreat in the mountains. The Spanish lady's operation was due to take place the following Monday, so I was hoping to have something positive to report to Tim after the weekend was over. She had two children, and we both were rooting hard for her. By mid-June, Junior had come back home from Chapel Hill and was able to continue his convalescence at home. Yvonne and I felt a little like celebrating his recovery, so off we headed to Linville Falls, North Carolina, where two of our friends had a gorgeous twenty-room lodge on a mountainside. We got a late start Friday and met seven of our friends waiting for us in the lobby around 9:30 p.m. There were psychologists and other professionals there, but more than anything, Yvonne and I were there to relax and have a nice time after one of the most stressful periods of our lives as parents.

After we checked in, we went down to the lobby and gathered around a small wood-burning stove. The building was made from pines that had been logged in the area, and you could see the beautiful grain of their wood on every wall. It was a cozy, wonderful place to talk. The first thing they asked me was why I had been painting so many birds. I had kept up with painting scenes from nature since I first started in 2008 when I was camping. Eventually I got in the habit of sharing the ones I liked best with friends on social media. Usually, my subjects varied, but for the past several months I had been painting hummingbird after hummingbird. For whatever reason, I associated these little sprite-like creatures with my efforts with Tim. The way their wings beat so quickly they almost vibrated, the fact that they had to continuously eat sugar or die, that sleep for them was the equivalent of hibernation, how slowly they perceived the passage time compared to us, their shimmering iridescence: everything about them was profoundly compelling to me. Painting was a way of studying them and getting closer to nature.

In any case, my answer satisfied them and our conversation sped on until one o'clock in the morning. We were all still having a good time, and one of us suggested we go try to see the Brown Mountain Lights. Brown Mountain was fairly close to us, and the group knew about a dirt road that led about four miles up to the Linville Gorge overlook. From the overlook, we supposed we could see the famous Brown Mountain Lights, a phenomenon documented over centuries, from Native Americans to the pioneers to today. The history is long and complex, but there have always been reports of orbs, lights, and other objects in the sky surrounding the mountain. I was curious, and they wanted to see the phenomena too, since they heard others around me often saw them too. If nothing else, we could catch a special glimpse of the Linville Gorge, what's called the Grand Canyon of the East.

We piled into my four-wheel drive truck and set out down the road to the dirt road that led up to the overlook. As soon as we turned onto the dirt, a brown bird about the size of a mocking bird appeared up in our headlights flying out of the forest from right to left. My best guess is that it was a brown thrasher. It then went around the back of the truck and passed by the passenger windows alongside us. Then, again, it passed in front us, ten yards in front of our headlights. The entire drive up the mountain, this bird kept circling us. There had been a lot of rain, which had washed out the road in several places. I frequently had to carefully nose forward so my passengers didn't get car sick from the jostling and so I didn't lose traction on the steep climb. Our slow trek up switchback after switchback took about forty-five minutes, and the whole time we were accompanied by our fluttering escort.

Once we got to the top, we all walked the last quarter mile to the overlook, and still, our friend kept up with us. We spent two hours at the overlook, in awe of the vast landscape stretching below us. Verdant swaths of leaves rustled in the moonlight. The Linville River, with its raging rapids below us, sounded like a quiet hush from our height. The stars hung over us like a tapestry. We saw Brown Mountain, but none of the lights. That bird stayed with us, as if hurrying us along on our sightseeing mission. At about four in the morning, we decided to head back to the truck, and lo and behold, our faithful companion came too. Going down the mountain we went a little faster, so it circled us less often, but when we got to turnoff for the main road, we saw it dip back into the woods exactly where it had emerged the first time. Whatever it meant, I was grateful the bird stayed with us. It seemed perhaps like a reward or acknowledgment of my efforts to get closer to nature.

∞

The next morning, Tim called me to ask how I thought the surgery on Monday would go. He and his team were on edge. Not only did their future funding depend on its success, but they had been entrusted with a human life on which to test their research. I told him about the bird the previous night, but we both needed a more specific sign. As we hung up, I told him I'd pray for something more definitive.

Two of the friends we had met the previous night, Cindy and Dave, happened to be the owners of the place and had to work that morning. One of our friends there had cancer and little energy at the time, so the plan for the day was to go with her on a small hike to Linville Falls. Cindy said she would skip work and go with us, but she had a headache and wanted to take a nap instead. The rest of us had a good time and really appreciated the company of our sick friend. The falls were gorgeous. I loved the feeling of being so deep in a valley, surrounded on either side by forest as though I were in the middle of a natural stadium that was teeming with life.

When we walked back into the lobby, Cindy was standing there waiting for us, her eyes big as saucers. Emphatically, urgently, she told us to listen. She said that after we left, she had walked to take a nap at their house, which was a two-story log cabin just behind the lodge. She went upstairs, lay down, and closed her eyes. Half-asleep, she felt something was off. It bothered her enough to look over at her nightstand. As her eyes adjusted, she noticed something strange about the coat rack beside the bed. It was moving. No, something was moving on it. Then it clicked. There was a six-foot long black snake coiled almost all the way around the pole. She shot up in bed. It was looking at her now. She screamed for her husband and ran out of the bedroom to get him.

As the rest of the group asked her a million questions, all I could think about was the image that came into my mind: a caduceus. I thought it was a snake wrapped around a staff, though in retrospect, I'd find that a single snake wrapped around a staff is actually known as the rod of Asclepius, a Greek god associated with healing and medicine. Whatever the specific symbology was, I knew immediately it was a sign for Tim, when the image of the caduceus morphed into a vision of the Spanish patient walking again. Not only that, the vision had come with the feeling that it would happen soon. Within minutes I called Tim and told him what had happened and that his patient would be walking again in sixty days.

Sure enough, the operation was successful and she was up and walking well before sixty days elapsed. I was thrilled when I heard the news. Helping Tim with this process was one of the most satisfying experiences of my life. Having had to work construction instead of attending UNC Chapel Hill, it was incredible to learn as much as I did and contribute to life-saving research. Naturally, I'll never know how much or little my drawings and dreams helped their efforts, but Tim said that they did, and that's more than enough for me to be proud of. My son was healthy again, and now this woman whom I'd prayed months for was returned healthy to her two children. Though my own health was in as much jeopardy as it ever was with my arthritis, I took solace in the well-being of others. What little I could do to contribute to it was everything to me.

One of the most maddening things about the years since this experience has been the secrecy imposed on me. Tim and the rest of them were in the habit of ignoring the comments and opinions of detractors who didn't know anything, but it remained difficult for me. Unfortunately for me, I am a man of my word and kept my vow of secrecy. I cared about people, even the ones who said I'd lost my mind, and it hurt deep down to hold in all these experiences with leading NASA scientists and doctors. I wanted to shout it from the rooftops every time a debunker waged a campaign against my family and me, and there were far too many of them. This book is my shout from the rooftops: the celestial world is all around us, interacting with us all the time.

CHAPTER 22

The town of Hope Mills goes all out for the Fourth of July every year. The party lasts all day. Everyone gets decked out in red, white, and blue, there's a long parade, and food trucks, face-painters, and balloon-animal makers populate the landscape as far as the eye can see. At night, people come from all around to watch the fireworks rise and burst over the lake at the center of our little town. Every year the show grows bigger, brighter, and longer, throwing brilliant colors and booming shockwaves over the water and through the air.

Our house was fifteen minutes away, but that quickly turned into an hour of traffic given how congested the roads would get. My arthritis was making it difficult to even get out of the house, so the proposition of braving the crowds for an event I'd seen all my life wasn't too appealing. Apart from that, we could see the fireworks from our house, about five miles away. Emily and I figured we'd be happier at home so we planned a night doing arts and crafts together as we watched a movie.

She was always painting or drawing or doing something else creative. Naturally we picked *Independence Day* and settled into my study.

Meanwhile, Junior was feeling better than he had in a long time. It was as though a heavy weight had been lifted from his shoulders, and it was beautiful to see him move without his illness. I could see it in his face, in the way he walked, how he talked to the rest of the family. Out of the hospital with a new lease on life, he had a first date that night with a girl to watch the fireworks together. He wanted everything to go smoothly and warned us that afternoon not to talk about UFOs or anything strange around her. He and his date stopped by the house on their way to town and the whole family dutifully kept their lips sealed, and the sight of them together was heart-warming.

Jeremy and Ryan headed off to their friend Nick's house for a pool party. Nick was a lifelong friend who lived just down the road, strangely enough in the same house my first wife grew up in. Yvonne went off on her own while Emily and I started the 1996 classic film. It was fun to revisit movies like this and see how their conceptions of alien life and the subsequent government response lined up with my experiences. Emily sat on the floor working on a painting as we sat together.

Night fell around nine o'clock, and a barrage of fireworks in our neighborhood and downtown began. Meanwhile there was no end to the sound of explosions coming from the TV. Eventually the booms and reports grew so loud I could hardly pay attention to Will Smith's efforts at saving the world. At 9:30 I paused the movie and asked Emily if she'd want to go with me to McDonalds for ice cream and I could get a coffee. The booms were getting louder and more frequent as the show ramped up toward its grand finale. The roads were about to get flooded to a standstill in a few minutes, so now would be our last chance. She said yes and started to put away her paints and clean her brushes. I walked down the hall to ask Yvonne if she wanted anything while we were out. It turned out she was in the shower, so I called through the door and said that Emily and I were going out for coffee and ice cream.

Then I decided to go outside for some fresh air to wait for Emily. On my way out the door I called to Emily that I'd be out by the truck, which was around the corner of the house. A minute or so passed and I was about to get in the truck when I heard her yell, "Dad! What is that?!"

I looked around and didn't see anything, then I closed the truck door and rushed over to her, standing on the back patio pointing upward. Beside her I saw what I had missed the first time: a giant orange house-sized orb hovering just over the trees. The instant I saw it I knew it had the same size and shape as the orb that took me for four hours on January 8th, 2007. A hickory tree right next to the house must have been blocking my line of sight by the truck. It held still, but its shape slowly morphed from sideways oblong to a round-edged cube. Its cycle of subtle shifts in shape mesmerized us. After gradually drawing itself inward from a tic-tac-like shape to the rounded cube, it would suddenly spring outward. On top of changes to its general shape, it had a pattern of shaded concentric circles within it, telescoping inward as if it were offering us a glimpse deep inside. These concentric circles were also in motion, giving us the impression we were moving through like a tunnel. Of course, we were standing still on the grass almost a quarter mile away from it. Above and around the orb, the fireworks finale five miles away flitted around it, dim in comparison, like a bouquet of distant sparklers surrounding the core of a nuclear reactor.

I was reminded of Diana Pasulka's descriptions of seraphim and how that word, usually taken to mean "angels," literally translates as "the burning ones." The exploding shells and various colors of the fireworks beyond us "burned" as a log in a fire would, but in contrast, the orb was doing something beyond burning. It did not seem to be spending fuel or exerting energy as it cast its radiance over the tree-line.

After watching it for a couple of minutes, I told Emily to stay there while I went to get Yvonne. Emily needed to stay with the orb since it had appeared to her first. I called Yvonne from the hall saying she better come fast. She rushed to the back porch in a towel and the moment she saw it, it darted away to the north like a spooked animal. Emily checked her watch and said it had been hovering and shifting for five whole minutes, either keeping an eye on our house or enjoying the fireworks alongside her. Emily and I were curious if anything else was out there, so we hopped in the truck and drove down the road to McDonald's.

When we got back after getting caught in a little traffic, Junior and his date were sitting on the front porch talking with Yvonne. Emily and I were worried at first when we heard him talking about UFOs, the one subject he had warned us not to talk about. Yvonne was a sharp and conscientious mother, not one likely to forget such a request. Our worry turned from confusion to relief when we heard the excitement in his voice as he explained what happened.

He was driving his date back to the house the long way to avoid traffic when they saw an orb hovering over a field. His date was baffled. They slowed down to get a better look at the brilliant orange ball of light. No one was setting off fireworks below it and the show in town had ended. When they got to the closest point that the road allowed, about a hundred yards away, it shot off up into the sky.

Junior was elated. The whole rest of the drive home, he explained what had happened to him and the rest of us over the previous seven years. It was the first time he ever felt comfortable telling anyone about the phenomena, much less a first date. He was out of the hospital and now here he was taking pride and enjoyment in these unexplainable moments. Seeing him finally able to share, and enthusiastically at that, I could tell his sorrowful, suppressed burden was beginning to lift. His date nodded and smiled and shared in his wonder. It was one of the most beautiful things I've witnessed as a father.

Before we knew it, Ryan and Jeremy had come home from Nick's pool party. Forgetting about Junior's warning, the first thing they said as they walked up to the porch was that they'd seen an orange ball of light streak over them while they were in the pool. Gathered on the porch, with faint wisps of smoke and other pyrotechnics hanging in the air, we shared all our stories again. Whatever the broader intentions of these "burning ones," that night they brought our family together in a way I had always hoped and prayed for. All of us were awestruck in our own ways, but no one was alone.

CHAPTER 23

Tim invited me to a rocket launch at the Kennedy Space Center in Cape Canaveral that fall. The August beforehand, a heavy package came in the mail stamped CONFIDENTIAL and PROPERTY OF THE U.S. GOVERNMENT. There were dozens of pages of documents for me to read and fill out. I had to gain an adequate security clearance before they would allow me into the facilities that Tim wanted to show me. It was a special window of opportunity because the woman in charge of the space center was temporarily allowing visitors into restricted areas that were usually off-limits. The forms took me weeks to fill out, and afterward I had to go through several interviews with Tim. No stone was left unturned: I had to account for virtually every moment of my life. I had to track down childhood friends, past teachers, distant relatives, employers, employees, and the travel histories of basically everyone I ever interacted with. Whatever Tim was going to show me, it was hard for me to believe that this vetting process had to be so airtight.

By mid-September I got the news I wasn't deemed a security threat, sleeper-cell, or under the influence of any foreign governments. Then came a long series of instructions and rules for what to do on the base, since I would be walking around in an active military environment. Mission control is one of the most highly secured rooms in the world, so it was an honor to be invited. I was more than happy to abide by these extensive rules. I was thrilled. The men I'd watched walk on the moon as a six-year-old had begun their journey from this marshy strip of land off the east coast of Florida. I would get to encounter the reality of space travel, the people, technology, and thunderous roar of our upward human leap. It was delivering the first test-flight of the crew module portion of the ORION Multi-Purpose Crew Vehicle by a Delta IV Heavy rocket.

I drove twelve hours from Fayetteville down to Cape Canaveral on a Monday, stopping often along the way to stretch my stiff joints and go over the guidelines for the visit. I was hoping my arthritis wouldn't act up and keep me from going on the scheduled tours. The launch was scheduled for Wednesday, and the weather looked good. I was one of eight people Tim had invited, the rest of whom were scientists, military personnel, medical researchers, and aerospace engineers.

I arrived at the hotel in Titusville where we were staying that evening and met Tim and the rest of our group. We gathered around the patio fire pit as we talked casually getting to know one another. The ocean air was damp and heavy as Tim passed out cigars for everyone. Just as with my family's briefing when he showed us the material, he was the consummate professional in his presentation, giving us both written and verbal guidelines for how to move through military spaces. Much of it was simply social etiquette. For instance, brigadier generals were to be addressed simply as "general," followed by their last name. Similar dictates for our comportment followed for scientists, researchers, and engineers, as well as their respective domains. Tim crossed every t and dotted every i in making sure his guests moved through the space center as smoothly as possible. Though the launch wasn't manned, millions of dollars, the future of the space program, and even lives were at stake in the event of a major catastrophe. Tim's integrity and accountability had a strange way of making me feel safe and a little unsettled at the same time. His brand of life-or-death seriousness lent a certain solemnity to the visit.

One of the scientists, Pete, worked in a different division at NASA managing their high-altitude WB-57 aircraft. In his thick Texan accent, he talked about these unusual planes with long, broad wings that can cruise on the thin air of the upper atmosphere. He explained their current project was the observation of missile tests, both to improve the missiles and study missile defense systems. It was clear that if anyone in the government was sure to regularly see UFOs, it would be the man in charge of these reconnaissance planes. We hadn't done anything yet, but I was already deeply impressed by the group.

Because the massive complex would be on lockdown the day of the launch, we spent Tuesday exploring as much as we could. We all met for coffee that morning in the hotel lobby. Tim told us he would be busy preparing for the launch, so Pete would be our tour guide for the day. We piled into a white Ford van and began the long process of security checkpoints and screenings. Stepping out into the bright Florida sunlight, a guard slipped a credential over my neck. Looking around at the vast and magnificent structures around me, I was struck with wonder. Just a few years beforehand I had vowed to never speak about the phenomena again when the lady appeared to me. Now I was at the planet's jumping-off point into space alongside some of the most qualified and credentialed UFO experts on the planet. With no college education and a body full of birdshot and scars, I had somehow joined the ranks of people with multiple PhDs, patents, and the highest security clearances that existed. The surrealness of the experience was only beginning to sink in. If anybody knew anything about the phenomena, it had to be these people.

I caught Tim in the parking lot before he was due to head off for a meeting.

"Tim, I'm flattered, but why on earth did you need me on this trip?" I asked. He trained his dark, focused eyes on me and his face went blank.

In his efficient, deliberate manner of speaking, he said, "We see them, but they don't seem to want anything to do with us. For some reason, they like you. They let you see them and experience them. We need to learn why." With that, he said goodbye to the rest of the group and turned to walk toward one of the unmarked buildings around us. All I could do was smile to myself and think of the lady's message: that she and her emissaries would remain with me forever on this mission to keep speaking about what I saw. From that moment on, all the doubt I had about belonging among the scientists and researchers went away. However, this was happening, I could feel I was being guided according to the lady's plan.

Pete proceeded to take us from launchpad to launchpad, pointing out the sites of major missions and rockets. The various names and numbers started to blur together in my head, but the scale and complexity of what I saw was staggering. At the center of the various launchpads and structures was a behemoth called the Vehicle Assembly Building, painted with the American flag and the NASA logo on either side. Originally intended for the housing and assembly of four Saturn Rockets at a time, it is the eighth largest building in the world by volume. Its doors take a full forty-five minutes to open and close, and it is rumored to have its own indoor climate. On foggy days clouds gather and it can rain indoors. I have never felt smaller than I did entering that space. A mere speck on the floor looking up at lights, staircases, and machinery across baffling distances, I noticed there were none of the usual reference points one would use to gauge size and scale. Left to our own devices for a few minutes, I walked around in a daze looking at the endless walkways, colors, and lights. It was almost too much to process. I had never experienced anything like it and never have since.

Next, we boarded the crawler, a massive vehicle used to transport rockets from the Assembly Building to the launchpads. When built, they were the largest self-powered vehicles in the world. We walked around massive treads and climbed up into the beast. We saw a control room where some of the thirty people required to operate it worked. I couldn't help but think that I was inside one part of every astronaut's journey into space.

After lunch, Tim called to say he was free to take us to the next part of our tour, the Astronaut Crew Quarters located in the Operations and Checkout building. This is where every astronaut spent the weeks leading up to the launch with their families undergoing rigorous medical exams. After their missions, they stayed there again for another round of medical checks. Every NASA astronaut that ever went to space spent weeks in the quarters quarantined with only family members, a small staff, a doctor, and a den mother. The den mother met us at the door and let us in. She explained that she had worked there for over thirty years, spending many astronauts' final days with them before sending them off to the final frontier. In the whole existence of the facility, from the 1960s to that day, she said only three hundred people had been granted access to the rooms in which we were standing. One president had visited, and no members of congress.

When I heard that, I could hear Tim's voice from two years before: *Why you?* It was beyond me, and I was okay with that.

The den mother led us around, pointing out the very chair Neil Armstrong had suited up in before stepping foot on the moon. Behind it was a series of instruments that measured the functionality of his space suit. There were bedrooms, conference rooms, a large dining room, and a kitchen. The air was heavy with history.

After taking some photos in the press conference room, we left Cape Canaveral for a seafood dinner on the beach. I took the opportunity to pull Tim aside and ask him again, "Why me?" Again, he looked me dead in the eyes.

"Chris," he said with the most deadpan gravity. Everyone who has ever been in those rooms has been to space. They brought something back with them, and it's still there. Now, you have felt it too, and it has felt you. Everything will be different now."

To this day, I have not forgotten his words because my relationship with the phenomena has only grown richer and fuller. When we were saying good night, he told me I needed to focus on singing a song to myself all the way through security. Just as in the woods with Chase and Pete when we lost time, he said it would prevent my mind from being read. I went to bed that night exhausted and amazed, trying to process everything I had seen.

∞

Just as the morning before, Tim escorted us into the Kennedy Space Center and left us with Pete and the instructions to be at mission control at ten-thirty sharp. The security was twice as extensive as the day before. We passed by dozens of men with M-16s as we were ushered through rooms with ominous black one-way glass and asked various questions. I tried my hardest to keep playing the song in my head. Eventually, after staring us down for a moment or two, an armed guard opened the huge metal door that led to the control room. It was a marvel to see such a complex array of professionals working together to prep engines, observe the weather, and the million other infinitely minute details needed to send a satellite into a precise orbit. There was an hour before launch and an excited buzz in the room. We met the general in charge of the operation and watched as everyone went diligently about their work.

After a half hour, Pete drove us to the launch site. It was a beautiful, clear day. Driving over, the reality of space travel sank in deeper than ever. The men and women I had just seen were going to send a rocket up into that endless blue. I teared up thinking of the profound courage required by all these endeavors, the unimaginable trust required for one's fellow man, the sacrifice every spouse and family member made in allowing their loved ones to leave. Looking at the cameramen and reporters under military escort, I was grateful to not deal with the stress of watching a manned mission.

A military official shouted to all of us to be ready to run to the vans, all of which had been left idling with their doors open so we would be able to escape if anything went wrong. Tim had told us the night before that several cavalier people had their cars melted after leaving them too close to a launch.

The only people closer to the launchpad were in underground bunkers monitoring the launch systems. The rocket itself was tall and skinny with a coned nose aiming straight up. The minutes slowly ticked by with our eyes on the clock as a dull roar slowly ramped up. Eventually there was a small trail of smoke at the base of the rocket. Then like a shockwave, it sounded unlike anything I'd ever heard coming to life in the distance. I could feel my chest rumbling and vibrating as an unimaginably bright light flared from the base of the rocket. As the deep roar grew and grew, I lost my breath. This 183 foot-tall, 1.3 million-pound rocket was actually lifting itself upward. Slowly, it seemed to gain traction with the air and accelerate upward at a steady rate. A wave of wind and heat hit us, and I prayed that nothing bad would happen. Leaving its trail of smoke, we watched it rise and rise into the blue in which it eventually disappeared. There it was. What was towering over us minutes beforehand was now a white speck we could now only believe was up there.

I was exhausted from two long days walking around with worsening arthritis pain. I missed my family too, and didn't want to spend another night in a hotel, so I decided to drive the twelve hours back overnight and rest when I got there. That way at least I would avoid the traffic I had faced on my way down. My family was expecting me that Thursday evening, but I figured I could surprise them. It was a long, lonely night on the road and my headlights hid the stars. As the miles ran by underneath me, a steady ache grew in my joints that at least did me the favor of keeping me awake. Dawn started to come on as I diverged northward and inland. Bleary-eyed and stiff, I saw the sign for Hope Mills and found myself smiling at the name despite how awful I felt. There was hope here. For all that had happened to my family, there was still hope.

When I saw the house, I felt something weird come over me. I braked to turn from the asphalt road to the gravel road, and the feeling got more ominous. I heard the tires crunch the gravel and out of nowhere I felt my heart break. A titanic sorrow grabbed me and pulled me down. My eyes were wet. I was gasping for air, sobbing. I thought of Nelly. I knew she was gone.

I walked in the back door with a lead heart and grief in my eyes. Emily was on the couch and was shocked to see me nine hours early. I saw it in her eyes and told her I already knew, she didn't have to break any news except how it happened.

"She was hit by a car, Daddy. She died two days ago and we buried her in the backyard. We'd have told you but we didn't want to ruin your trip. How did you know?"

"I don't know how I knew. I just saw it when I pulled into the driveway. She doesn't even know she's gone," I said, then sat down and let myself cry until I slept, hungry, bereaved, aching, exhausted. Later that week one night I was in the backyard standing over my best friend's grave, crying. I was telling her to go to the light, that everything was okay now, that I'd be seeing her soon. I felt something and looked up right as an ivory-colored orb flashed on at me. I knew it was her. I took out my phone and she let me take one last picture of her.

CHAPTER 24

My correspondence with Diana Pasulka stayed strong and I related everything to her on a regular basis. Talking with her was always enlightening, and just about all my stories sparked some reference or parallel to an ancient text. In our conversations, I realized how the interconnected nature of the phenomena also extended into the past. People have always seen what I've seen, it's just that the words for it vary according to the cultures and religions. The possibilities of a book or a movie deal with the screenwriters seemed to have stalled for the time being, but we were optimistic.

Tim wanted to meet Diana ever since I told him about her. Diana, however, was wary of interacting with powerful government officials. She said the focus of her studies had made her enemies in a few academic and religious communities. Like me, she had a family she needed to protect from ridicule, so naturally I understood. After two years of hearing stories about my interactions with Tim, when she heard about my trip to the astronaut crew quarters, she said she felt comfortable enough to meet over the phone. Clearly there was not a malicious or foolish bone in Tim's body. After introducing them to each other over email in early December 2014, the three of us had a long phone call. The two of them hit it off immediately, and their relationship would eventually change the course of Diana's research and career.

In mid-December I received a mysterious early Christmas present. The mailer it came in was unmarked and had no return address. I didn't suppose I was enough of a target for anything like anthrax, so I went to my study to open it. The first item to fall out was a pristine white napkin. I flipped it over and saw the Presidential seal surrounded by the words Camp David and Presidential Retreat. Afraid to stick my hand in not knowing what was inside, I kept gently shaking the envelope over my desk. Next was a thickly-embroidered mission patch for the launch I had attended. It was circular, with a series of abbreviations I didn't recognize, but I did see the name ORION.

The last item I shook out was a small jewelry box. I opened it to find a twenty-four-karat gold pin with a distinct triangle inside of a circle. It was almost exactly the same shape I had seen on the chest of the beings at our home in 2007. I picked it up and it was surprisingly heavy. There was nothing written on it, nor any other distinguishing features. One day I would learn that this symbol is a closely guarded secret among those like Tim who work with the phenomena. It was known as an

O.P. pin, short for off-planet, given to those who had direct experience with the phenomena. A small circle knows about them, and an even smaller circle has them. It was a good Christmas present, though I hardly knew who to thank for it.

∞

That winter my appointment with a rheumatologist finally came around. For all these years, the difference between regular arthritis and rheumatoid had remained somewhat unclear to me. At my first appointment with this doctor, they took a blood test to confirm I had rheumatoid, in addition to fifty X-rays of my joints. They went ahead and officially diagnosed me with degenerative arthritis and osteoarthritis.

My next appointment was two weeks later, when I would receive an official decision on my rheumatoid status. I was not optimistic. Of course, the first thing the doctor said upon entering the room was that I have a moderate to severe case. The doctor was serious. I was worried. They had more tests to do and as I waited a nurse handed me a pamphlet. To this day, I resent this pamphlet and wish I had never seen it. Its language was stark, brutal, and punishing: lifespan reduced by ten years, blindness, multiple organ failure, debilitating pain, fatigue, and the treatment was chemotherapy. None of this information had ever been communicated to me. I was shocked and horrified, alone and feeling trapped in that exam room. The doctor brought out the X-rays to show me the irreversible damage in my joints. My prescribed treatment was weekly doses of methotrexate, the chemotherapy drug with awful side effects, as well as weekly immunosuppressant injections in my stomach. It felt terrible to agree to a regime of self-poisoning, but the little relief I found just barely made it worth it. Besides that, I had to do everything I could to stay alive for my family, and the potential for organ failure was unacceptable no matter how awful the chemo was.

I spent early 2015 trying to adjust to this treatment and keep my weight up. A southern Baptist bible college two hours away invited me to a dinner to give a talk to a class that was studying the relationship between UFOs and Christianity. On the one hand, it seemed like the lady and her beings were more on my side than ever, but on the other, I knew I had to be careful. No matter how accepting and kind they were, I was afraid that because of their commitment to a bible college would label me a heretic doomed to hell. I had faced plenty of those accusations and did not want to face another.

The more I talked with Diana and learned about the history of world religions, the more certain I became that the phenomena were a worldwide and angelic presence. Native American folklore described the appearance of white stone canoes flying overhead. There were multiple reports of glowing, flying ships all through the eighteenth and nineteenth centuries: one report even described a ship dropping anchor down into a London chimney. These western accounts are just the tip of the iceberg. Diana said that one of the biggest stumbling blocks for people when it comes to reckoning with the phenomena was a mistranslation of the word *cloud* in both the old and new testaments. Alternate, and sometimes flat-out wrong, translations were substituted for the word *cloud*. In most of these cases, the intent of the translator was to make the text easier to comprehend and therefore believe in. Instead of *clouds*, words like weather, rain, sky, angel, and voice were used. Of course, it would be easier for a reader to believe that an angel spoke to someone rather than a cloud, or that lightning lit up the sky rather than a brilliant glowing cloud. With all of these texts, Diana and I discussed the likelihood of these clouds being orbs like the ones I was seeing. Some seemed like a stretch, but most of them struck a deep, resonant chord in me. I recognized orbs in what I read with total confidence: their playfulness, strangeness, consistent inconsistencies, colors, intensity, and mental connection were right there in the scripture. The history of religious wars was especially troubling to me. It broke my heart that all people on earth shared this ability to connect with the phenomena directly but were told it was against the rules. To paint with a very broad brush, various politically-affiliated religious sects and institutions have told us that they alone hold the keys to religious experience, meanwhile casting all outsiders as damned in the eyes of their god. This profound spiritual division among people has caused endless misery, isolation, dehumanization, and violence. The orbs were always here and open to all of us, ready to give us the signs and messages we need.

Southern Baptist bible college students would have to be unusually open-minded to entertain such ideas, but I hoped they would try, and feeling the lady on my side, I accepted their invitation. If they got hostile, I could always leave or get quiet and eat their barbecue. I have a deep respect for all people who seek God, whatever their religion. It's merely a flaw in their belief systems and institutions that leads to so much unnecessary pain, sorrow, and violence.

I was due in Goldsboro at 5:30 on the first of March at a well-loved barbecue restaurant. I had only talked with the dean of the college, who was also the teacher of the course, so I had no idea what I was getting into. When I walked in the door, a couple of people recognized me and led me back to a private room where we could eat and talk. I was surprised to find a room of people about my age and older, not the young ministers in training I was expecting. There were about twenty students, including the dean and myself, standing around a group of tables that had been pushed together in a long rectangle formation. A seat was open for me in the middle, and as I made my way there, I noticed a book had been set in front of the chair next to me. Its cover read *Ultraterrestrial* and had a little green man on it. It gave me a bad feeling, but dinner came first and the smoky old place smelled unbelievably good. We all sat and ate facing each other and I had a nice time talking with my neighbors.

When we had finished and put away our plates, the dean who was sitting next to me stood up, holding the book.

He launched into an introduction for me, mentioning the Discovery episode and bits and pieces of what had happened since. When he finished I stood up and began to tell my story and all that the TV episode had left out. I got to the part where I was hiding in the reeds from the two orbs. I told them how I looked up and saw the third one above watching me, and how afterward I recollected parts of being taken.

I had just begun my story when the dean stood up again, cleared his throat, and started to explain to the class what he thought had happened to me. He raised up his *Ultraterrestrial* book and started lecturing us about the demons, negative forces, and dark energies that overtook us that night. He had obviously prepared a long list of citations and bible quotes to defend his claims. This ruffled my feathers a bit but I sat down and let him finish his spiel. I continued my story where I had left off, recounting the details I had repeated so many times before. Ten minutes hadn't passed before the dean stood up again, whipped up in a frenzy, shouting at the group how he knew I had been taken by a demonic force, my delusions, the willingness with which I had received the devil into my heart.

I'd have been upset and scared, but just about everyone else in the room was looking at him with the same confusion and embarrassment I felt. The room fell silent. I didn't know how to respond so I just sat back down. Before I knew it, a group of kind older ladies had surrounded me telling me not to mind him. I looked over at the dean and he and a few of his friends were just staring at me. I didn't want to hang around for long, and noticing this, the ladies invited me to one of their houses down the road for cake and ice cream. I rushed out and before I knew it, I was sitting in Monica's living room, getting to know a whole group of people who clearly felt bad for how I'd been treated. It was a beautiful feeling to be surrounded by support after facing such a fire-and-brimstone rant. It turned out Monica had made a beautiful cake too, and I felt like this was the room I was really meant to visit that night. They were curious about the rest of my story, so I picked up where I'd left off. Every few minutes, one of them asked me a question, never out of doubt and skepticism, but out of curiosity and open-mindedness.

As I was talking, I noticed a woman slumped in the corner of a couch on the far side of the room hadn't spoken a word. She was much younger than the rest of us, and it saddened me to see such a young person look so sad. For some reason, I decided to rush through a couple years to tell the story of my father's brush with kidney cancer in 2012. I explained how in the span of a few weeks, a kidney riddled with cancer according to one hospital turned out to be medically insignificant by another. I talked about praying and the initial stroke of luck that UNC had the new scanning machine. Then I talked about the family waiting on the back patio for the results to come back, how when my mother smiled and teared up, I raised my hands to thank god, how between my hands appeared a pearly silver Tic Tac-shaped orb.

As soon as I mentioned this orb, a number of women gasped and looked pointing over my head, wide-eyed and shocked. Three of them immediately asked, "Did you see that?" one after the other. Out of nowhere, the sad young woman on the couch leapt up and hugged me, saying, "I just knew you were going to talk about kidney cancer!"

It took me a moment to process what had happened. The women explained they had all seen bright flashing lights over my head as I told this part of the story. The young woman introduced herself as Sharon Debonis, saying that just a year and a half ago, one of her kidneys had to be removed due to a chemo-resistant cancer that had swelled it to the size of a softball. Very recently, the same chemo resistant cancer had appeared in her other kidney. Understandably, she was devastated. She said that if the chemo didn't start working, that would be it for her. It was an incredibly emotional moment I'll never forget.

The whole drive home, I could think of nothing else but her vacant defeated stare, sitting slouched on the couch. I prayed for her nonstop the whole two hours. *Heal Sharon. Be with Sharon. Fill Sharon with hope and love. Give Sharon a sign if it be your will.* I pulled into the driveway exhausted and stiff from the drive, but my dreams were vivid and energetic. I dreamed about Sharon, how she was touched by the phenomena and this would not be the end of the road for her.

The next morning, I went to gather eggs from the chicken coop and check in on our forty hens. Most of them laid at least once a day, so it was an intensive daily chore for us. I was going from cubby door to cubby door, lifting these warm gifts out one or two at a time, when I looked down and felt a weird shape in my hand. It was a kidney. That was all I could think of. This was the sign for Sharon. I dropped everything and took photos to send her to give her the hope I knew she so desperately needed. All the rest of that day I kept praying for her off and on, hoping along with her and for her.

The very next morning I got a call from her out of the blue.

"Thank you," she cried through tears and sobs.

It just so happened that Sharon had an oncology appointment to check in on how things were progressing. Her blood tests had come back with a miraculous result. Her platelets were back to normal levels and a scan of her kidney showed the cancer had shrunk to tiny, negligible speck, just as my father's had.

I can't speculate what effect my meeting her had, what matters to me is that I had managed to give a scared soul some hope. I reflected that praying for my father and sticking together as a family was a similar process to how I felt about Sharon. Maybe the flash of hope that changed things for him was switching hospitals, or maybe he simply believed because we believed alongside him. I don't know what gave Junior the willingness to come forward with the pain he was in because of his kidney infection, but I can't help but understand the lady's appearance in our house as an image of hope itself. Maybe Junior came forward because he allowed himself the hope of feeling better, instead of suffering in silence. Three people in my life had kidney illnesses, and three were healed. All I can say is I opened my heart to the sky, to the truth of what I saw, and asked for healing from the core of my being. Whatever was out there listened.

To this day, Sharon is cancer free.

CHAPTER 25

Larry Frascella, the host of the 2012 Gathering, called me out of the blue two days before the Fourth of July, 2015. We spent the first few minutes of the call talking about our plans for the fourth. Yvonne and I were excited to have the children back from college and everyone together again. There was no end to the changes they went through every time they came back after a time away, and it was always a blessing to see their faces.

Larry said there was a twelve-year-old boy named Brandon who needed my help. Brandon lived in Washington D.C. with his parents and suffered from a quickly worsening genetic mitochondrial disease. The doctors said he would be lucky to make it to thirteen, and they had the wealth and connections to see every kind of expert in the world. Brandon's mother, a doctor, and his grandfather, a well-known cardiologist in New York, had run out of experts and specialists to consult with. The Make-a-Wish foundation had just approved Brandon's application, but the family wasn't ready to give up yet. They knew Larry and Larry knew me, so there I was in my study in Hope Mills, realizing I was this innocent child's last hope.

It was a Thursday night and I was looking forward to the holiday weekend, so I asked him if it couldn't wait till Monday. Larry said he wished it could wait, but every day Brandon was getting worse. The most concerning symptom he was exhibiting was an inability to digest food. He was losing the nutrients he needed to live quicker than he could take them in. Having felt similarly from my long illness with Crohn's disease, I felt sympathy for the child. My heart sank as I imagined him, weak and laid up in bed while his friends were out playing. I remembered Tim Taylor telling me to use whatever gift I had as often as I could and as long as I felt the energy of the lady on my side. Just as the lady wanted me to share what I saw, I felt she also wanted me to share the energy she had touched me with. A Fourth of July party was just a party, after all, and I knew I'd see my family again.

"Larry, you get me there. Send me a plane ticket and I'll see you tomorrow," I said. I asked a few more questions about Brandon and his illness so I could go ahead and start meditating and praying for him. He told me a bit about the role of mitochondria in the cell and the laundry list of other symptoms he was suffering. He had already been placed on a feeding tube, which was the last and most extreme treatment available. I went to sleep that night with a dozen medical terms cycling through my mind. I never knew what to expect or hope for: all I could do was care, try to feel the weight of this family's sorrow, then expose that sorrow to the lady's light.

The next morning, I walked out of baggage claim in Dulles Airport and met Larry waiting in his black Mercedes. He helped me with my bag and we started on the forty-five minute drive down to Old Town Alexandria, Virginia. He gave me more information about the family and how he knew them. They were Jewish and had a long history with conventional medicine, so this turn to a holistic approach represented a major shift. Put simply, they were out of options.

Eventually I saw the Washington Monument poking out over some buildings and knew we were close. We entered a gorgeous old neighborhood where every tree-lined street was draped in American flags and bunting. Just a few years beforehand, my community called me everything from a liar to a maniac to a drug-addict, and now here I was, recruited as a last resort for one of the most respected and influential families in America—all because of what I had seen and felt, and what I dared to assert was true. There is a hidden world around us asking to be recognized. It's up to us to open ourselves to the possibility of seeing it.

Brandon's parents met us at the door and gave us an amazingly warm welcome. They led us to a fine, spacious living room beside their kitchen where I saw Brandon. He was small for his age, and pale, but with a broad, easy smile. I could tell in an instant how brave he was being, how much he wanted to hide his suffering from his parents, and how much hope he felt at this new kind of opportunity: the relief of treatment outside of a hospital or clinic. This stubborn refusal to share one's pain was all too familiar to me.

We talked for an hour about my experiences and how I came to helping the sick. I kept looking over at Brandon as I talked, feeling strangely drawn to him. I said that Tim Taylor had encouraged me to help as many and as often as I could. Brandon never took his eyes off of me and seemed to absorb every word. Most importantly, I acknowledged that I didn't know how healings worked or happened, nor did NASA, and this was why Tim wanted me to continue my efforts. From my experience with Sharon, I knew that hope, prayer, and focus were all important parts of the equation.

Brandon then started to talk about how his illness affected him. He was an amazingly polite and gracious young man. There were none of the rude outbursts, depressive silences, or meltdowns one would very reasonably expect from a twelve-year-old boy who'd been told he was terminally ill. Occasionally he couldn't help but betray a sign of how weak he felt: a little wince raising a water glass, a certain weariness in his expression, a slow reaction to something his parents asked him.

As afternoon turned to evening, I kept asking the holy spirit to guide me in my head. There was no recipe for a healing. She hadn't given me any guidelines. I could only hold her image in my mind and guess. The sensation isn't unlike tuning a guitar: somewhere in my thoughts about her is an unmistakable note I try to get in tune with. It feels like an infinite flow of generosity, compassion, and understanding. It's an emotional posture, a mental stance, and a way of seeing all at once. As I asked in prayer over and over again, I started to feel an energy build in me that felt almost electrical. Along with this buzzing came the thought that if I gave Brandon a hug, he would receive the energy he needed.

Brandon's mother served a wonderful dinner and I began to get tired. The day before the Fourth of July had been a long busy day of travel. Fatigue from my RA was starting to set in too. Curiously though, while I felt physically drained, this electric-feeling buzz was growing stronger. It was as though it would build until I carried out the impulse it was seemingly linked to, so I made a note to myself to make sure I hugged him before I left. I supposed goodbyes would be a natural time for that.

Brandon and I hugged for a few moments before Larry and I left for our hotel. It had gotten late surprisingly quickly. As I held his small, frail frame, I prayed silently:

Heavenly spirit, this child is so special.

He is the most humble person I have ever met.

Surely he deserves a second chance.

Help him, watch over him, and guide him throughout his life.

Give him this chance. Heal him.

∞

It was almost 1:00 a.m. when Larry and I were checking into the hotel and I got a call. It was Brandon's mother, ecstatic, exclaiming how thrilled she was that her son had two full helpings of food after I left. She said she hadn't seen his energy and appetite reach those levels for months. All I could say was he was a special boy, that I believed he would be okay, and that I would keep him in my thoughts for as long as it took.

Brandon's parents would become lifelong friends of mine. Just a month later, my whole family received invitations to Brandon's bar mitzvah in October. It was sure to be an extravagant occasion in New York City, but more than anything I was excited to see my young friend again. It ended up that Yvonne, Ryan, and his girlfriend Jennifer (now his wife) were the only people in the family who could get away from work and school that weekend. The four of us boarded a plane for Philadelphia one night in early October to spend an evening with Larry and his wife. Ryan loved meeting the man who hosted the Gathering that he had heard so much about.

The next morning, we were off to New York. A shiny all-black Suburban with tinted windows ushered us into the city. Our towering hotel was just south of central park. Uniformed bellhops ferried our bags up to the rooms while we checked in. Everything was taken care of for us, and it was staggeringly generous of Brandon's family to provide so well for some guy from North Carolina they only met once. Our room had a beautiful view of the city, its checkered streets and avenues.

That afternoon, Yvonne, Jennifer, and Larry's wife planned shopping, nail, and hair appointments for the next day while Ryan and I walked around taking in the sights. Hot dog stands, the park, the Plaza hotel. We were mainly killing time before an important meeting. Brandon's parents had invited us partly so I could meet a man named Jim Semivan. I had heard a few things about him, that he was the James Bond of the CIA and he wanted to meet me, but when I did some research that afternoon, I started to get a little nervous. He had a twenty-five-year career as an operations officer, essentially a spy, and retired as a member of the senior executive service. Unlike Tim, Hal, and other high-level government officials I'd met, Jim's interest in the phenomena was not strictly scientific or spiritual. It was personal. It seemed quite unlikely that any aspects of the phenomena could be used for spy craft or antiterrorism efforts. Regardless, government people treated me with far more respect and understanding than the civilian UFO community, and there was no reason to expect a deviation from that pattern. He was a friend of Brandon's family and in town for the bar mitzvah as well, so I assumed our meeting would be at least somewhat social.

At 6:30, we rode the elevator up to the thirty-fifth floor and saw our conference room. There were caterers setting up a buffet and laughing. I led Larry's wife, Yvonne, Ryan, and Jennifer in as the sun set. The vast skyline was starting to glimmer. Lying like a monolith, Central Park stretched away from us, its deep shadowy green spangled with street lamps. After a few minutes, Larry and two other couples walked in and we all made our introductions.

I assumed they would want to hear my story the way most people do, directly from me, in my voice. It always brought a tension into the room that felt like being put on trial: every new listener eyeing me, trying to discern truths or lies in my voice. I had told my story many times and still remember it as vividly as yesterday, but undergoing this cross-examination demanded a great deal from me emotionally. It took energy and focus to do justice to every detail, and I felt a deep sense of duty to my family to say it right. I had no clue what the stakes were for this meeting, what these two couples knew about the phenomena, or how they would react. In any case I was glad this time I had my family and Larry there to support me.

The caterers brought out wine for everyone and served an incredible buffet. As we talked, I immediately became comfortable with Jim and breezed through the story. I brought my computer along and had it hooked up to a projector so I could show images and videos I'd taken of the phenomena, the burnt tree, my trip to the Kennedy Space Center, and the rest of my family. Since the lady came in 2012 and gave me the ability to capture phenomena, I had amassed quite a library of these. As I talked, Yvonne, Ryan, and Jennifer would jump in to confirm what they saw. I could tell by the way Jim was focused on me that he believed me. The other couple, friends of Jim's who worked at the Justice Department, were listening intently as well. As usual I ended up crying despite my best efforts not to. Whether believed or disbelieved, it is heartbreaking for anyone to have such a big part of one's life called into doubt. That night in New York, high above the city, they were tears of joy.

Out of kindness and concern, Jim's wife Deborah, who is a doctor, came and comforted me. She said she understood how difficult this must have been for us. When I finished, Jim started talking in great detail about his own experiences with the phenomena dating back to the first years of his career in intelligence. Not only was it still shocking to see another government official speak openly about these subjects, it simply felt good to be believed. I almost regretted having my guard up at first, but my daily experiences getting attacked and threatened on social media had made me careful. I felt closer than I'd ever been to that elusive goal I'd pursued since contacting MUFON: vindication. All the online hobbyists and skeptics who claimed to know everything would know the truth if they could have been in that room. I wanted more than anything to shout about this meeting from the rooftops, but that would have to wait. Sharing these stories requires a delicate web of trust, since all who share them put their careers and families on the line. I knew all too well how damaging breaking that trust could be, but it took all I had to honor it. The night ended but Jim and his wife would become lifelong friends of ours.

All the women left early the next morning for a busy day of shopping and pampering before the bar mitzvah. Jim, Ryan, Larry, and I just felt like strolling through the city. I had the best time talking with Jim that day. We quickly got past small talk and discussed our biggest questions about the phenomena, our government's response, and each other's lives.

While we were walking together down a busy street, he asked me what I missed most in the world. I told him I wanted to fly again. Getting recertified to fly was expensive and time-consuming, and next to impossible with RA and children that needed tuition and other support. He stopped on the sidewalk, looked me in the eyes smiling, and said, "Chris, you will be there again." I will never forget the flat certainty of his statement, how it filled me with hope, even comfort, knowing that I could believe it if he did. The change that simple sentence wrought in me was a small miracle.

We walked around a long while sightseeing and by midafternoon it was time to go back to the hotel to get ready. We dressed in our nicest clothes and Yvonne and Jennifer looked beautiful having seen a world class hairstylist and makeup artist. I was excited to see Brandon again and was hoping his big day would go off without a hitch. After meeting the rest of the group in the lobby, we got in three blacked-out Suburbans to ride to the synagogue on Madison Avenue.

I had no idea what to expect from a bar mitzvah, but I knew it was an important coming-of-age ceremony for Brandon. The temple was magnificent and packed. We sat together shoulder-to-shoulder watching him recite from the Torah in front of everyone he knew. I was so glad to see him looking less pale and speaking confidently. We'd find out later that his performance was flawless. Through all his illness, he had kept up with his study of Hebrew and the Torah. After finishing, the whole temple stood up to give him a standing ovation. It was a beautiful outpouring of love for a child I knew deserved it so much.

Next was a party in the basement ballroom underneath the synagogue. It was a spacious and beautiful room with linen tables, a dance floor, and a band already playing as we entered. As I walked with Jim, he told me that the room was going to be full of intelligence people, prominent doctors and lawyers, and Mike Morrell, the former deputy director of the CIA. We found our table next to Jim and Deborah's and had a wonderful dinner. Then the party started.

It was unbelievable how everybody suddenly got up and started dancing. Looking at my family dancing and laughing in fine clothes in a beautiful room, I couldn't help but feel the guiding force of the lady. After so much rejection and shame, my pursuit of the phenomena had brought us to this joyous moment.

Suddenly there were shouts and screams behind me. I looked around trying to figure out what was happening. The band stopped playing. Deborah was gripping my shoulders telling me to come quick and help him. Among the shouts I heard the word *doctor!* I didn't know who she was talking about, but I got up and noticed a man at Deborah's table slumped forward with his face down. There was a group of people everywhere around him trying to revive him. Deborah led me to him through the crowd. Everything was happening so fast and I wasn't sure what to do, so I simply laid my hands on his shoulders. Through the man's coat I could feel he was completely limp. I was planning on saying a prayer for him until a doctor came, but before I could say anything he shot up, gasping for air, stunned by the crowd surrounding him.

Deborah stared at me and told me I saved him. It's true I had felt the lady's presence just moments before, but I don't claim to have had any effect on him. These things simply happened, and there are times I feel her unmistakable energy flowing through me.

The rest of the party went smoothly. We said congratulations to Brandon and it warmed my heart to see him at the center of such a triumphant and loving celebration. Again, I can't claim to have done anything for Brandon, but things did slowly turn around for him after our meeting. Over the years, our families have vacationed together and remain in touch. Today Brandon is a sophomore in college.

CHAPTER 26

It was a busy and humbling time. Whatever was in control of where I was headed next was working overtime. The only thing I could be sure of was that there was no way of predicting it.

I must have made enough of an impression on Col. John B. Alexander when in Philadelphia investigating the pope's assassination plot, that he asked if he and his wife could come to Hope Mill. I was honored to accept, and they were on our doorstep just two weeks after my trip to New York City and Brandon's bar mitzvah. It so happened that they were coming on the weekend my family was planning on celebrating my birthday, since it fell on a Thursday that year. The kids were thrilled to meet him, having seen him on television many times over the years on various History and Discovery channel shows. He remains about as famous a person can be in the UFO paranormal community, and was also a highly respected member of the military and intelligence communities.

He and his wife Victoria came over briefly on Friday night just to say hello to everyone and plan the next day. They were tired from their long flight from Las Vegas and went back to their hotel. The next morning, the whole family was gathered waiting with a million questions. When he arrived the first order of business was to show him the burnt tree and all the other places I had encountered the phenomena. Each time I showed someone the property it amazed me just how often and how varied these experiences were since that first night coming home with Junior when the dogs started barking. I related to him the experiences of the first night as well as twenty or so of the most significant encounters of the previous eight years. Our whole family history was bound up in the land. I was introducing him to my family as much as I was to our unexplainable experiences. Most important to John and me at the time however was the burnt tree, which had lent me the information that brought us together. After an hour or two walking around and explaining what had happened, we headed back to my study where the whole family crammed in to hear his stories.

To put it briefly, Colonel Alexander was involved with the most unconventional and elite corners of the U.S. military for almost all of the latter half of the twentieth century. The story of America's rise to become a world superpower was profoundly intertwined with his career. Clearly this was a man that people in power had trusted with their most dangerous questions and materials. I've come to believe that the horseshoe theory applies in cases like his and Tim Taylor's: there comes a point at which duty, genius, and stoic rationality can take you no further, and seemingly impossible, antithetical answers become more and more likely, despite all your previous commitments and codes. John and Tim shared this unflinching receptivity, a pose I myself struck many times during my near-death experiences and most challenging encounters with the phenomena. It takes a certain combination of faith, vigilance, and steel to really accept, and I saw that in John as he told us about stories that Indiana Jones would have cowered at. His wife Victoria had accompanied him on many of these adventures—scuba diving with great white sharks, bushwhacking through the depths of the Amazon jungle, riding on horseback a hundred miles into northern Mongolia to learn from nomadic reindeer herdsmen's ceremonies—and nodded in agreement as she sat with us. John had brought his laptop with us and showed us pictures of all they had seen and done.

Hearing all this, I felt no small amount of pressure to deliver on his expectations of seeing phenomena during his visit. I knew that the selfish demands of convenience and John's view of me were the last things the phenomena and the lady would heed, so I tried my best to let go of this anxiety. I was merely a guide on a whale watch, I thought to myself. If no whales show up, well, then no whales show up. Still though, I prayed and asked the phenomena to appear to John. What harm could it do to pray and ask? As the saying goes in Matthew, "to him who knocks, and keeps knocking, the door will be opened." If there were anyone in the world who needed to see what I saw, I knew it was him. He had the connections and experience to make a real difference in terms of getting the message out.

By mid-afternoon we were all talked out, and John and Victoria headed back to their hotel to rest a while before dinner. We ordered Chinese takeout and they met us again around 5:30 that afternoon. We had a great dinner together with our special guests. It wasn't long after we finished eating that John pulled me aside and forced the issue. I knew John would want to go to the river, but I also knew the property was under new ownership, and judging by my general reputation in town, I had no reason to expect we would be greeted warmly. Whether people assumed I was demonically possessed or looney, I still did my best to steer clear of them. The property was still farmland though, and far enough away from houses that I figured a brief visit wouldn't raise too much suspicion. I told him alright, give me a few minutes and we'll go.

Now I faced another problem. Of course all the kids would want to go, and I wanted them to come, but on the other hand I knew I owed it to both John and the lady to give him the best possible chance of an encounter. On top of that, there was the practical matter that multiple cars would raise even more alarm from passersby and neighbors. Judging how to have an experience is a tricky calculus that proceeds more by gut instinct than anything else, though over the years I've guessed a few guiding principles. The one I'm most sure of is that large groups, say more than ten people, almost never have an experience. I can only explain this by saying that every time I have an experience, there is a deep personal attunement to my emotional state, the words of my prayer, and those for whom I pray. A focus settles over me that I suppose a big enough group of people can't synchronize adequately enough to mimic. The second principle is precisely this intentional focus. The mind can't be worried or preoccupied with dishes left in the sink or how awful the next day at work will be. One has to offer oneself wholly to the present moment. The third is that one can't harbor anger, hatred, violence, or anything negative and damaging when trying to observe the phenomena. If it could be said that they have a personality, it is playful, thinks far beyond our intelligence, and abhors all things base and cruel. I have this sense because of the desperate place I was in when they first appeared, and how they show kindness and the delight of their appearance to those deepest in the depths of hopelessness and despair.

As I was thinking about who to bring, I remembered something Tim Taylor told me the first time we met. He said it was just like the bible verse, "Where more than one is gathered in my name, there I will be." For whatever reason, this memory gave me the impulse to bring only Emily along with John and his wife. I felt all my children were magnetic for the phenomena, but she was the youngest and it simply felt right. It had rained recently and I didn't have my old truck anymore, so John, Victoria, Emily, and I took their rental car on the ten minute drive to where it all happened January 8th, 2007.

Light was beginning to wane when we pulled into the dirt drive. My stomach sank with nervousness. I wanted so badly for John to see something. We pulled up to the same old gate over which I'd mistaken my first orbs for two suns. With no way to unlock it now, and with ditches and furrows on either side of the road we didn't want to ruin, we got out and walked down to the river as I rehashed what had led up to that evening. I was relieved to see the same stand of trees was there, and the path that dog legged right and south alongside the river wasn't too overgrown. It was about as muddy as it had been in 2007 though, and the going was slow. Just as I'd acted as tour guide in the backyard earlier that day, I pointed here and there: where I'd hidden in the ditch, where in the sky the orbs had appeared, where Junior said he'd first seen the eyes of the beings, and finally the clearing where we'd built the fire. I felt clever. As long as we didn't spend too long by the river, we would end up back at the car around the edge of darkness, and it felt like favorable conditions for an experience. A little chill came over me remembering the guys and Junior's fear and confusion that night. Here were the same pines, oaks, hickories, and gum trees, eight years older and casting longer, deeper shadows. It hurt to remember the look on his face when I pointed to the spot in the tree-line where he had been hiding, paralyzed with terror. The sun set. Twilight was fading to darkness and we decided to head back after twenty minutes talking by the river.

It was harder to step gracefully through the dark muddy tunnel the fallen autumn leaves made even more difficult to traverse. A little light from the opening to the field shone through at the end of the path to help guide us. Once we got to it and I saw the road leading a quarter-mile up the gently sloped hill, a chill came over me. I felt like I was back in 2007, with next to no money to support my family and a terrible illness that kept me from working. I snapped out of it and kept walking, though I kept half-expecting to see two orbs appear over the cattle gate in front of John's car. He'd backed it in I suppose in case we had to hightail it out of there.

Again, there was the place I stood when I realized there weren't supposed to be two setting suns. There was the spot where I dove into the reeds. I prayed the last fifty feet of the walk, but nothing had shown by the time we got to his car. Still though, I felt a trace of the lady's energy in me, and I did my best to let go of all the expectation and pressure. I already knew that my meeting John had been preordained somehow, but I had no way of telling if we'd see anything that night. I recalled over and over my visions of her. In my mind, I repeated her words that I had a mission: simply tell what I saw. Everything beyond that, she would take care of. I believed it, and reminding myself of this promise helped me relax and focus. There wasn't a cloud in the sky. That was a good sign.

When we got to the car, there were still some vestiges of light on the western horizon that dulled the stars. Noticing this, John asked if we couldn't just wait a while until night really fell. We weren't in any rush to leave, and no one had driven up to ask us what we were doing on their land, so we stayed by his car. Slowly, the stars began to come out in earnest. We were lucky where we were, since Fayetteville's light pollution wasn't all that bad compared to other cities. To this day, a clear night sky never fails to fill me with awe and gratitude.

Victoria was tired from the long day and trudging through all that mud, so she got in the back seat on the passenger side to rest. Emily sat beside her and chatted with her but kept the door open with her feet hanging out of the car so she could see more of the sky. John was leaning against the driver side front fender looking up, and I was between him and Emily leaning against the closed driver side door. John and I talked as the darkness deepened as he pressed me on the finer points of my previous experiences. It was an exacting and precise series of questions, but it showed he was serious and I was happy to answer them as best I could. A while after it had gotten as dark as it was going to get, the old familiar charge came over me. I was as sure of it as I am rain is wet. My hair stood on end. I had to stand up from leaning against the car: I was buzzing with this energy. I couldn't stand still.

In the south, especially in wooded areas, the sounds of crickets, other bugs, and the wind through the trees is only slightly diminished from the blaring soundscape of summer. I had spent my whole life listening to this volume wax and wane with seasonal daylight and warmth. From the time I was five and my father brought me on hunts, I remember being told to be quiet and listen. I remember the importance he placed on every sound we heard on those hunts: a twig breaking, a bird chirping a certain way, the frequency and tone of the dogs' barking. Soon after I felt this jolt come through me and I was almost vibrating, every sound from the woods around us stopped. It was like a switch had been flipped. We were in total silence.

Quickly I asked John if he heard that and he said no. At the time, I'd forgotten about his hearing aid and was confused. Then, of all things, the sound of dogs barking, from both north and south of us along the river. I remembered there were houses along it but not that many or that they kept outdoor dogs. They had that strange fear in their voices. It was happening. It had to be. It was just a matter of time. Then came an owl, loud and close. I remembered my first encounter at ten years old looking one dead in the eyes just a week before my back was blown open by a shotgun shell. I was overwhelmed amid this chorus's alarm when the charge heightened in me. That same adrenaline and focus took charge in me.

I knew then, they were above us.

I took a step forward so John would see me out of the corner of his eye and pointed up. I said, "Oh, I think they are here."

He stood up from leaning against the hood. He looked up where I was pointing. I was sure Emily was looking too. There were the familiar constellations. A few seconds passed as the stars glimmered back at us. A few more seconds passed. Nothing, though the energy had me almost shaking as I craned my neck upward. A few more seconds passed. Right where

I was looking in the sky, a brilliant orb flashed in front of us, pulsating for two or three seconds a white beyond white, bright beyond bright. Before any of us could say anything, it shot off in a streak of light to the south. John gasped and then let out a yell, "Oh my God!! Victoria, did you see that?" She was on the opposite side of the car with her door closed and didn't make it out in time, but Emily had seen. I looked back and saw her jaw hanging open.

After a few moments in silence trying to process what we'd seen, John took out his phone and walked away. We waited a while as he made some calls. I'd learn later that Jim Semivan was among those he dialed. Tears welled up with happiness and gratitude. It was an unusually bright and beautiful ball of light, and it had come at a time when I most needed it.

John came back to the car and we headed home. Everyone was ecstatic. John even managed a smile but I suspected it was one of the few times in his life that the phenomena appeared. He told us that of the two genuinely unexplainable encounters he'd had in his life, this was by far the more staggering and significant. The fact that I had felt and anticipated its arrival totally floored him. He said he had spent more than fifty years pursuing the exact relationship I demonstrated. Apparently, I had what those in these circles refer to as a "temporal connection," which John explained was what they called a telepathic connection with a nonhuman intelligence.

Later I tried to explain what the feeling was that clued me in. The physiological descriptions were much easier to describe than my emotional state. The closest thing I've felt was in my most moving experiences in church. In prayer, in song, thought, a similar tingling jolts through my body, bringing on goosebumps and making my hair stand up. It had happened since I was a child. To this day, I'll get the feeling out of nowhere and go outside with my camera: they'll be there waiting for me or I'll wait a while and sure enough they arrive. I'll pray and think of those close to me. Many witnesses, some of them government officials, have watched this process play out.

Watching John and Emily describe what they'd seen and what had happened to the rest of that family, I couldn't help but smile. The dangerous and mysterious military man they'd always seen on TV was in their living room, affirming their entire childhoods. A hint of what I felt standing in the field a half hour ago came over me: call it the spirit of God, call it love, the room was full and glowing with it. You'll know it when you see it.

CHAPTER 27

*Perfume and incense bring joy to the heart, and the
pleasantness of a friend springs from their heartfelt advice.*

—Proverbs 27:9

A full year of rheumatoid arthritis treatments kept me at
home for most of 2016. We kept seeing and documenting the
phenomena with increasing frequency, but with the difficulty of
travelling it was easiest to have guests come to our home. It was
a long and difficult year. By the end of the summer, Yvonne and
I had come to the conclusion that we could no longer maintain
the property we'd lived on for more than twelve years. There
was simply too much grass to mow and too many chores that
my aching joints couldn't keep up with. I didn't want my kids
saddled with these burdens. We were all devastated to be leaving
a house that had so much history, but we were out of options.

Jim Semivan and his wife Deborah visited on my birthday
weekend a year after John Alexander's visit. It was a relief
that Jim would be able to see the house and property before

we moved, since there was no telling what would happen to the house and the burnt tree. Jim and Deb arrived and we all went out to lunch together in town. Junior, Emily, and Jeremy hadn't met him yet, and everyone was excited to ask him questions about his career in the CIA.

Jim is a remarkably intelligent and observant man, no doubt from his decades spent in pursuit of information crucial to our nation's security. The one person at the table who didn't ask any questions was my son Jeremy. Jeremy's relative silence prompted Jim to ask him direct questions about his academic interests, which ended up having a fair amount in common with Jim's intelligence career. After a long back and forth between them, Jim asked Jeremy flat-out, "Why are you embarrassed about your father?"

It was a surprising turn in the conversation that Jeremy didn't really know how to respond to. I was a bit shocked too and looked over at my other kids pretending not to hear his question. Jim meanwhile launched into a passionate defense of the phenomena, citing worldwide instances of unfair persecutions of experiencers dating back to the ancients. Jeremy had experienced the phenomena many times, but opinions of others ate at him in a way my other children didn't experience. Jeremy was at the vulnerable age of fifteen in 2007, and he had the hardest time. In high school he became withdrawn, and once he was in college he hardly ever came home. It was too much for him to deal with these people, and even his aunts, uncles, and cousins could be hostile toward us.

Jim continued asking my kids questions as a full picture of their social environment emerged. The detail and scope of the abuses they each suffered saddened me deeply. It was difficult to sit and listen to, but there was no ignoring what was now the whole table's conversation. It seemed that there was no grade, class, sport, or extracurricular activity that wasn't overshadowed by the fallout of that one night in 2007. It was all out in the open for us to reckon with together. It seemed like an impossible task.

Jim paused. Commandingly, he said there was going to be a skywatch that night, and that the kids were to invite everyone they knew. He told them to prioritize their classmates and peers who had been the most cruel and doubtful. He wanted to have a word with them. Then he sprang into action, giving my kids orders like they were new recruits at Langley. Lunch was over and the four kids spread out all over town getting the word out.

Yvonne and I drove Jim and Deb to show them the cabin we were moving to. It was smaller but far more manageable for us. The cabin was tucked away next to a pond that Jim and I stood beside, looking out over the water. I was worried about how the phenomena would react to the move. Orbs had followed me all over the country, but still I hoped and prayed they would appear on the other side of town. As always, I took care to not take anything for granted. The pain and exhaustion of RA was wearing me down, but this property promised some relief.

I was talking with Jim about all of these changes when he said my life was just like the book of Job. That struck a chord in me. It was true that I had suffered greatly, won and lost a fortune, and even lost family too. A shiver ran through me as I remembered everything Job went through. If there were some wager between God and Satan about me, I knew I was lucky that the scale of my suffering was not as extreme as Job's.

Then he told me that he was aware of a study. He couldn't divulge what exactly the study was or how he'd heard of it, but he did tell me that for people who had experiences with the phenomena, a positive change always came twelve years after the first encounter. Every single person in the study had been somehow blessed after that span of time. He said that all I lost would return, my aching joints would improve, and my family would be blessed with happiness and success. January 8th 2019 was still over three years away, but looking in his eyes I was convinced. A breeze rippled across the unfamiliar pond. There was a little hope on the horizon.

Back at the house it was getting dark. The children were still buzzing around, talking to friends and sending out messages to everyone in their phone. Outside, I gathered wood for the fire pit. I never knew how long a sky watch could go, so I had quite a pile ready.

By dusk a small crowd had accumulated around the fire, lured by rumors of a man from the CIA who wanted to discuss my claims with whoever had questions. The faces of my children's friends and enemies glowed in the night air. Some I recognized because they'd been in the living room the day before, and some I hadn't seen since my kids were in kindergarten. Three of the friends were new graduates of Fayetteville police academy all arriving in their squad cars. Whatever Jim was planning on saying, it would fall under the scrutiny of an audience of about a dozen people, only half of whom I really knew. Out in the distance, I could see the burnt tree as it faded into the night.

Jim stood up and cleared his throat. The group went silent. He introduced himself, detailing as much as he could about his career in the CIA while hinting at everything he couldn't disclose. He was a practiced and steady public speaker, with a direct gaze searching the fire-lit faces for information. Having worked as a spy, he knew how to read people. In a voice of absolute certainty he detailed how significant this case had become. NASA, the CIA, the FBI, the NRO, the Vatican, and every division of the defense department had their hands in this, he said. The white house and other world leaders had been briefed on the events that took place on the very land we stood on. He denounced the Discovery channel episode as a ridiculous and exploitative piece of entertainment that did us a huge disservice.

As he was talking, a profound sense of warmth and gratitude came over me. This was exactly the kind of direct vindication I had always wished for. I never really worried about what other people said and thought about me, but it almost ruined me to hear about the humiliation and ostracism my kids went through. It would have been overstepping and possibly worsening the situation if I had ever tried something like this, though I had wanted to on many occasions. It was my birthday, and Jim was giving me the gift of a lifetime. Junior, Jeremy, Ryan, and Emily were smiling. No cloud of shame hung over them. It was honest, unmistakable pride. Tears of joy welled in my eyes. I drew a breath of relief I hadn't felt in more than a decade.

With such a large group, no phenomena appeared that night, but something far more miraculous and important happened. After that night, things changed for the Bledsoes when we ventured into town. This time, the rapidity with which rumors spread worked in our favor. The severity of the accusations waned as more and more people began to realize the harm these jokes and rumors had caused us. I had the impression they thought of me not so much as demonically possessed, crazy, or addicted, but simply a man who saw things he couldn't explain.

My relationship with Jeremy improved dramatically, as he had faced the worst of the ridicule in middle and high school. Emily and Ryan had been young enough that their circles of friends had somewhat more charitable responses. The whole family got closer together as a result of this one night, which banished so much of the pernicious shame and resentment that had dogged us for so long. We began to defend and support each other in ways that weren't possible before. Finally, these deep wounds could begin to heal. I owe a huge debt of gratitude to Jim for this kindness. Today, my kids bring their friends over to watch the phenomena, and when we go out at night and look up, we all look together.

∞

While Jim and Deborah were visiting, Jim told me that Tom DeLonge from the rock band Blink-182 had formed a new company to research and disclose information about UFOs called To The Stars Academy (TTSA). Jim mentioned that Tom and I should meet.

Two weeks before Christmas, Yvonne and I were having dinner at a local Mexican restaurant when my phone rang, it was Tom DeLonge. I could not believe it! A famous rock-star calling me in a Mexican restaurant. I immediately got up from the table, leaving Yvonne sitting there alone, and walked out to my car in the parking lot so that I could talk privately. Yvonne finished her meal in solitude.

We had a great conversation that ended with an invitation for me to come meet him in California. Tom spared no expense flying me first-class to L.A. and had me stay in the most luxurious hotel in downtown Hollywood. I was taken aback by his hospitality and kindness.

Friday morning came and I met Tom along with Chad and Carey Hayes to discuss the possibility of a film project. The meeting was held at Tom's personal talent agency in Hollywood. After that meeting, we decided to meet up the next day in Encinitas, Tom's hometown.

The following morning, the two-hour drive south to Encinitas was beautiful. When I arrived, I checked in to a hotel facing the ocean on the northern city limits. The rhythmic sounds of the ocean were soothing. It turned out to be a great day, meeting for lunch with Tom and some of his friends, one being Bill Tompkins. We talked a great deal about the phenomenon and my ability to interact telepathically with it and record it on camera. Later that evening we ended up having a sky watch on the beach where we witnessed several orbs.

Tom's interest was piqued when I told him about some material I had in my possession that had dripped from orbs. I also told him about two friends of mine that had some of what they thought was molten metals that had come from orbs.

After an interesting couple days meeting with Tom and other wonderful people, I was on a plane headed back to North Carolina. I couldn't believe how just four years earlier I was ready to quit it all.

A few months passed and it was early spring when Tom called to ask me about the metamaterial I and my two friends had. I told him I would work on it and get back to him. Eventually I was able to convince Benny F. and Larry C. to meet with me and Tom in Columbus, Ohio. Lue Elizondo would be joining us as well. Benny, Larry, and I had in our possession metals that we witnessed dripping or being ejected from orbs.

I met Tom and Lue at the airport in Columbus. I was happy to see them and had hopes the meeting would go well. We rented a car and headed to visit Benny and Larry. They were ecstatic to be having lunch with a famous rock star and Lue, who was at that time gaining popularity. Lue ended up receiving all of our off-world material and returned to California with Tom.

The metals would go on to be tested in laboratories and none of us, Benny, Larry nor I, have seen them since. I was told the materials have been classified and will not be returned.

CHAPTER 28

After Jim Semivan's visit, three long years passed. RA, the immunosuppressants, and a relentless schedule of methotrexate chemotherapy had hobbled me. My hands—the tools I'd used to build countless houses, an airplane, a garden, and raise a family with—had become virtually useless with pain and swelling. My younger children in college were dealing with the stress of deciding on a career that would pay off their student loans. Yvonne and I stayed close with all of them and shared the weight of these concerns. I needed help buttoning my pants, and the going was slow wherever we went.

I continued to experience the phenomena at least a couple of times a week these years, whether flashing glimpses or extended stays I tried my best to capture them on my phone. The lady and her beings were still with me, which kept me focused on the twelve-year anniversary date Jim had told me about. Easters and Christmases remained among the most significant experiences of the year. In my mind, I knew I just had to make it to January 8th, 2019 and some kind of blessing would come. After Jim's visit, we gave up the land I'd spent so much of my life on and moved into the cabin. It was closer to town so the stars were less visible, but it was much more private and tucked away than the old house. It was a great relief that the phenomena kept occurring there. Many in the community believed that the orbs and beings are location based or tied to a certain space, but there was no change in the frequency or feeling of my experiences after the move. I don't know how or why, but there is something in me that excites them and brings them out of hiding. Eventually, I would learn that I had the ability to imbue certain others with this ability to catalyze their environment, causing orbs and beings to appear. With these people, it sometimes happens that we see the same or similar orbs at the same time despite being hundreds of miles apart.

These years, I wanted my children to succeed and find happiness, I wanted the ability to operate my own body, and I wanted to keep spreading the word of what I knew. Of these three things, the first two proved too much of an obstacle for me to work on the third. I largely stopped attending UFO conferences and other events because of the difficulty I had traveling. The RA-related fatigue prevented me from doing interviews or talking for long periods of time. It was a demoralizing time, but I also knew things had been far worse not so long before, so I kept my head up. A few times, when I was with a relative who had always doubted me, an orb would wink at them over my head and their jaw would drop.

The phenomena's childlike, trickster behavior was a steadfast delight in tough times like these.

∞

The holidays came and went like a carousel after Jim's visit, and after the third year I was bursting with anticipation for January 8th. My RA had worsened to the point where I was worried for my overall health. I was haunted by the pamphlet I'd been given that described a laundry list of fatal illnesses, and especially the reduced lifespan for RA patients. More than anything, I wanted to be there for my children who were going through a critical period, first entering adulthood.

On the night of the eighth, I went out to the pond where Jim had first told me under his breath about the study and the twelve-year pattern it revealed. I looked above the water remembering his exact words. A few clouds drifted by. Then I remembered that first night twelve years before, how distant and yet so near. My despair-then-shock, Junior's fearful face, the orb over the bend in the road where my first wife died, the dogs howling, and finally falling asleep in my truck beside my son: all these scenes became deep parts of me.

I watched and waited. My knees ached, then burned, then screamed with pain. Still, I stood and prayed for relief. After hours, none came. I went back inside and went to bed, doing my best to remember there was a plan. I trusted deep down that the increasing number of appearances were leading to something. I remembered Tim Taylor's advice to pay attention to my dreams and write them down, so that was where I placed my hope that night and for many nights to come. There was always Easter coming around the bend.

∞

The weeks dragged on until finally April came. Orbs had continued to appear, and I eventually came to the conclusion that Jim's study was merely an estimation. I remembered his encouragement to pray for myself. I was so long in the habit of praying for others in greater need than myself that it seemed hubristic and selfish to do so, but I had tried everything else so I gave it a tentative try after a particularly bad day with RA symptoms. It was difficult at first and felt like trying to learn a new language. I tried hard to remind myself why I was praying for myself: to be a healthy, present husband and father.

My hope grew as Ash Wednesday, Maundy Thursday, and Good Friday arrived, but I was careful not to *expect* anything. I believe it's crucial to be as receptive and present as possible. Yvonne and I spent a nice evening together that Saturday night. I was still getting used to the slightly different perspective I had on the night sky, and went out that night after dinner once it got dark. Tonight was the night. Every year since 2012, they gave me a sign the night before Easter. It was nice to live beside a large pond: in addition to the usual flora and fauna of the area, there was the occasional splash of fish making a turn at the surface or a turtle easing itself into the water from a log. I got myself a chair, figuring it could be a long night. I had been praying for myself more and more assuredly, and I hoped this would have a positive effect.

I sat there well past midnight. Nothing happened. A painful push-and-pull happens nights like these, despair and fatigue wrestling with my attempts at a positive receptivity. I prayed for everyone I could think of in addition to myself, and still no sign came. I went to bed exhausted and woke up the next morning even more exhausted, stiff, and demoralized. I could hardly walk. I felt I'd done something wrong, and now my RA was worse than ever.

Two thoughts kept me from true despair. The first was that it didn't seem to me that the nature of the phenomena was in any way punitive. My family and I may have been tested, but whatever my mistakes, it wasn't like the lady or her beings to use pain as a tool. The second was that whatever the significance of Easter in relation to the phenomena, I had a sense this annual appointment might occur any time surrounding the day itself. Still, it was a sad and quiet day, and after dinner I lingered in the house, not wanting to disappoint myself again.

I sat with Yvonne as she read her email, listening to waves of cricket sounds through an open window. Then it came over me, that same unmistakable electric charge that makes my hair stand on end and my whole body tingle. I'd felt it many times before, and almost without fail I would walk outside to meet an orb hovering over the house. They were here. Later than I thought, but they had come. I told Yvonne I'd be back in a while then walked out the back door.

∞

With eyes aimed straight up and swollen joints, I stumbled my way to the edge of the pond. The water is convenient because the lack of trees opens up a broad view of the sky. Sure enough, on the other side of the pond, two hundred feet above the eighty-feet tall pines, was an orb. It was an unusual appearance because it seemed to have been waiting for me to walk out the back door. Most of the time, an orb will appear and flash simultaneously where you happen to be looking.

A moment after I locked eyes on the ball of whitish-blue light, it started to descend. Spiraling down in a corkscrew motion, it flashed rapidly and brilliantly, changing colors in a white-yellow-orange-red cycle. It closed the two-hundred-and-eighty-foot distance in about five seconds at a constant speed. It paused for a moment on the needle-strewn shore just forty yards opposite the pond from me. I felt the tingling charge intensify as it got closer to the ground. Suddenly it started shooting up and down, while still changing colors on the same white-to-red spectrum. It would rise about ten feet then fall back down to the ground. The most apt comparison I can offer for this motion is that it reminded me of an excited child that can't control their emotions.

I had rarely felt such a charge in my body. I knew a meeting was about to transpire. I took a few steps to the water's edge and fell to my knees praying that I would not get hurt. All my friends in the government had warned me not to get too close. Diana Pasulka had even suggested that my RA was analogous to the stigmata that plagued Saint Francis of Assisi. Despite this concern, and that I was shaking like a leaf on a tree, there would be no running from such a sight. I needed relief from RA so badly it was worth whatever risk was involved.

Staring wide-eyed at this orb rising and falling, I began to see the outline of a tall being. Somehow, the orb was contained within its body, as if its motions and colors were a part of its expression. It was a tall, majestic figure with seemingly broad shoulders, though there was nothing quite physical about it. It was as though I could make its shape out only via the indirect light cast by the orb. After a few seconds of this pattern, I thought I ought to get my phone out and start filming.

Careful not to lose my connection with the being, I swiped and pressed the touch screen as quickly as I could to get to the video recording app. It took longer than it should have because I kept looking up to maintain whatever end of the deal I was meant to hold up. Suddenly it started to approach me, gliding over the water. In my rush and excitement I finally managed to press the record button and aimed it across the lake, holding it below my chest. I continued to look directly across the pond and to my great relief, my recording hadn't changed its behavior at all. I was thrilled to have pulled this off but scared that it was getting too close. The lady told me she would help me with witnessing the phenomena and sharing it with the world, and I knew that finally this would be my best shot at it.

The being came to rest at the center of the pond and I felt at peace. It would not harm me. Still, the orb within it rose and fell at a steady tempo while changing colors. I knelt in awe of this grand, translucent being just twenty-five feet away from me. I could feel the hair on my arms pricking like needles while adrenaline coursed through my veins. Watching it hover just over the water flashing its mesmerizing colors, I thought to check whether the angle I had the camera at was still working. I was stunned to look down and notice that a whole ten minutes had passed. I could have sworn that not even a minute had passed. I looked back up at the being as if to keep it there, then back at my phone to make sure I hadn't misread the time. I hadn't, but then I noticed that in my initial rush to record, I'd neglected to actually start a recording.

The moment I pressed record it went totally dark. I was crushed. Then there was a flash where the being had stood, but dimmer and smaller. For the next seventeen and a half minutes, I recorded this periodic flashing on and off. I was spellbound. It had to have known I wasn't recording, which was why it allowed itself to be seen so openly. The form it took after I pressed record was less impressive and a bit more cautious, but still it shocked me to be given such a long and close-up capture of what was usually such a fleeting experience. This was no doubt the fulfillment of the lady's promise of help with witnessing and recording.

The final flash came, and as had happened the first Easter in 2012, a uniquely powerful exhaustion overtook me. On top of RA fatigue and an adrenaline crash, I felt profoundly drained. It was all I could do to drag myself to bed in a daze.

I might have called everyone I knew to tell them if it weren't for this exhaustion. All I could think of was sleep. As soon as my head hit the pillow I was out like a lightbulb.

∞

I awoke the next morning still dazed. A flood of visions rushed through my head that I could hardly process. I was full of convictions and understandings that I didn't remember being told. Like the first time seeing the lady, it was as though I'd been programmed like a computer.

The messages came through in brief phrases. "We will allow you to film us more and share with witnesses. Share the truth. Difficult times ahead."

Famine, plague, and unrest were just over the horizon. My work was now to prepare for this in addition to getting the word out about the phenomena. I wrestled all that week with how to tell my family and friends without alarming them too much. It was difficult for me to reckon with such an ominous message coming from phenomena that I had always known as benevolent and good. Armageddon seemed like a bit of a stretch, and I didn't want to risk our reputation or scare people if there was a chance I was misinterpreting the message.

By the following Sunday, I knew what I had to do. First I told my family. They took it well without panicking. I hadn't done an interview since 2012, so I had accumulated a long list of podcasters and publications that I'd turned down. I sent emails to all of them that day, and within six months I'd given ten interviews detailing my experiences and offering this warning. My understanding of these troubled times was that people would need to stock up on food and prepare to live at home without the help of modern comforts. It wasn't so much a doomsday prophecy where toads would fall out of the sky, but a broader warning.

After one of my podcast appearances, a scientist in California sent me a thousand-dollar Sionyx camera with night vision recording capabilities. I took it as a sign from the lady to keep trying to record the phenomena. Other cameras have come since then, and I've built up a small arsenal that cumulatively have captured thousands of images and videos.

Around Thanksgiving that year after another podcast, a scientist named Dr. Bob McGwier wrote me a beautiful letter asking to meet me. Like Tim Taylor, he had worked at the cutting edge of technological military research for many years. He was a professor at Virginia Polytechnic Institute and State University (Virginia Tech) and served as the director of its Hume Center for National Security and Technology. He also had a PhD in mathematics from Brown University, so he seemed like exactly the kind of scholar-government official hybrid that I had such good luck with in the past. I wrote back saying it would be an honor for him to come in December.

The Friday after Thanksgiving that year, Hal and Katie Povenmire were due for a visit. Hal had been one of the first government officials to show up on our doorstep. Over the years we had grown quite attached to the towering burly genius NASA had sent to debunk the Cape Fear River incident. When he couldn't, he became our friend, offering us the support we needed so much in the early years. It had been a while since we'd seen each other, so the whole family was looking forward to seeing them again.

Friday night came with no word from either Hal or Katie, and we started to worry. Eventually, Katie called to say Hal had fallen in the bathroom and was in a coma. We were all devastated. It was terrible timing. We all wished we could have seen him one more time and it put a huge damper on the holidays. Hal passed away a handful of days later, on December 6th. We will always remember Hal for his kindness and generosity to my family when we most needed it.

∞

I wrote to Bob and postponed his visit until January. He and his wife Sharon came on a Friday night and planned to leave Monday. The weather was terribly stormy the first two nights, so we stayed in and got to know each other. They were a wonderful couple and we got along great.

Sunday it started to clear up. After an early dinner at a local restaurant, we got home just after dark. We talked for just a few minutes in the living room when that charged feeling started to come over me. I got distracted from whatever it was I was thinking and doing: in my head all I could think was *they're here waiting for us.* Immediately I asked Bob and Ryan if they wanted to come outside for a look.

I went to get my Sionyx camera then led them to a little patch of ground beside my workshop that gets darker than the rest of the property. It has a nice broad view of the north and north-eastern skies. The three of us stood in the cold looking up at the night sky, and the tingling persisted, making my hair stand on end. I handed Ryan the camera and told him to be ready if anything showed up.

Minutes passed. A white-blue orb flashed to the west just over the trees, then traveled slowly to the northeast. I pointed and we all saw its silent trajectory as it glided through the air above us. Bob shouted and Ryan captured it on camera. Eventually to the northeast it vanished, blinking off. Bob was ecstatic. We kept watching and recording. A few minutes later Bob gasped and pointed over and around my head, saying he saw several tiny flashes of light like a lit sparkler. Others have reported seeing these, though I've never caught a glimpse. Sometimes they are described as sparks or little yellow flames.

We walked back to the house beaming. I was as sure as I ever was that I was carrying out the lady's plan as she intended. Without knowing why, I told Bob that the phenomena would be following him home. My only guess as to how I knew that was intuition: some people have that kind of magnetic draw while others don't. Bob and Sharon left the next morning for Blacksburg.

Just a week later, I got an excited call from Bob. Apparently, water was materializing out of thin air on the floors of his house, on Sharon's clothes, and on their bed. I heard fear in his voice and reminded him that they wouldn't harm him. I told him that they were there to help them in one way or another that we cannot understand. After another week, I got another happier call from Bob, who said that Sharon's stroke symptoms had all but disappeared. We talked a while and tears of gratitude welled up in me.

In February 2020, Yvonne and I traveled to San Francisco for a conference I was speaking at. My RA was still so bad Yvonne had to push me through the airports in a wheelchair. It was my first public appearance in years, and I was grateful that it was scheduled because my sense of dread was growing. My dreams told me that times of trouble were coming. I included these warnings in the talk I gave, but again was careful not to be an alarmist since this message from the lady wasn't as clear as previous ones.

After we got back home to Fayetteville, we started to hear reports of something called coronavirus. When I heard that word, I was convinced that this was what the lady had been warning us about: suffering, death, locked doors, quarantine. I was terrified for myself as well. My RA treatments had gotten me down to 150 pounds, and among my many medications were immunosuppressants, which I had been on for six-and-a-half years. I knew I was fragile and booked an appointment with my doctor in early March. Covid was close to getting to North Carolina, but the appointment was important enough to keep.

We talked and my doctor recommended quitting my immunosuppressants and prednisone. By mid-March I was totally off of both. Eventually Yvonne, Emily, and Emily's husband got sick with the virus, and I had to quarantine out in my workshop. Eventually everyone in the family except me got Covid. I spent six weeks alone out there, and slowly noticed my joints weren't aching quite as much. One morning I looked down at my hands and hardly recognized them because the swelling had gone down so much. By the end of those six weeks I could walk without a cane. I was gaining weight and even managed to button my pants. The worst of the pains recently had been in my hip, and that too became far less bothersome. At every turn, I found myself free of pains I had forgotten I was suffering. I had more energy and could play a more active part in family life.

It may have been that my medication was in fact causing my symptoms, and that getting off them was what changed things. I was sure however that it was Jim's advice that I pray for myself that did it. My family was overjoyed to see my improvement, and it was an incredible comfort during a period of great suffering throughout the world.

CHAPTER 29

Ask and it will be given to you; seek and you will find;
knock and the door will be opened to you.

—Matthew 7:7

Colonel John Alexander wrote to me in September 2021. Over the years, we had our usual conversations about our experiences with the phenomena, but this time there was a rare urgency in his email. He wanted me to get in touch with David Broadwell, who had a communicative experience with the phenomena in Northern Virginia. I was happy to do John a favor and put it on my list.

Since 2019, I have had many people reach out for so many different reasons that it's hard to keep track of it all. Covid lockdowns and the general chaos of these years has made it even more challenging, and before I had realized it, a week slipped past. Then John called to ask if I'd talked to David yet. I said I'd do it immediately. I was about to talk for the first time to the man who would become one of my closest confidants and collaborators.

David picked up the phone and even as he introduced himself, I knew there was something different about him. He possessed a boundless energy and an indomitable enthusiasm. He had a real workmanlike focus and a good heart. As serious as he was lively, he was well-informed and had a family he clearly adored. I liked everything about him and just sat back and listened as he told me his remarkable story.

On a clear day in June 2017, David was driving on Rt. 7 in Northern Virginia when a thirty-five-foot white disk-shaped object appeared in front of him. Hovering silently around two thousand feet in the air, the object seemed as though it specifically wanted his attention. David had never seen anything like it before and was immediately drawn in. As he watched, he noticed two smaller spherical white orbs to the left and right of the disc. The three of them moved in subtly different manners, independent of one another, but seemingly connected at the same time. It was a quiet morning in the blue ridge mountains, and the only sounds were the wind and the occasional car whooshing past. Then as soon as it was there, it was gone.

David remembered he was only two miles north of Mt. Weather, a U.S. government facility that plays a major role in the continuity of government. It is where the highest level of civilian and military officials will be relocated in the event of a catastrophic national disaster. It is the location of

FNARS, a high-frequency radio system connecting most federal public safety agencies and the U.S. military with the rest of the states. FNARS allows the president to access the Emergency Alert System. At this base is also an underground facility designated "Area B" and is where Supreme Court justices and congressional leadership were evacuated to after the September 11 attacks.

Unsure of the significance of the UFOs' proximity to Mt. Weather, David was even more baffled because they bore no resemblance to any aircraft. A pilot and aircraft owner himself, David had flown in this area for over twenty years, and he knew what he was looking at was no aircraft and that it was precariously close to the Air Defense Identification Zone (ADIZ) encircling Washington, D.C.

David told his daughter what he had seen and to be on the lookout from her bedroom window whenever she could. Obsessed, he was convinced it would return. He told her there was a "knowing." Two weeks later, while driving on the same road just north of Mt. Weather early in the morning, he felt an inner sense to look over his left shoulder, and when he did, it was there. The same object was in almost the same place and altitude, hovering silently. David stopped his car in the middle of the road and got out to walk toward it, leaving his door wide open. The whitish disk-shaped orb was stationary, sitting quietly in the clear blue sky. David was transfixed by it; even more powerfully than the first time, it seemed as though the object was communicating something and seemed to acknowledge David. He had the distinct impression that the object wanted him to know it was there.

David stood frozen in the middle of the road, his car running and door open. After about a minute of intense connection, the orb began to move off to the right slightly tilting as it did and then dematerialize, vanishing into the air as though it were cloaking itself. It just disappeared. David was deeply moved by the encounter. There was an intelligence about this object, and he felt as though some line of communication had been opened.

David began making inquiries, confiding in a friend who was an electromagnetic and optoelectronics engineer at the Office of Naval Research where he worked. He also contacted the FAA manager at Potomac TRACON, the radar approach air traffic control facility in charge of the Washington, D.C. airspace, and inquired if they had any reports of UFOs in the area of Mt. Weather. Response: negative. He spoke with Chris Mellon, former Deputy Assistant Secretary of Defense for Intelligence about his telepathic experience. He spoke with Bryan Bender, senior national correspondent for POLITICO who submitted a FOIA request, #2019-009871, on his behalf to the FAA about the sighting "over or near Mt. Weather." Several months later, David got a call from Chris and Bryan that the FOIA request came back. It stated, to no one's surprise, "Our search revealed there are no records responsive to your request."

∞

David had the revelation that telepathy was the linchpin. Obsessed with the communicative aspect of his encounter, he spoke to John Alexander, who mentioned me. I was moved by his story, but not surprised. I began asking him the typical questions that I have asked so many people who reach out to me. Particularly, I wanted to know about any trauma in David's past. The most important thing I have discovered over the sixteen years since I first saw the orbs is that the majority of experiencers have some level tragedy they are struggling with. Sure enough, David told me of some personal details regarding the health of his wife that nearly wrecked their world, and that it was in the midst of this when he began to experience the phenomena.

As we talked on the phone, I felt an intense connection with David, as well as that beautiful, familiar energy. The sound of the forest began to ring in my ears, and I knew they were waiting for me. While still on the phone with David, I grabbed my camera and opened the door. Immediately the sky was alive with light. Beautiful orbs were everywhere, or what ancient text calls Chariots of Fire. I began filming and told David about how excited the heavens were that we were talking to each other. I knew instantly that they wanted me to meet David, I had never seen such a reaction before.

I was full of electricity.

Just as excited, David walked outside of his Virginia home and looked up. Above him orbs began appearing and flashing, just like above mine. It was as though they were signaling to us both—above his home in Virginia, and above mine in

North Carolina. Right away he asked if he could come visit, and I readily agreed.

∞

A week later we were sitting together in my living room. It was a Sunday and we spent the day sharing stories and getting to know each other. Emily was there with her husband, Jack, as well as Yvonne, and we all enjoyed David's company so much that time just flew by. Eventually afternoon turned to evening and Emily and Jack went to pick up dinner from a local restaurant. Yvonne was working in the kitchen and David and I were sitting across from each other in the living room. We were having a deeply personal conversation about an experience when suddenly an energy began to surge through me.

I looked up at David and said, "They're here."

Immediately he jumped off the couch and bolted out the front door, and I was right behind catching the storm door as it was slamming back. He got outside just a few feet and looked straight up. There, directly overhead, was a slow-moving and very beautiful bright orb. It wasn't very high, maybe four hundred feet, and we stood there in awed silence watching.

Eventually I said, "There are usually three."

And sure enough, a few moments later a second one appeared behind the first, travelling in the same direction at the same speed, and then a third. David reached in his pocket, grabbed his cellphone, and began filming. He looked at me and said, "My God Chris, John told me you had a connection with them. This is incredible."

Eventually Emily and Jack returned and we went back inside to eat. As we were finishing up, David suddenly had an idea.

"Chris," he said, in a flash of inspiration, "I have got to get you to Monroe."

I had no idea what he was talking about but he explained that the Monroe Institute was the premiere center for research into the deepest aspects of consciousness. Using all manner of technology, especially audio-based experiments, the institute had pioneered consciousness research and was committed to the exploration of what is beyond space and time.

At this moment, the idea for a secret gathering at Monroe was born, one that would harness the sound technologies of the institute to explore the experiences we had been having. These technologies are specifically designed to enhance the ability of remote viewing and telekinesis, and we hoped that if we could gather a group of highly-attuned UFO experiencers, we might enhance and better understand this pre-cognitive state.

I was excited by David's enthusiasm, and he set off to bring the conference into being. Meanwhile we agreed that we would continue our own experiments of coordinating our experiences of the sightings. It had become apparent that every time I spoke with David on the phone, we would witness the phenomena at the same time. Is this what Albert Einstein famously referred to as "spooky action at a distance" —quantum entanglement—the ability of separated objects to share a condition or state?

David purchased the same camera as I have, and we synchronized our settings. I would focus my camera at a certain place in the sky, and David would do the same at his home in Virginia. We would leave our phones on speaker so each could record the same conversation in both locations. Soon after meditating and focusing on this agreed-upon location, there would be a flash of light over my head, and at the same instance one over David's head at an altitude low enough that it would be impossible for us to film the same object 400 miles apart. In one instance, while David and I were on the phone experimenting, he filmed an orb flash overhead and yelled "Flash!" and I filmed an orb flash instantaneously at ground level twenty yards in front of me. This was definitely spooky. Did we just record separated objects sharing the same condition or state? Is the phenomena trying to communicate with us? This footage was presented to Col. Alexander.

PhD Jeffrey Kripal once said, "In the past we interpreted the UFO as gods, goddesses, angels, demons, and today most would interpret the UFO as an advanced form of technology. Why is it that we don't interpret the UFO today as gods, goddesses, angels, and demons?" While I don't have academic credentials, postulating theses, or speculative papers, I do have real, genuine videos of the phenomena witnessed in real-time by government officials and lay people alike, from young to old. My videos show interaction, plain and simple. The videos now number in the thousands and are increasing exponentially for reasons I do not know.

∞

Soon David was able to obtain permission from the Monroe Institute board to hold a private, invitation-only conference in May of 2022. The goal was to bring together a group of experiencers and researchers that share the same intention, and over a five-day period use Monroe's technologies to interact with the phenomena. It was an eclectic bunch that finally gathered, ranging from a Hollywood actress and psychic medium to a world-renowned UFO explorer. There were ex-military, including John Alexander, a government employee, a distinguished professor, a podcaster, hippie, Bank of England financial analyst, an Argentinian, and a big strapping cigar-smoking Texan thrown in for good measure. In short, every kind of person was there, all united by their experience with the phenomena and a passionate desire to learn and explore.

Emily and I arrived together and it was nice to meet all these incredible people. There was clearly a huge deal of energy and excitement for the days to come. The Monroe Institute is a beautiful and magical place set isolated in the mountains of Virginia close to Charlottesville. Out back is a large grassy plane that slopes down towards the distant mountains. About a hundred yards down the hill sits a huge, six-foot-tall quartz crystal.

The first evening there was our group of twenty people sitting in a semi-circle just talking, waiting for dark. Suddenly I felt an energy I am all too familiar with. I looked at John Alexander and told him and David that Emily and I were going to walk down to the crystal. We made our way to the giant crystal and went around behind it to the opposite side. We leaned back against this unusually warm rock that had been heated all day by the sun's rays. As the darkness fell the temperature was dropping so this rock felt unusually good helping to keep us warm.

I lifted my arms and said a few words in private asking for interaction that night and all week. I could feel their presence as I stood there. I lowered my arms and instantly a huge white flash appeared above the mountains we were facing. I found it hard to be in a large group where the intention seemed scattered, but here with just Emily it was easier to focus, and I was glad that we had been given a good sign. The night continued on and many orbs appeared high, though they kept their distance.

Each day would start off with a wonderful breakfast followed by presentations and discussions about the phenomena. We participated in guided exercises of telekinesis, spoon bending, remote viewing, and pre-cognitive exercises that were accompanied by sound meditations. These sound exercises were one of the most amazing things I have ever experienced. They were conducted in private cubicles called Controlled Holistic Environmental Chambers (CHEC units). These were also where we slept. Each CHEC unit is a small, cube-like structure that blocks out all light. It has high-fidelity speakers built into the wall on either side where your head rests that introduce specially designed sound frequencies to alter the brain's electromagnetic environment (entrainment). These frequencies are designed to synchronize the right and left cerebral hemispheres.

After one particular sound exercise, everyone came out from their CHEC units weeping. A small group of us met in the hallway looking at each other wondering what just happened. Rob Freeman, the world-class UFO explorer, came out of his room, wiped a tear from his eye and said smiling, "You won't get that online." We all began to laugh. It was a beautiful moment.

On the fourth day after lunch, David mentioned that Dr. Ross Dunseath, a scientist from UVA, wanted me to participate in an EEG experiment. I followed him to a specially-designed copper-clad room made for Joe McMoneagle's remote viewing work, and then into an adjacent office. There a woman named Nancy McLaughlin-Walter was sitting at her desk, preparing a computer and a wiring machine. I had never had an EEG and had no idea what to expect.

Ross and Nancy sat me down in a comfortable chair next to the desk with the computer equipment. Nancy began preparing a complex wiring harness that had to be stuck to my scalp with thick gel. Before long my hair was covered in what looked like gobs of Vaseline. Nancy then attached electrodes all over my head, neck, and fingers. It reminded me of the lie detector test MUFON surprised me with, though this was far more sophisticated and, of course, much more professional and kinder.

Once the electrodes were secure, Ross started connecting the wiring harness to the computer. They turned it on not saying anything much and after a few minutes of wiggling wires and rebooting the computer I began to realize this thing wasn't going smoothly. I just smiled and thought, *if they only knew how many kitchen appliances and circuit breakers have failed around me!*

Ross and Nancy kept fiddling with and rebooting the machine, but nothing seemed to improve. It was apparently picking up the left side of my brain, but nothing else. They unplugged the leads and were surprised to see the left side of my brain was still registering on the computer with nothing connected.

"You have defeated our machine," Nancy said smiling.

Ross walked away for a moment and came back with a brand new machine in the box. He opened it up, connected the new wiring harness, and rebooted. Again, no luck—it could only read the left side of my brain. They plugged and unplugged everything but still it wouldn't work.

"I can't believe it," Nancy said, "this is our most reliable machine."

Almost an hour passed trying to get these two machines to work. Finally they unhooked everything and pulled out a third one. This machine was old and had a rubber cap with thirty-two leads.

"If you defeat this one," Ross said, "you will be Superman."

They fired up the old machine and it began to work perfectly. They let it warm up for a few minutes, then said they were going to hand me two objects. They wanted me to relax and just picture what was in each. For the first, Ross handed me a small, square plastic box that looked like a square fishing hook box but you couldn't see through it. I held it a moment and envisioned a small square which resembled paper of a postage stamp. All the while they were glued to the monitor.

He reached out and took it back only to hand me another identical looking box. This time was different. I saw a bright blue flash with the outer edges having a gradation of colors morphing blue to green to white. I felt as though there was a living, glowing insect inside. At this point they were satisfied with the data they had recorded, and helped me out of the electrode-embedded shower cap. As soon as Ross unhooked me, I made a beeline for the shower with hopes I could get a ketchup bottle full of Vaseline from my hair before dinner.

What I did not know was that David had received from Dr. Harold Puthoff a tiny piece of metamaterial that, given its construction and composition, is believed not made on earth. A renowned physicist, Dr. Puthoff's work dates back to the Stanford Research Institute (SRI) and the once classified CIA funded Stargate Program. Hal also conducted extensive experiments with Uri Geller back in the 1970s. I had just taken part in a double-blind EEG experiment at the Monroe Institute using material supplied by Dr. Puthoff. I was flabbergasted. The second box, which I described as feeling alive, contained the metamaterial. Later that day,

David told me that Uri Geller had a similar experience with a piece of material that Wernher von Braun handed him while at the NASA space research laboratory, Goddard Space Flight Center, just outside of Washington DC. Uri described the slender twelve-inch-long metallic piece as having a color like he had never seen before, pearl-like, almost translucent with greenish blue hues. Holding it he told Wernher that it felt "like it was alive", that it was "breathing."

Each night after dinner everyone would return to their rooms for sound exercises, and then we'd reconvene for nightly sky watching. Everyone had been hopeful during these sky watches, but very little was appearing. I wanted the phenomenon to show up, but felt that everything was being hampered by all the science and an endless sort of skepticism. Two individuals in particular seemed eager to discredit any glimmer of the phenomenon.

I prayed about it off and on all day trying to figure out the best way of handling the situation. The final evening, Emily and I walked down to the crystal again and stayed there a few minutes before returning to the large group. As we did, a calm came over me and I said to the two skeptics, "Look, just please open your mind and don't automatically try to debunk everything you see." I told them let the energy flow without judgment and they may be surprised at what happens.

It was getting late and finally one of the skeptics came up to me and apologized.

"I'm sorry, Chris," he said. "You have opened my eyes to something I couldn't see."

I stood up feeling the greatest joy because my prayer was being answered. I reached out and hugged him and said I was sorry too. And just then, at that very moment, someone shouted, "LOOK!"

We all looked up to see a flashing orb. It was timed perfectly to the two of us apologizing to each other. Rob, a world explorer on the hunt to film the phenomenon, had a $200k camera array set up twenty-five feet away. He filmed that orb for an hour sporadically pulsing, and while the star field moved out of the frame, the orb never budged. It was our last night together, and a beautiful way to end a transformative week.

The last sixteen years have been a tremendous test of my faith. But this story does not end here. It continues with you. Do you want to experience the phenomena?

All you need to do is humble yourself before the heavens. This simply means go outside and look up. Connect your heart and mind as one, humble yourself, and say out loud, "I am here." It is not more complicated than that. God, the universe—whatever you want to call it—did not make it difficult to connect. You don't have to follow some set of formal instructions, learning fancy words and acronyms to experience the phenomena. It is between you and God. Just pick one spot in the night sky, surrender yourself, and say, "I AM HERE." And don't give up. Stay positive. This is just the beginning.

ACKNOWLEDGEMENTS

I want to thank Yvonne for sticking by my side and showing me what true love is.

I want to thank my children who inspire me every day.

I want to thank David Broadwell, my friend and fellow traveler, whose loyalty and tenacity made this book possible.

I want to thank Hayes Cooper for helping me write my story and always listening with compassion.

And most of all, I want to thank God.

www.UFOofGOD.com

Printed in Great Britain
by Amazon

57816880R00209